"*Bedroom Rapper* ranks insanely high on my list of artist/musician memoirs. As a Black person who came up in a predominantly white indie music scene, I wish that this book had been around when I was starting out if only to say, it's gonna be rough, but stay weird, stay you, and we'll all be the better for it. A fantastic portrait of a genre defying artist who (consciously or not) blazed a trail for so many who are doing it today."   —Tunde Adebimpe, TV on the Radio

"Rollie Pemberton just gets it. He writes memoir with the insight of an essayist and criticism with the firsthand experience of an artist who's been through it all. Whether he's delving into hip-hop genres like trap and grime, the elusive magic of a good DJ set, or meditating on the lost art of music reviewing, he always seems to cut right to the core— because he's lived it. He's gone from Edmonton beer halls to the office of poet laureate, partied in lofts with Grimes and posted his music on bygone blogs. He's been taken advantage of by an exploitative and extractive music industry that profits off of Black creativity and sur- vived to write the tale. And he recommends a ton of good music along the way. A must read for Canadian music fans."

                    —Richard Trapunski, *NOW Magazine*

"Reading *Bedroom Rapper* is like hanging out with that friend with the great record collection who turns you on to things you feel like you should have known but somehow missed. You can feel Rollie's excite- ment, his eagerness to share music that matters, to shine a light on a part of the Canadian music scene that has, for a long time, not gotten the attention it deserves. It's so rare to read a book that builds up the mythology of Canadian music scenes (and, yes, that includes HMV)— and such a treat to read one that's so much fun.

    This is the kind of book that begs to be read next to your stereo, or while wearing headphones, so you can follow along with the soundtrack

Rollie provides. It's an education in hip-hop, and it's a Canadian music story that needed telling. A perspective that Canadian music desperately needs!"   —Raina Douris, Host, *NPR's World Café*

"Charting the highs and lows of his remarkable journey from attic-bound experimentalist to award-winning MC, Rollie Pemberton remains as ruminative, engaging, and forthright in the margins of *Bedroom Rapper*— as poet, journalist, critic, musicologist, documentarian, DJ, and more—as he is on the mic."   —Calum Slingerland, *Exclaim!*

"Rollie is a writer whose authenticity defines his work, making *Bedroom Rapper* a book that's as beautifully compelling as it is sharp, honest, and insightful. His voice is powerful and empathetic; his re-tellings are vivid, heart-wrenching, and strong. An absolute privilege to read, and a story I can't wait to keep following."

—Anne T. Donahue, author of *Nobody Cares*

"Read this if you're a hip-hop fan. Read this for a delicious behind-the-scenes. Read this for a coming-of-age book unlike any other. This memoir by Rollie Pemberton is open, funny, sharp, and filled with storytelling treasures. It's a beautiful love letter to life as an artist in Canada as well as an incisive critique of our culture. His storytelling is raw and polished at the same time, the mark of great art. We all stan Cadence Weapon!"

—Hannah Sung, co-founder of Media Girlfriends

"I was immediately charmed by Rollie's tale of cutting his hip-hop teeth in Edmonton, a city that gave him a unique vantage point where he could absorb influences from the U.S. and the U.K. in the same breath. *Bedroom Rapper* tells the tale of a precocious, intelligent musician finding his way during the rise of Internet forums and online discovery, at a time when the record industry itself hadn't fully caught up with the artists who were changing it, like Rollie himself. His boundless curiosity is palpable all throughout the book."   —A-Trak

BEDROOM RAPPER

CADENCE WEAPON ON HIP-HOP, RESISTANCE AND SURVIVING THE MUSIC INDUSTRY

ROLLIE PEMBERTON

McClelland & Stewart

Hardcover edition published 2022

McClelland & Stewart and colophon are registered trademarks of
Penguin Random House Canada Limited.

Library and Archives Canada Cataloguing in Publication

Title: Bedroom Rapper : Cadence Weapon on Hip-Hop, Resistance, and
Surviving the Music Industry / Rollie Pemberton.
Names: Pemberton, Rollie, 1986- author.
Identifiers: Canadiana (print) 20210394676 | Canadiana (ebook) 20210394684 |
ISBN 9780771051883 (hardcover) | ISBN 9780771051890 (EPUB)
Subjects: LCSH: Cadence Weapon, 1986- | LCSH: Rap musicians—Canada—
Biography. | LCGFT: Autobiographies.
Classification: LCC ML420 P395 2022 | DDC 782.42164092—dc23

Book design: Matthew Flute
Jacket art: courtesy of the author
Typeset in Berling by M&S, Toronto
Printed in Canada

McClelland & Stewart,
a division of Penguin Random House Canada Limited,
a Penguin Random House Company
www.penguinrandomhouse.ca

1 2 3 4 5   26 25 24 23 22

Penguin
Random House
McCLELLAND & STEWART

To Mick,
thanks for always believing in me

CONTENTS

FOREWORD

by GABRIEL SZATAN

I'd imagine a healthy number of you hold this book in your hands explicitly because of the year Cadence Weapon has just had. There's no shame in that. *Parallel World* put jumper cables to Rollie Pemberton's career, sparking overdue recognition from the typically cold and indifferent music media (heartbreaking: the worst industry you know just made a great call). The "right album at the right time," it launched a wave of rejuvenation which resulted in front covers, news chyrons and a few shiny trophies for the mantlepiece.

Well, prizes are nice and all, but *Bedroom Rapper* would have been worth the ride anyway. This memoir isn't really about Cadence Weapon the rapper. It's about Rollie—at once the smartest guy in the room and someone who is disdainful of the metrics by which we measure "smart"—an erudite, funny, omnivorous music hound whose life has been speckled by encounters that seem too rich and rare to dream up.

Rollie's earnestly nerdy approach to everything from beat-making to self-actualisation should scan as deeply relatable to this book's likely audience. No matter what era you first came across him, *Bedroom Rapper* is littered with close-mic'd details—rhyming over the Flaming Lips, conjuring sunrise Larry Levan tributes for his friends, dropping The Roots on his classmates as St. Francis Xavier High School's *official* cafeteria DJ—which makes you feel like you've known the man all along, and maybe even spy a bit of him in yourself too. I mean, tanking catastrophically before Rihanna at a festival? We've all been there.

How Rollie recalls half this stuff is a mystery—seriously, try and remember all the computer software you were using two decades ago, or the exact names of your saved files, and you'll hit a wall pretty fast—but his attention to detail will hit the pleasure points of anyone who grew up or came up in the early 21st century. "This might be the most '00s sentence ever committed to print," he'll tell you at one stage, after having rapped "Paper Planes" on stage with Diplo. Truthfully? There are dozens of contenders within.

His storytelling not only revives a compendium of forgotten clubs, blogs and hits, but taps into the nomadic duality of a modern recording artist: an existence spent shuttling between late nights and early mornings, unceasingly needing to keep pace with a digital landscape that conjures fresh social interfaces, audio formats and marketing demands every year.

Although we realise now that we'd actually performed at the same London clubnight in 2007, Rollie and I first met properly in May 2012. He was on the road with Japandroids, then the reigning kings of chest-beating indie rock (who still slap, for what it's worth). The tour was winding through Nottingham, which you might say is the U.K. equivalent of Saskatoon or Denver: a large-ish city floating somewhere in the middle of the map, with lots going on but a comparatively light artistic footprint. The chances Rollie knew anyone in the entire English county of Nottinghamshire were marginal, but we happened to board on the same music forum so I offered up my place to crash.

Looking back, that bill was a curious pairing. For one, Rollie didn't employ the services of a wind machine on stage. Both acts were fond of late-night drinking and pondering life's great intangibles, but that wasn't remotely the vibe you were getting from a Cadence Weapon record at the time. Yet this was the peak of Cool Canada™, where all the DeMarcos and Bouchers of this world pallied together, so it made vague sense. I honestly just marvelled at the guy. Touring the world, hanging with rockstars and a Television Personalities tattoo adorning his arm? The six-year age gap between us felt chasmic.

Memory tells me the set went well, as Rollie galvanised bar-hugging early arrivals with some call-and-response chants, and ended with "Loft Party," a fun Meek Mill-referencing loosie that may have gone down even better if any of the white students in attendance were even peripherally aware of Meek Mill. A triple-grimace spread over my face after reading that this was precisely the kind of environment which made Rollie want to pack MCing in completely. Not only does Rollie explain 2012's *Hope In Dirt City* was something of a creative nadir, and that he was long since fed up with thankless support slots, but Cool Canada™ was a lazy trope and anyone who bought into it was surely an idiot. Sorry!

It's interesting to see how the grass is greener no matter which side of the Atlantic you're on. Contrast the pedantic British fascination of "cracking" North America with Rollie's wide-eyed appreciation of how Europe sires the arts with prime-time media coverage and lashings of braised chicken. Gradually, our narrator comes to appreciate that it's a healthier and potentially more fruitful endeavour to build on home turf, no matter how stubborn the soil can be (or how much he genuinely adores grime).

What's apparent throughout *Bedroom Rapper* is Rollie's strong moral compass and empathetic ear. He's one of few music writers who has successfully made the leap to minting a lasting catalogue of their own; a keen thinker who can conduct lectures, but is not pigheaded enough to assume they can't glean fresh insight, too. Once an overconfident teen critic who believed doling out bloody noses to aspiring rappers was a badge of honour, he's mature enough now to recant. It's just a shame his Game Boy Color reviews are lost to eternity.

Amongst tales of his path to poet laureate and eating egg fried rice with Ghostface Killah, Rollie dives into the drudge work of untangling personal history with alacrity. There are raw passages and whole years tallied as write-offs, yet in his hands, the past is less a grotesque animal and more a wellspring of future renewal. He captures the fits and spurts of culture taking place all around him, when the simple act of keeping rent money coming in is dizzying enough.

What charms me most about *Bedroom Rapper*, and why the book is so faithful to its author's personal qualities, is the honesty about not holding all the answers. Rollie stumbles through the world as we all do, forever writing, editing, revisiting and revising his thoughts before trying to braid them into something substantive; half a lifetime's worth of experiences collated on the Notes app. And in 2020-21, by focusing his writing directly on the scourges of city redlining, contractual entrapment, racial subjugation and the generally frayed fabric of society, this process paid dividends.

So, to arc round to my earlier point, I lied. Yes, the book would have been a pleasure without its most recent grace note—but oh, the validation! Whenever I think of idly scrolling down my timeline and seeing that caption of "Third time's the charm!!!" alongside the news that *Parallel World* had bagged the Polaris Prize, it straight up makes me grin.

You deserve it mate. Next step politics, right?

—*Gabriel Szatan*

1

BEDROOM RAPPER

My rap career started in math class. It was the year 2000 and I
was in tenth grade. Our classroom was a pale beige cube adjacent
to the principal's office. I was sitting at my desk in navy-blue
Adidas tearaways with neon-green stripes when a pugnacious
white kid with spiky blond hair named Devin tapped me on the
shoulder and passed me a crinkled piece of loose-leaf paper. On
it, he had scribbled four vaguely threatening rhyming couplets. It
was suggested that I should respond.

I was the archetypal introverted fourteen-year-old Black nerd
before there was a rich online subculture for us. The two kinds
of Black men at the time were Steve Urkel and Stefan Urquelle
and I was somewhere in the middle. I had still somehow developed a reputation for "being into rap." This certainly made me
stand out at St. Francis Xavier, a conservative, mostly white,
Catholic high school in the west end of Edmonton, Alberta, with

an upper-middle-class population and well-regarded hockey, soccer, and basketball academies.

Hip-hop had not yet swept up the youth of our city like it had in so many other urban centres around North America. Cultural trends usually arrived a little bit later in our Canadian prairie metropolis. The first CD I remember buying was the *Teenage Mutant Ninja Turtles* film soundtrack with MC Hammer on it. Rap was not played on commercial radio back then. In fact, the first person to play it over the airwaves in Edmonton was my father, Teddy "T.E.D.D.Y." Pemberton, back in the '80s on his show, *The Black Experience in Sound*, on the University of Alberta's station, CJSR 88.5 FM.

Teddy had relocated from Port Chester, New York, to Edmonton in the late '70s to settle down with my mother, Michelle. Everyone in our family calls her Mick or Mickee. Teddy opened a short-lived record store called Good Vibes at 11147 87 Avenue in the early '80s and eventually pivoted to radio. Many Edmontonians have told me over the years that his show was their earliest exposure to rap music, though some kids, myself included, watched *Rap City* on MuchMusic if they were allowed to stay up late enough to catch it during its nine PM timeslot. (I idolized the host Master T and got to meet him at an autograph signing at Kingsway Garden Mall.)

Being Black in the early '90s in Edmonton often meant engaging with contemporary African-American culture from a distance. Shows like *In Living Colour*, *Def Comedy Jam*, and *Martin* felt like beacons sent to me from my home planet. Any glimpses I managed to catch of BET when I got around someone with access to satellite TV were electrifying. I could sense that something big was happening just beyond my immediate surroundings. This feeling only grew when I was around my family.

My parents met at Shaw University in Raleigh, North Carolina, where they used to party with the Last Poets. After they dropped out of college, they drove around the States, following Parliament-Funkadelic from town to town until Mom convinced Dad to return to Edmonton with her to be closer to my grandparents. There was always music playing in our house. My mom played piano, and she and Teddy would put on funk and electro records by artists like Rick James, Whodini and Cameo. I would dance around the house alongside my older sister, Gena, and my younger sister, Sierra. My parents had strong opinions about music too. They used to call pop music "la la" if it didn't have meaningful lyrics. If a singer couldn't actually sing, they only had a career because of "studio magic" that corrected their vocals. Teddy and Michelle seemed personally aggrieved when their favourite musicians didn't get their due respect. They were big fans of underappreciated R&B singer Phyllis Hyman and were devastated when she committed suicide in 1995.

My grandmother was Dr. Marianne Miles, clinical psychologist and former president of the Psychologists' Association of Alberta. She was from Harlem. My grandfather was Rollie Miles, an athlete originally hailing from Washington, D.C. He moved to Canada to play baseball, was convinced to switch to football, and became a Canadian Football League hall of famer and a legendary three-time Grey Cup champion for the team now known as the Edmonton Elks.

This helped to make my grandparents, my mother, and her six siblings arguably the most well-respected Black family in the city. My mom was once falsely accused of stealing a record from Zellers by a mall security guard. After she told her father what happened, he had the chief of police drag the mall cop to their house to apologize. When people like Muhammad Ali and Duke Ellington came to Edmonton, they were introduced to Rollie and Marianne. After retiring from football, Rollie Miles worked at the Edmonton Catholic school board, became a member of the 1978 Commonwealth Games board of directors, and was a principal with the Alberta Human Rights Commission. When he died in 1995, a field in town was named after him.

That prestige didn't quite translate to financial security. My family was firmly working-class. My mom did clerical work for accounting and law firms and my dad hustled in a variety of ways, embodying the freelance lifestyle before there was a name for it. Much about my upbringing was unstable. Unlike my fellow students who lived in the same family home, owned by their parents, for decades, my parents rented and we moved from house to house with great regularity.

My family background didn't help me much at school either. My otherness was made clear to me by the time I was in first grade. It was my birthday and I got to go in front of the whole class and write my favourite things onto a large sheet of paper. When my teacher asked me what my favourite type of music was, I excitedly shouted, "Funk music!" This befuddled white woman was horrified. "Wh-wh-what did you say?" She thought I was expressing my appreciation for "fuck music," whatever that would be.

Later that same year, on the playground at St. Vincent Catholic School, a white kid took my Ninja Turtle action figure—Raphael, wearing an astronaut outfit—from me. I told him to give it back and he refused, holding it above his head out of my reach. And then he told me, "Fuck you, nigger." Later that day, I found a discarded astronaut arm with a green hand near the jungle gym. The school did nothing and my enraged parents removed me from St. Vincent. I tried Blessed Kateri for a year and then switched over to Velma E. Baker for the rest of elementary. Once again, I was one of the only Black kids; once again, I was bullied by white students. One time I put a kid in a Sharpshooter submission hold for picking on me. The principal called my parents. When we were out of view of the teachers, my dad high-fived me. I ended up making friends with some South Asian kids and we played community league basketball together for the Meadows with my dad as the coach.

I'm thankful that my family had a long history of Black greatness for me to draw positive inspiration from. But it was my relatives closer to my age who helped to connect me to what was going on in the present moment. I'd go to my cousin Mario's house and listen to Wu-Tang albums that built worlds that were just as vivid as any Marvel comic book I had read. My sister Gena had Redhead Kingpin posters on her bedroom wall. She would teach me new jack swing dance routines to Bell Biv DeVoe songs in the basement. But then I'd leave the house and all anyone wanted to talk about was k.d. lang. The cultural dissonance was like being stuck inside a snow globe, seeing the blurry edges of a more vibrant world calling to me from the other side of the glass.

Live shows by mainstream rap and R&B artists were few and far between in our city. Artists would only make the long trip to Edmonton if they were already big enough to play in a stadium. The first rap-adjacent show I remember going to was Boyz II Men and Montell Jordan at the Edmonton Coliseum in 1995 when I was nine years old. My mom bought me a ball cap with "This Is How We Do It" on the front from the merch table—I wish I still had it! In the years after that, I stayed plugged into the culture by reading magazines like XXL and *The Source* and watching rappers like Cam'ron and Ghostface freestyle on BET's *Rap City: Tha Basement*. By the turn of the century, at fourteen years old, I noticed that rap was incrementally breaking through in Edmonton. A couple hip-hop cuts would make it onto the Much Video Dance Party playlist when they'd set up in the gymnasium at school. I remember going on a student ski trip and every room in the chalet seemed to be blasting *Get Rich or Die Tryin'* by 50 Cent. The occasional track crossed over, but hip-hop fandom was still an exception at my high school.

And here Devin and I were at St. Francis Xavier, passing verses back and forth instead of learning algebra. Like many aspiring rappers our age, our rhyme styles were both heavily influenced by Eminem. *The Slim Shady* LP came out on February 23, 1999, right as I was coming of age. And if you were following rap then, the impact that album made could not be overstated. I got a promo copy of the CD from my dad. He had not been won over by this lewd white rapper from Detroit, but I was enamoured by his intense storytelling, technical skill, and clever, sardonic attitude. His music was like catnip for teenage boys. The thing that really blew me away was Eminem's use of multisyllabic rhyme schemes. He wasn't the first person to rap this way (Kool G Rap is the father of this style), but he refined the method for the twenty-first century. His lyrics were impish and his flow was playful. He deconstructed rap and turned it into a nerdy word game, some new rhyming version of Scrabble where you'd earn extra points for having the most intricate disses. You can see how this might be appealing to kids. I worshipped him while completely ignoring the virulent hate speech that made up so much of his content. I still remember one of the raps I wrote with Devin because it was such a transparently obvious Eminem imitation:

Watch me skydive while I drink a mai tai . . . bye bye!

This was a slice of ambiguously rebellious language about doing an extreme sport I'd never tried while consuming an alcoholic drink I'd never imbibed. I was way more likely to be chugging a frosty bottle of Mountain Dew Code Red while playing *GoldenEye 007*. Why didn't I rap about that? What happened to keeping it real? That wasn't really an option for an Albertan teenager with no real-world experiences. Like it did for so many other hip-hop fans, writing raps represented a world of imagination and escapism that occasionally required a slight reshaping of the boundaries of believability.

When I wasn't writing raps with Devin, I was publishing poetry and articles in the high school newspaper. I wrote a blind item column about house parties under a pen name, the Party Prince. But the most pivotal outlet for my evolution as a rapper was the internet. In the late '90s, the web wasn't really popping yet. At home, I had access to a Hewlett Packard desktop computer with Windows 95 and a 14.4k dial-up modem thanks to my mom's secretarial work.

I used the internet to download video game emulators and ROMs so I could play Super Nintendo games for free. But after years of reading monthly publications like *The Source* and XXL, my thirst for rap knowledge led me to find websites that broadened the breadth of my hip-hop acumen. I obsessively read reviews of rap albums on RapReviews.com. Eventually I found an online community of people who also rapped solely in text format. They called themselves textcees and their home was the message board on RapMusic.com.

As a teenager in a remote Canadian prairie city, there wasn't a readily accessible street cypher where I could hone my skills. So RapMusic.com essentially became my first rap scene. I discovered a no-holds-barred ecosystem of hundreds of aspiring rappers hurling insults at each other from all around the world. The board was overwhelmingly male and shared a distasteful, irreverent sense of humour with the Something Awful forums that started around the same time (think of these boards as a precursor to 4chan and Reddit). The rappers had usernames like Warbux, Okwerdz, and Poison Pen. The early internet bulletin board, complete with a black background, felt like a void you could get stuck in.

Most of the textcees were influenced by a cerebral strain of battle rap developed by artists like Eminem, Jedi Mind Tricks, and Canibus. Could you suggest your opponent was mentally stunted while also referencing hieroglyphs and pyramids? Then you'd be very likely to score high marks on RapMusic.com. My username was Antagon, short for antagonist. A working title for my first album was *Black Protagonist* and that was how I saw myself. Back then, a Black leading man was a rarity in media. In what was essentially self-directed, unrewarded, extracurricular English homework, I set about honing my skills as a textcee on a daily basis after school.

The board had forums for everything you could think of: discussing new album releases, romantic advice, sports, politics. But the primary draws were the sections for audio and text battling. There were even some real professional underground rappers on there, like Immortal Technique. This was a place where people rapped just for the sake of rapping. There was no financial goal or fanbase to be developed. You'd start a thread with someone else and post verses one after another and other users would determine who had the best punchlines and cleverest lyrics. They had tournaments and crowned champions.

While trading disses was the main attraction to the board, I also found myself interested in the forum that focused on storytelling. This area was also competitive; the winner was the user who wrote the best story as a rap verse. Storytelling is one of the pillars of rap lyricism, arguably the element that has made the art form such a rich oral tradition. Artists like Slick Rick, KRS-One, and Chuck D made storytelling ability a necessary part of any rapper's repertoire. Furthermore, in the mid-'90s, there was a trend of using personification to tell stories in rap songs: Common's "I Used to Love H.E.R." was a literal love song to hip-hop; "I Gave You Power" by Nas was written from the perspective of a gun; Organized Konfusion's "Stray Bullet" followed the path of an errant gunshot. This style lent itself well to the text format so many people on the board experimented with this technique. It's something I still use to this day. Most importantly, the storytelling forum was a place where I could be creative without having to put other people down.

Already a huge dork who once got 100 percent on an assignment by rewriting *Hamlet* as a contemporary teen gross-out comedy, these forums were right up my alley. After trying my hand at a few text battles and getting some positive feedback from other users, I worked up enough nerve to connect one of those super-long pale grey computer microphones to my mom's desktop and start recording myself rapping out loud with my human voice. To minimize the popping sound I made when saying letters like *P* and *B*, I fashioned a homemade pop filter out of a reshaped wire hanger and a spare pair of my mom's pantyhose.

I'd send these tracks to my friends over MSN Messenger, upload them to SoundClick, and post them on the board in search of constructive criticism. J. Cole and Earl Sweatshirt used to write verses on boards just like I did. Drake used to post on HipHopCanada.com under the username DrakeHotel; Tyler, the Creator was a regular on the HypeBeast.com forums. Nice to see some of the most bar-centric artists of our time were huge nerds like me, chopping it up online before they made it big.

And then I met someone on the message board willing to produce for me. We created my first song together. It was called "Payroll Takin' tha Toll" and it sounded like an Ultramagnetic MCs demo from 1987 that was rejected for being too weird. By this point, I was calling myself Payroll, a play on my first name and my vast earning potential. Our song sounded incredibly dated, despite being made in the twenty-first century by two people with access to comparatively advanced digital audio equipment. I breathlessly rhymed about my lyrical supremacy with no consideration for the boundaries of the confounding, irregular, and yet rudimentary beat I was rapping over.

From there, I tried my luck at audio rap battling on the board. I was terrible, jamming way too many words and syllables into each bar, a problem that arises when shifting from rhyming exclusively on the page to rapping out loud. I would grab whatever instrumentals ripped from 12-inches and CD singles that I could find on Kazaa and step into the arena. Anything was fair game: weight, appearance, sex, location, whatever. Knowledge was power and anything you knew about a competitor became the foundational clay of your diss track. My heart was never really in the battle scene though, and soon I shifted away from the message board entirely and started getting serious about recording some real rap music.

Around this time, I came up with a new name. Payroll just didn't fit. First off, I nor anyone else I knew had any money. And it didn't really jibe with the anti-commercial stance of the rappers who influenced me. I noticed that whenever I'd fire up an instrumental and freestyle, I would end up unconsciously returning to one particular mantra: my cadence is my weapon, my cadence is my weapon. I prided myself on having a variety of ways of presenting my vocals when I rapped. I shortened the mantra and became Cadence Weapon. It was my shorthand for music as a weapon, rap as a vehicle for change.

At our family Christmas celebration in 2001, I declared to my uncle Brett Miles that I'd started rapping. In most families, this statement would be met with rolled eyes and skeptical expressions. Not mine. We went to my aunt's basement so I could kick some rhymes for him in private. Uncle Brett was an accomplished jazz saxophonist who had previously lived in New York, performed with James Brown and recorded on sessions for Mick Jagger. He was a heavy musician. He'd started a band called Magilla Funk Conduit that gigged around town. He had long stringy dreads and a vibrant array of technicolor daishikis. If there is a patron saint of funk, he probably looks something like Uncle Brett. His wife, Dani, was an accomplished dancer. They were the first adults I knew who were making a living through art. After hearing me rap, Brett was amazed by my vocabulary and started calling me Thesaurus Jones.

Brett invited me to join his funk band as an additional vocalist. The following year I performed with him at local venues like the Sugar Bowl and Sidetrack Café and got free glasses of cranberry juice and some pocket change. I couldn't believe my luck. This was my introduction to the stage. I'd go on holding an index card with the first word of every verse I had previously memorized written on it just in case I forgot something. I was just jamming with my uncle and his friends back then, but performing live became one of the great passions of my life.

I started to chat with producers from the message board on ICQ. I eventually stacked up enough original instrumentals from a beatmaker called Taj Mahal to record my demo, 2003's *Soldier Speech* EP. I was seventeen years old. The tracks he made were relatively conventional loops, a mix of the same sample-heavy beats you might hear on a late '90s underground rap album, along with imitations of the chipmunk soul trend taking over the mainstream; the sound fell somewhere between Rawkus and Roc-A-Fella. To be honest, the beats never really suited me, but production wasn't my focus back then. I just wanted to hear myself on record. My idea of pushing musical boundaries at the time was rhyming over a loop of "The Gash" by the Flaming Lips. I was already deconstructing Pharoahe Monch and Aesop Rock verses for fun and had clearly decided that using big words was my answer to every problem:

> *Used music, trashcan rap status in a new movement*
> *Loose truants, broken microphone zone, delusion*
> *Union unit, metronome abusers known as metafusion*

Such a nuisance, found truth in televised revolution
Evolution, what you're using, vanity mirror redundance
Sanity fears my function, outlandishly sears assumptions
Banality leers combustion, only confused choose to lose a muse
Refuse to abuse fools, they'll infuse views into the news

You can hear the hiss on my vocals from the cheap microphone I was using, as well as unintentional room noise because I was recording my verses in my HMV friend Vanid's tenth-floor apartment underneath a mountain of couch cushions that we used as a recording booth. I was heavily influenced by Nas at the time, who inspired me and so many other young hip-hoppers by releasing his epoch-defining debut *Illmatic* when he was only twenty years old. What Vanid and I made was far from perfect. The quality of my performances fluctuates wildly from track to track. Sometimes, trying to rap fast like Myka 9 or Busdriver, I sound out of breath. My verses on the EP are claustrophobically cluttered, self-indulgent, and way too clever for their own good. I had not yet developed a consistent musical identity and instead pushed a vaguely political, morally authoritative stance that was based on pretty much nothing.

Still, Vanid and I both agreed that it was pretty damn good for a seventeen-year-old. So, I set about burning it onto CDRs and selling it out of my backpack to my friends at school, my family, and random strangers. Yes, that's right: I was once the man on the street asking passersby if they love real hip-hop.

My first girlfriend, Lisa, helped me spray-paint the adhesive labels for the discs on the floor of her basement, creating unique purple and pink gradients that looked like deep space nebulas. Lisa and I vibed because we were the only kids we knew who listened to the Strokes and Yeah Yeah Yeahs, bands who inspired my eventual performance style and personal aesthetic. The paint dried and made the labels rise up a little; I worried that they'd get stuck in people's car stereos. Lacking any sense of decorum or understanding of the performer-audience boundary, I managed to throw a couple mixtapes on stage during the Blackalicious show when they played at Red's in West Edmonton Mall.

When I'd tell folks that I was a rapper, I often received a look of confusion. For those of a certain age, rap was crap. Misogynistic, violent, ignorant, retrograde. Especially to those people living in a racially homogenous prairie province that had replaced thousands of years of Indigenous music with a few decades of country western. To the uninitiated, all rap music was gangsta rap. Most weren't aware that alternatives existed. What I considered to be a vibrant tapestry of divergent styles and unique perspectives was a monochromatic, hateful blob to most people in my immediate environment. As a result, much of the early part of my career involved me giving people a quick tutorial on hip-hop culture and my place in it.

Despite failing to take the rap world by storm with my hastily recorded demos, I nevertheless kept at it and ended up rapping at my high school graduation. I wrote some verses about how cool it was to graduate and performed in an ivory suit. I also had a cane. To paraphrase Pusha T, I was wearing so much white, you might think your holy Christ was near. A few days later, I was sitting in my living room playing NBA *Street* when I got a call from my sister Gena in New Jersey. Our father had collapsed and died while working as a baggage handler at the airport.

My parents had been separated for a while and he had been living with my sister. He was encouraged by my mother not to come back for my graduation because of the fraught state of their relationship. His death was sudden but it wasn't a total surprise. He had been diagnosed with glomerulonephritis, which had led to kidney failure and forced him to go on dialysis. For as long as I could remember, my dad was getting his blood cleaned by a machine every other day. He often jokingly referred to himself as being "half-dead." Maybe that was his way of preparing us.

I would visit him in New York in the summers and we would drive around listening to Hot 97. I remember hearing Clipse's "Grindin'" for the first time while sitting in the passenger seat, hearing him laugh at the outrageous street boasts in the song as he yelled out, "These boys watch too many movies!" Teddy's death was devastating to me because I'd always felt that he wished I was more like him. I had a complicated relationship with my dad. I never got a chance to show him who I really was. To most people, he was the life of the party. He cruised around town in a vintage chestnut-brown Jaguar and rhapsodized about his love for Borsalino hats and alligator shoes. Back when he was a teenager carousing around upstate New York, his friends nicknamed him Broadway. He was a big city guy; he even worked as a Manhattan cab driver as a summer job during college.

On his radio show, he was an idiosyncratic, multigenre DJ several decades before it became fashionable. He had the audacity to open his shows with the *2001: A Space Odyssey* theme. Then he'd follow it up with "N.Y. State of Mind" by Nas. He snuck into Woodstock as a kid and became obsessed with Jimi Hendrix. He still played songs like "The Wind Cries Mary" and "All Along The Watchtower" among modern rap and R&B tracks well into the '90s. He befriended the reggae group Third World, serving as the inspiration for their song "Low Key-Jammin." He was famous for his gift of gab, the combination of his syrupy effortless delivery and unforgettable one-liners. The outros for his radio show—typically delivered over the opening strains of Phyllis Hyman's "Waiting For The Last Tear To Fall"—were silky smooth and impossibly epic. He could make Fab 5 Freddy sound pedestrian by comparison:

> *Just like a flick of the Bic, it's all over with!*
> *You can reach for your green crayon and your colouring book*
> *and check it, E-Town, it's been a rock down!*

A larger than life, near-mythical figure to anyone who encountered him in Edmonton, he had no qualms about coming to my junior high convocation sporting a DMX . . . *And Then There Was X* promotional long sleeve T-shirt. Other kids befriended me just so they could come over to my house and be around my dad. Teddy was an incorrigible flirt. He had more hustles than Hustle Man. Mostly, he sold weed. Our basement was a grow-op. Sometimes he would have my sisters and I turn on the lights and sprinklers. He would've been amazed by the legal marijuana industry today. He'd take me to Northlands racetrack to bet on horses or we'd pick football teams on Sports Select. He got into real estate and dodged bill collectors like Barry Sanders hurdling linebackers.

Teddy was quick with a joke but he also had a quick temper. He yelled at us a lot. Most of my earliest childhood memories involve getting screamed at: for emptying out a box of Raisin Bran in the garbage, for opening the door while the car was moving down a desert highway, for anything. I got slapped upside the head from time to time. He used to call me stupid.

There was one time when he was yelling at Gena about something and tried to suggest she wasn't smart. He said "Well, you know what? L is for dummy!" and we all burst out laughing. He meant to say "G is for dummy." This became a running joke in our family for years.

There was often humour tied up in the anger, making it hard to dislodge the emotions from each other. That was just growing up; no one would've called it abuse back then. I always felt like I wasn't really what he was hoping for in a son. I was introverted and nerdy with an unkempt afro. I didn't really care about how I dressed or being appealing to girls when I was younger. I was occasionally slow to understand things and painfully shy. I cried a lot as a child, and I felt he wished I were tougher. I had rapped for him over the phone but was always reluctant to share anything more with him, fearing that he would judge me harshly.

I performed a poem dedicated to him at his funeral, a small affair in suburban New Jersey. His death inspired me to open up and express myself more, suddenly freed from the constant fear of disappointing him. After the funeral, I took a semester off instead of starting university, to save money and work on music. I reached out to some internet producers to put together a proper album and it ended up being an unexpected musical turning point. I hit up this one producer I knew from Finland on ICQ and asked him to make me a beat using a sample of "The Stroke" by Billy Squier, a painfully cheesy '80s pop-rock single that had a surprisingly decent drum break in it. I went to Money Mart and expeditiously sent the producer one hundred Canadian dollars via Western Union money order after he sent me a short unusable snippet of what the beat might sound like.

Suddenly, our communication broke down. He ignored me, stopped answering my messages, and never supplied me with the lame beat that I'd paid for. Defeated, a stray thought crept into my mind: Couldn't I just make this beat myself? I fired up Soulseek, downloaded a low bitrate mp3 file of "The Stroke," and then pulled up the Sound Recorder program from the Accessories folder in Windows 95. Sound Recorder was the most basic recording application you could possibly use. It makes GarageBand look like the TONTO synthesizer.

It was not designed for making music. It had no visual interface or sequencer to let you see what you were doing. I would load up a file, copy a time selection with a sound in it, go to the end of the track, scroll past the silence at the end of the song, paste the sound *there*, and then repeat this process until I had created a beat with some semblance of musicality. The herky-jerky mess that resulted from this process sounded a bit like the experimental compositions that people actively try to make today.

Around the turn of the century, hip-hop producers were becoming just as popular and influential as the artists who rapped over their tracks and I found myself inspired by many of them. Timbaland's beats were electric and otherworldly, full of syncopated alien rhythms that felt as if they were beamed in from a distant, funkier future. The Neptunes took the schoolyard immediacy of kids pounding on the lunch table, blew it up, and made it widescreen.

The way that RZA and Prince Paul could reconfigure stray howls and grunts from ancient funk and soul records to turn them into a warped sample orchestra transfixed me. After reading an article about how 9th Wonder from Little Brother made beats with a program called Fruity Loops, I dug around the dark corners of the internet and connected to a torrent holding a cracked copy of the program.

The thing that set FL apart from other production suites of that time was the fact that it was user-friendly and intuitive. People who used hardware to make beats took pride in how difficult the gear was to use. The colourful interface and short learning curve made FL feel more like a really addictive video game than a studio tool. I fooled around with it a few times without creating anything of consequence until one particular session changed everything. It was the middle of summer and I lived in my mother's attic. I was sweating in oppressive, stifling heat. I was playing around with some bass synth preset sounds and started layering what sounded to me like a rocket blast hitting a battleship from the inside of a submarine. It was watery and undulating.

The rhythm track I created for it was strange and somewhat illogical. It didn't start with a kick on the one, and the percussive elements were what was driving the rhythm. It was cold, mechanical, icy. It certainly didn't sound like any rap I had ever heard before. It was electronic but I didn't have any sonic reference that I could compare it to. Looking back, you might say that I was making grime or techno. It probably sounded a bit like video game music, which was a huge inspiration to me.

At the time, it felt completely new. I couldn't help but feel an exciting connection to what I had just made. I had no training, couldn't read music, and wouldn't be able to tell you what key the melody was in. But something about this beat made me want to rap and so I rhymed over it for a couple hours. This wasn't like when I rapped over beats I got from some random European guy I'd never met before. This was my music. I saved the file as "depthcharge.flp." In my mind, I was officially a producer.

From that point on, when I wasn't working or listening to music, I was teaching myself to make beats. I'd take the loops I made in FL, export them, and then sequence and arrange them with another simple program with a silly name that I illegally downloaded, Cool Edit Pro. Did I care that my tools of the trade were stolen? Not really. Rap music probably wouldn't be here today if it wasn't for all those turntables and mixers looted during the N.Y.C. blackout in 1977.

And sampling, the process of using elements from old recordings, is one of the cornerstones of the genre. My years of using the internet to hunt for obscure samples to chop up beyond all recognition helped to refine my taste in a way that wasn't possible locally. Free access to cutting-edge music software balanced the playing field so that an untrained kid living in the middle of nowhere with little to no resources had a chance to compete with major label artists with big budgets and professional studios.

In each session of experimentation, I was coming up with different tricks and discovering new ways to sculpt sound. Around the same time, I was starting to get noticed by the local rap scene, which did in fact exist. A couple DJs named Marc Pause and Sonny Grimezz invited me on their radio show at CJSR and I rapped live on air. Rumours swirled about this young rapper who was the son of T.E.D.D.Y. I went over to Marc's house and recorded some verses for a mixtape they were making called *Hot Sauce*.

They took me under their wing. I'd help carry their crates of records into the bar for their weekly hip-hop night at the Black Dog, a popular pub in the Whyte Avenue area that would later hold much significance for me. Standing in the bar's dank basement in the crush of hip-hop heads in puffy jackets, for the first time ever it felt like I was finding my people. But right before I turned eighteen and could legally explore Edmonton's nightlife further, I was forced by my mom to try out university. I wanted to stay in Edmonton and go to University of Alberta for English but was persuaded to enrol in Hampton University—my sister Gena's alma mater—to study journalism.

Going to an HBCU like Hampton is considered a rite of passage for many African Americans. Established in 1868 in Hampton, Virginia, HU is a member of the unofficial Black Ivy League. Going to Hampton was intended to bring me closer to my Black roots and immerse me in Black culture. It's true that I did appreciate the African-American history course, where I learned things that would've never been covered back in Canada. Joining the Hampton chapter of Amnesty International was also pretty influential. We took part in letter writing campaigns and went to the National Mall in D.C. for a protest where Mumia Abu-Jamal spoke from prison on a large screen. But my overall experience at Hampton didn't quite have the desired effect.

Dropping me into a monoculture in a foreign country just emphasized how different I was from everyone else. I made a couple friends, including my homie Brandon who would take me with him to hardcore shows in other towns. But everyone else just thought I was insanely weird. Which I was. I used to blast Aphex Twin in my dorm room, which probably sounded like sheer alien noise to everyone else in the building. And the idea that I was a Canadian rapper completely perplexed everyone (what a concept!).

There was also a pervasive culture of conservatism there that didn't resonate with me at all. You had to take off your hat whenever you went inside a building. If you wore dreads and were in business school, you had to cut them off because according to the faculty, you could never get a job looking like that. Most of the other kids went to church every Sunday and a surprising number of my fellow students were Black Republicans.

Spending the summer of 2004 back in Edmonton put these differences into even sharper relief. I started working at a vintage clothing store, Divine Decadence, and made friends with artsy kids that I had more in common with. We'd hit up the strip on Whyte Avenue and drink ourselves silly at the Black Dog, the Strat, and Savoy.

I spent most of that summer dealing with a musical nightmare scenario caused by my mom's new partner. Sebastijan was a Bosnian man in his late thirties whom she met at a jazz club. He loved Black culture. Maybe a little too much. He occasionally spoke with a blaccent. My mom would even give him cornrows, to the chagrin of her children. He was young at heart, even more immature than I was. He used to sit around the house and play all manner of video games when he wasn't working at a metal processing plant.

When I'd come back from Hampton, Sebastijan told me that a virus had somehow infected the family computer. It had to be wiped clean. This was the same desktop that I had been using to work on the beats for my debut album over the previous year.

All of the session files, samples, and instrumentals I'd made during that period of time were gone. I hadn't backed anything up. I didn't even get a chance to record my vocals over any of the beats. It was a colossal setback. I couldn't believe I was going to have to start from scratch.

I spent the rest of the summer remaking what eventually became my debut album. It was a multitiered approach and it took me months. In some cases, I remade entire compositions from the ground up. I collected half-finished beats and ideas that I'd sent to friends over MSN Messenger. I then used these low-quality mp3s as the foundation for new versions of the same songs, sometimes sampling the old files for the new beats.

But this experience inspired me to add entirely new parts to certain songs, such as a new synth melody during the third verse of "30 Seconds," the beat change-up on "Turning on Your Sign," and additional samples on "Holy Smoke" and "Vicarious." Though I initially felt crestfallen about losing everything, being forced to revisit my compositions turned out to be a blessing in disguise. Piecing the beats together in a fragmented process gave the instrumentals a ramshackle, patchwork quality that I liked even more than the originals.

Before I went back to school, I set out to record my vocals at an outside studio so there was no chance of a mishap like a computer crash derailing me again. Uncle Brett had recently introduced me to Nik Kozub, the head of local label Normals Welcome, lead member of the electro band Shout Out Out Out Out, and producer extraordinaire. I was aware of him from hanging around Listen Records; I'd seen him come by to talk shop or drop off tickets for a show. After being invited to Nik's studio to record some verses with Brett for the Magilla Funk Conduit album *Just Dance*, I managed to score some additional studio time for myself. Uncorking what felt like a lifetime of views, stories, and opinions, I went Super Saiyan and recorded the vocals for most of the album in a single one-day session.

These sessions were far different from the ones for my demo. Nik's place was a real studio, for one. It was in the basement of his dad's home, but it was a high-tech operation with all the bells and whistles. His father was the leader of the band Wilfred N and the Grown Men so music also ran in his family. Nik himself was already pretty well known for being the bassist in the band Veal. This wasn't the kind of place where I'd have to record under couch cushions (no offence, Vanid). My vocal performance was much improved as well. I had continued writing and rapping while I was away in Virginia, and the time spent alone in my dorm room gave me the space to refine my lyrical perspective.

Hurly fuckin' burly, it's the dirt merchant, I hurt persons
People and the populace, your scene screams of opulence
Dominance, surely, I'm surly, sick
I'm making ships sink 'cause kids think they're fly in pink like Kirby
And early riser birds on the worm watch
Stop, drop, and roll for any soul who might hold Glocks
They cold-cock the sore hearts to pour drops of life force
They sold pot and show rocks in core spots in strife-torn
Ghetto landscapes, how can you plan fates
Around the dope man's hopes and his personal mandates?

These tracks had a socially conscious edge that my first songs didn't. My thoughts were expressed more clearly. My technique was sharper, and for the first time, I had someone engineering the sessions who actually suggested that I attempt my verses more than once. Rhyming over my own beats was invigorating. I was finally rapping with confidence and some serious attitude. I came away ecstatic about what we had worked on, though not knowing what exactly I would do with it.

Returning to Hampton that fall did nothing to dissuade my instinct to leave school. My journalism classes seemed geared towards people who wanted to be TV newscasters. I wanted to write about music and there was nothing in the curriculum to encourage that. Perhaps I might've experienced the same challenges at Howard or Morehouse. Maybe things would've gotten better if I'd stayed at Hampton longer. As it was, the whole experience just made me lean into my freakiness even more. I'd leave campus and go for walks alone. On one such trip I happened upon a group of hippies having a noise jam at their house and I joined in, chanting on the mic. They were a bunch of freaks and I felt a kinship with them based on the fact that they were doing something outside mainstream culture.

More than anything, I wanted to focus on making music. I became obsessed with the thought that someone else would make an album exactly like the one I was making and that I had to release what I had worked on as soon as I possibly could. I linked up with DJ Nato after the semester ended and recorded "Black Hand," "Sharks," "Oliver Square," and "Julie Will Jump the Broom" at his home studio.

It was 2005. I dropped out of university and went back to Edmonton. I was sleeping on my mom's couch at her apartment downtown. This very easily could've been the end of my story right here. I knew that the music I was making was interesting and unique, but I didn't have any indication that I was on the right path. My mom gave me an ultimatum: I had a year to try to make it work with music, but if there was no progress by then, I'd have to go back to school. A few days after I had returned home from Hampton, Uncle Brett called and asked me if I would open for his band at the Sidetrack Café.

Performance has always been a family hallmark. One of the first Christmas gifts I can remember getting from my parents was a Fisher-Price microphone. One of my earliest childhood memories is of standing in the middle of my grandparents' living room, my family sitting around me in a circle. Someone put on a James Brown song and I spontaneously performed a wildly frenetic dance as my family clapped and laughed. I started crying because I thought they were all laughing at me and only stopped after Grandma gave me some grape Life Savers.

On most holidays, we'd crowd into the basement at Grandma's place or my cousins' house in St. Albert and take turns singing songs on Auntie Monica's karaoke machine. Her machine used cassettes and we had to read lyrics from the booklets that came with the tapes. Now she has access to every song ever made through YouTube and we read lyrics off our iPhones. Probably the first time I ever rapped was when I successfully attempted a hearty uncensored rendition of Snoop Dogg's "Gin & Juice" at the age of eight. I quickly developed a repertoire of signature songs that I still sing to this day, none more significant than my take on Frank Sinatra's eternal version of "New York, New York."

We all have our go-to tracks. My sister Gena does a crowd-pleasing version of "Real Love" by Mary J. Blige while my mom enjoys singing a jaunty, old-fashioned lounge version of Amy Winehouse's "You Know I'm No Good." My family performs karaoke like it's a truly creative endeavour. The point is never to merely do justice to the original recording. It's about taking the song to a different place, adding a bit of yourself in there, transcribing someone else's song with your own handwriting in a bolder typeface. It isn't just a fun family activity either: romantic partners and new additions to the family are expected to take part. A lack of participation is frowned upon. Beyond the typical karaoke antics you might expect, we also engage in a contest-within-the-contest that we call the Competition.

A tune is selected, and one by one, we take turns performing it. Typically, the song in question is "And I Am Telling You I'm Not Going" from the Broadway musical *Dreamgirls*. The recorded versions of this song are plenty bombastic, filled with gospel histrionics from Jennifer Holliday and Jennifer Hudson, but we attempt to raise the stakes even higher. Rolling around on the ground, running around the room, jumping from couch to couch, crawling over each other, howling as loudly and for as long as possible: anything goes when it comes to the Competition. Unlike most other competitions, there isn't a prize or a conventional winner. We just try to outdo the person who came before us. In a way, we all win just by competing. It's my spontaneous James Brown dance routine updated for an older age bracket. As a family, we liked to stretch the boundaries of what "singing a song" can mean for our own entertainment.

It was only fitting that my inaugural public performance would take place alongside someone in my family. I played my first ever

Cadence Weapon show as the opening act for Magilla Funk Conduit. I still have video of the performance. Rocking a bald fade and sporting a dark grey graffiti T-shirt with a multicolour striped short-sleeve button up on *underneath* (what?) as well as a black bandana tied around my right forearm (huh?), I ran through most of the songs I'd recorded at Nik's studio the summer before, with Uncle Brett beside me as my hype man. The crowd was sparse—new friends from the vintage store where I worked, Lisa, my family—but it felt like I had just rocked the Apollo Theater. Cadence Weapon wasn't just this secret world that I talked about sometimes: it was real.

◆

No longer just a depository for bootleg Nintendo games, the internet had become exponentially faster in just a few short years and had birthed sites like SoundClick and MySpace that could host music and easily connect you with fans and other musicians. This was also the music blog era. Everyone had a blog, including me. I started mine, *Razorblade Runner*, back in university. I would upload my favourite rap songs of the moment and write about them.

It developed a bit of a following; for a while, I was much more well known for the blog than I was for my music. Back then, some of the top mp3 blogs were just as influential as the biggest Spotify playlists are today. Labels would inundate blogs with music, hoping to get coveted placement on some random person's homepage. It was a brief period of industry disruption where individuals had genuine leverage in determining what music would become popular on a worldwide scale.

One such site, *Fluxblog*, was run by a guy named Matthew Perpetua. If you take a look at his site today, one of the first things you will see is his proud claim of *Fluxblog* being "the very first mp3 blog," started way back in 2002. While primarily focusing on weirder stuff on the electro pop spectrum, he occasionally posted rap and other genres that piqued his interest. I was blog friends with a few people like him and we'd exchange music we liked. In early 2005, I emailed Matthew and asked him if he might be interested in posting a song I'd made called "Oliver Square."

Years of listening to rap anthems about every corner of New York and Los Angeles left me longing for a similar song about my hometown that my friends could relate to. It was a no-brainer that I should make a song about Edmonton. But what aspects of the city would I rap about? There wasn't much in the way of civic pride when it came to our town. It was a country music outpost on a mainstream level and home to a few decent hardcore bands on the underground side. Certainly nothing in the rap world. Edmonton is most famous for having a really large mall and being home to Wayne Gretzky's Oilers dynasty. In many ways, it's Canada's answer to Denver: a nondescript, frigid capital city in a flyover province.

But to me, it was a glittering metropolis with a seedy underbelly that was ripe for rapping about: drunks trying to break into your car while you're still on the road, users smoking drugs out of pop cans at the West Edmonton Mall bus station, shady cab drivers who might break your arm. I mined my limited nightlife experiences, highlighted by a raging house party I threw while my mom was on vacation in China that devolved into an all-out brawl.

Edmonton can be a rough town. Lord knows why I ever went to any house parties in the first place. They would inevitably get busted up. Gangs would target the parties and steal video game consoles and DVD players. More than once, I ran out of a house screaming and covering my eyes because someone sprayed bear mace inside. I even witnessed a machete fight on the front lawn of a picturesque suburban home. The juxtaposition of a prairie city that was outwardly wholesome but carried a sinister under-current was and still is intriguing to me.

The *Fluxblog* post dropped on January 24, 2005, and the response was instantaneous and positive. I was suddenly inundated with label interest for my weird little song about Edmonton. It even got me commissioned by Island U.K. to remix a Lady Sovereign track! She was on *Run the Road*! A real U.K. grime artist! It was my first significant rap money, and as a sign of the times, I wasted much of it on a bottle of Alizé, a Bearbrick, and a pair of Nudie Jeans.

"Oliver Square" started picking up radio play in town, getting requested on the Bounce 91.7 FM. People saw themselves in it. This song shouting out the strip mall that housed the McDonald's I once worked at was actually resonating with people! It was a raw, unvarnished look at the city and it came from a place of truth. All of this showed that there was interest in the sound that I was cultivating. In March, a blog friend named Aaron Newell sent "Oliver Square" to an indie label based in Toronto called Upper Class Recordings.

The label was founded by two former major label employees who branched off to start their own company together. There was a business manager who kept the money side of things organized and a music manager who I dealt with more frequently. I was primarily interested in signing a record deal because I needed to pay five hundred dollars in studio expenses to get the files for my album. The label seemed cool and was mostly known for albums by indie rock groups. I really vibed with the music manager, a fellow music nerd and anglophile. He was a musician as well.

We hadn't signed anything, but they sent me a cheque to get the album mastered and started doing work on my behalf. They got some T-shirts made, made sampler CDs to pass out at SXSW, and started applying for grants for me. I wanted to capitalize on the momentum I was building so I cobbled together a few bootlegs and remixes, a couple loose tracks from the album sessions, some instrumental suites, freestyles, and other odds and ends I'd made over the past year and released it as a mixtape called *Cadence Weapon Is the Black Hand*.

By this point, my production was becoming much more robust and structurally complex. Remixing "Oh" by Ciara and Ludacris, I prioritized the acapella and hollowed out the track by removing the original's poppy lead melody and replacing it with an evil-sounding square synth that sounded like a buzz saw. The chorus arrives and there's a sound that resembles a robot being tasered at the beginning of every bar, and the square synth envelopes the entire track, like lava tumbling down the side of a volcano. The first half of the second verse is dominated by a dizzy-sounding, off-key synth line with heavy glide on it. And then for Ludacris's verse, I recast him as a futuristic techno preacher by surrounding him with interlocking hypnotic electric organ lines. It's certainly indebted to U.K. grime, but there was something obtuse and bugged out about my approach that made it sound unique.

The mixtape got reviewed by *Pitchfork* in March 2005 and received a decent score of 7.8. I started getting emails from people around the world asking to buy it and quickly had a relatively busy mail-order business going selling mixtapes. In typically Canadian fashion, this American attention led to the first press I ever received in my own country: a May 2005 *Edmonton Journal* feature by Sandra Sperounes entitled "Weirdness Is His Weapon" in which I utter the words "I'm very blog-centric."

Things progressed quickly with Upper Class. They were a small operation but they had major label distribution and key industry connections in Toronto through their experience working at larger labels. They flew me out to Toronto in September to meet them, hang out for a couple weeks, and perform at their label showcase at the Gladstone Hotel. Despite not having signed a contract with me yet, they soon started producing CDs of my debut album. It came out in stores on December 6, just two months before my twentieth birthday.

I decided to call the album *Breaking Kayfabe*, a term I'd learned as a fan of professional wrestling. It meant to break character, to cut through the facade of how you presented yourself to the audience. If you were a heel and you decided to hug the good guy in the ring, you were breaking kayfabe. Rap reminded me a lot of wrestling. On the album cover was a drawing by local artist Ashley Andel based on a photo of me making the snarling face I would make when I made a particularly nasty beat. It was unadulterated and raw, my way of showing that I would never pretend to be someone I wasn't with my music. I'd come a long way from rapping about skydiving with a mai tai.

The album received rapturous reviews in *Eye Weekly*, NOW *Magazine*, *Chart Attack*, and many other publications. The *Globe and Mail*'s Robert Everett-Green gave it four stars and said it was "full of brittle beats that rattle and buzz like the one part of the societal machine that signals the collapse of the whole." I was covered on MuchMusic's *The New Music*. *Pitchfork* raved that *Breaking Kayfabe* "revels in clashing the two worlds of hip-hop together, the self-awareness of Rollie's underground-leaning lyrics spilling over gargantuan synth riffs and decidedly non-boom bappy beats." Fame wasn't one of the reasons I started rapping, but all of a sudden, I was being recognized. After years of stumbling through the process of finding myself as an artist, I was popping like a motherfucker.

I became a rapper in a gradual, unplanned way and I feel like I'm better off for it. Despite the increased access to tools for creation and distribution that artists have today, a story like mine feels somehow more unlikely than it did back then. Now, rappers arrive fully formed, media trained, manicured, and developed by controlling interests before they've even posted a song online. They announce themselves in incongruently big budget videos with major labels lurking behind the scenes to maintain the crucial illusion of independence.

All my floundering around, the uncertainty of floating in the weird corners of the internet, and my local scene are what helped me to create a sound that was truly individual and has given me longevity. And one of the great things about discovering a new artist early on is that you get to see them grow and change and try new things and make mistakes and hopefully come into their own. It makes me sad to think that there's less room for that kind of spontaneous growth nowadays.

A few days after my album came out, I was interviewed for a *Maclean's* article about how advances in technology were democratizing media production. The writer played up the atypical way in which I created my music: "But between touring, he still works out of his bedroom. It's the revenge of the amateur . . . Through the portal of the home studio, the bedroom is a mouse-click away from the Big Time." In the accompanying photo, I'm holding a first-generation iPod with some ragged Sony studio monitor headphones around my neck.

Portrait of a bedroom rapper. This wasn't the last time that my music would be framed in this way. It felt like a misnomer, a form of disrespect. I'd recorded my album in a real studio! The article suggested that there was a homemade, unprofessional quality to what I was doing. But looking back, it's not something that I'm ashamed of. It's true: all of this started in my bedroom, that claustrophobic, sweltering attic where I redirected the trajectory of my entire life. I was a Black kid growing up in the most unlikely place for rap on the planet. I see it as a badge of honour now.

2

REMAIN ANONYMOUS

To paraphrase the title of a classic rap covers compilation from 1997, In The Beginning, There Was Rap. In the late '70s, community centre parties in the Bronx featured DJs alongside masters of ceremonies who would rhythmically talk over the music. They would shout out their neighbourhoods, their friends, their clothes, and whatever might be happening at that particular moment. This was anticipated and directly inspired by Jamaican reggae sound system culture, which goes back as far as the 1940s. It was as if these emcees were the narrators of inner-city life. They quickly went from a functional aspect of a party to a primary attraction themselves.

In the early '80s, these DJs started getting signed as recording acts and in order to properly translate the vibe of their events, they'd bring along their emcees. Two such groups were Afrika Bambaataa and the Soulsonic Force and Grandmaster Flash and the Furious

Five. In 1982, both crews released singles that represent the two stylistic poles of rap that have continued to compete and contrast ever since. You can hear the entire future of hip-hop in these two songs. A former gang member, Afrika Bambaataa inextricably connected his music career to his efforts to reform a group of street gangs into a spiritual movement he called the Zulu Nation. One of the first hip-hop songs to use the Roland TR-808 drum machine, which became a sonic standard for the genre, Bambaataa's "Planet Rock" is a cosmic electro rap jam with beats, sonic elements, and computerized voices inspired directly by electronic pioneers Kraftwerk. It was a revolutionary hybrid of sounds that influenced several future genres like freestyle, Miami bass, ghetto-tech, and Detroit techno.

But for a song that's a prime example of an early mainstream triumph for rap music, the rapping isn't really the point here. What you hear are several emcees crowding the recording booth, shouting vaguely positive, pseudo-spiritual aphorisms ("Love, life, live!" "Let your soul lead the way!" "It's time to chase your dreams!"), saying their own names or commanding you to dance in a way that anticipates the "jack your body!" directives of house music. The most memorable lyric from the song is when Pow Wow says, "Zih-zih-zih-zih, zih-zih-zih, zih-zih-zih-zih-zih-zih-zih!" You can draw a direct line from that moment all the way to Future's meme-baiting "la-di-da-di-da" verse on 2018's "King's Dead." Sometimes rap is just about what sounds and feels good, synthesizing the essence of a good party into a few well-placed nonsensical words.

The other side of the coin here is by comparison a far bleaker affair. "The Message" by Grandmaster Flash and the Furious Five was the first mainstream conscious rap single, a narrative about the pressures of urban life that matched a journalist's attention to detail with a novelist's figurative verve to solidify rap's position as a true art form and help to dispel the notion that this music was just another fad. A sludgy blast of boogie funk with a spoken word breakdown about police harassment that echoed Stevie Wonder's "Living for the City," "The Message" was certainly danceable. But if you stopped to listen to the words, you might realize that you were hearing a voice that had never been heard on the radio before, the Black kid on the street speaking about a corrupt world that was right in front of you but commonly ignored. It was an update on the street corner soliloquies of Gil Scott-Heron and the Last Poets writ large. The song features a procession of grim characters: "Smugglers, scramblers, burglars, gamblers, pickpocket peddlers, even panhandlers," a "zircon princess" who is forced to become a sex worker, "junkies in the alley with a baseball bat."

The socially conscious approach of rappers Melle Mel and Duke Bootee was also commercially viable: "The Message" was the fifth rap single in history to go gold and it made it to sixty-two on the *Billboard* Hot 100. Several decades later, many of the lyrics are still incisive and relevant to city life in America. Lyrics like "It's like a jungle sometimes, it makes me wonder how I keep from going under" are the foundational clay from which many other rap songs have been made. The attitude and spirit of "The Message" can be heard in the impossibly dense conceptual narratives of contemporary rap artists like Kendrick Lamar.

Through these two songs, you can see the dual powers of rap: the ability to move bodies and the ability to move minds. In Jeff Chang's book *Can't Stop Won't Stop*, he describes the "aesthetic tensions" of hip-hop culture as being a struggle between "representation versus abstraction, roots-rocking versus avant-vanguardism." He points out that "the same dialectics had played out between 'The Message' and 'Planet Rock,' and would continue with Chuck D and Rakim, Marley Marl and the Bomb Squad, N.W.A. and De La Soul." Over the years, rap has proven to be a good tool for both of these objectives, sometimes simultaneously. But more often than not, these seemingly contradictory goals have splintered the genre into divergent directions, the helixes of hip-hop's DNA becoming further mutated by regional, economic, and sociopolitical differences.

The mid- to late '80s gave birth to a glut of imitators of both of these groups. But there were also prominent evolutions to their ideological stances over the decade. Gangsta rap melded street culture and vivid storytelling as artists like Schoolly D, Ice-T, N.W.A., and Too Short talked about social injustice and the state of their (often Californian) communities while never failing to keep the party hype. Their lewd jokes and profanity were inspired by the Redd Foxx, Dolemite, and Blowfly records they had sneakily listened to as kids. The confrontational rapping of Rakim, Big Daddy Kane, and Kool G Rap went on to influence the hardcore rap scene of the '90s. On the other side of the divide, conscious rap gave birth to political rap, which focused on social issues and Afrocentricity and mostly eschewed the overt misogyny and gratuitous violence of gangsta rap. Pioneering groups in this subgenre include Public Enemy, Brand Nubian, Poor Righteous Teachers, and X Clan.

Throughout rap history, you'll find crossover between these two worlds. Ice Cube left N.W.A. to work with the Bomb Squad and Public Enemy. Boogie Down Productions started making more politically and socially conscious music after Scott

La Rock's murder. The seeds for underground rap were sewn in the late '80s as well: 1988's *Critical Beatdown* by Kool Keith's group Ultramagnetic MCs as well as Beastie Boys' *Paul's Boutique* and De La Soul's *3 Feet High and Rising* in 1989 birthed alternative rap.

Depending on who you talk to, the golden age of hip-hop is generally considered to be from the late '80s into the early '90s. This was when rap no longer had to search for its identity or justify its purpose and settled into its signature sample-based sound, forming a canon and concrete rules for future artists to abide by or subvert. It's an era defined by several classic albums, such as Dr. Dre's *The Chronic*, Wu-Tang Clan's *Enter the Wu-Tang (36 Chambers)*, and De La Soul's *Buhloone Mindstate*. Gangsta rap exploded into a worldwide phenomenon with g-funk artists like Dr. Dre, Snoop Dogg, Warren G, and 2Pac in the West and hardcore rappers like Raekwon, the Notorious B.I.G., Mobb Deep, and Jay-Z in the East. Independent labels in the South like Rap-A-Lot Records, Suave House, No Limit, Cash Money, Swishahouse, and Hypnotize Minds were selling thousands of albums in their communities, creating a below-the-radar scene of uncompromisingly thugged-out tracks that didn't stay underground for long.

At the same time, there were also socially conscious groups like A Tribe Called Quest, Jungle Brothers, De La Soul, and Black Sheep that were direct descendants of the Zulu Nation (one of the members of the Jungle Brothers is even called Afrika Baby Bam). They formed a similar conglomerate in New York called the Native Tongues. Collectives like the Dungeon Family were keeping it weird in the South, featuring groups such as Goodie Mob and OutKast. In California, there were major label alternative rappers like Del tha Funkee Homosapien (Ice Cube's cousin and lead rapper from the Hieroglyphics crew), Ras Kass, and Souls of Mischief.

While this generation of emcees were all selling records on mainstream labels with big-budget music videos on MTV, there was another parallel world of rap developing beneath the surface. An open mic night in South Central Los Angeles called the Good Life Café became the incubator for several influential underground rappers such as the Pharcyde, Jurassic 5, and most importantly Freestyle Fellowship.

In a just world, the members of Freestyle Fellowship would be household names. Aceyalone, Myka 9, P.E.A.C.E., Self Jupiter: four emcees who made two overlooked albums in the early '90s that had an outsized impact, stylistically influencing future generations of rappers from both the mainstream and the underground. Part of the larger Project Blowed crew, they were more like a jazz quartet than a rap group. Their voices were their instruments, twisting and warping their words in unpredictable, spontaneous ways as if their verses were trumpet solos.

An improvisational background that encouraged creativity influenced their flows, which seemed to mutate rapidly, sometimes within the span of a single verse. Myka 9 was a huge inspiration to me, famous in the underground for his quick chopping style of rapping (as evidenced on "5 O'Clock Follies" in 1991) later popularized by chart-topping artists like Bone Thugs-n-Harmony and Busta Rhymes. 1993's *Innercity Griots* is their masterpiece; it harnesses the experimental potential of rap without sacrificing tunefulness or playfulness.

On the East Coast, there were the Soulquarians, a bohemian group of rappers, singers, and producers affiliated with the neo-soul movement whose members included Common, the Roots, J Dilla, Erykah Badu, and D'Angelo. The Lyricist Lounge open mic series, which started taking off in 1997 on Manhattan's Lower East Side, helped spawn a series of compilation albums on Rawkus Records, one of the primary independent labels for the underground rap movement of this era. Started in 1995 by Brian Brater and Jarret Myer with financial backing from Rupert Murdoch's son James (quite ironic for a label full of anti-capitalist rappers), Rawkus helped to take alternative rap to the next level. The label released albums by artists who shaped the sound of underground rap, such as Mos Def, Talib Kweli, Pharoahe Monch, and Big L.

Rawkus's *Soundbombing* compilations were showcases for left-of-centre rappers who weren't being marketed by bigger labels. Sometimes these rappers weren't underground by choice: major labels didn't know how to promote them. That was the case with Pharoahe Monch. His group, Organized Konfusion, had been signed to Priority earlier in the '90s, and he resurfaced as a solo artist on Rawkus. *Soundbombing II* featured former underground battle rapper Eminem fresh off the release of *The Slim Shady LP* but before he became a household name. It also featured "Patriotism," an excoriating political harangue by Company Flow, the group helmed by acerbic rapper and producer El-P who went on to run the influential underground rap label Definitive Jux and later formed the duo Run the Jewels with Killer Mike.

Much of this was in stark opposition to the mainstream rap of the late '90s. Following the murders of Tupac Shakur and the Notorious B.I.G. in 1996 and 1997 respectively, major labels slowly retreated from the wanton violence of gangsta rap, forcing rappers to tone down the gun talk and shift their focus to aspirational tales of materialism. This ushered in what is often referred to as the Shiny Suit Era, named after the luminescent outfits worn in popular music videos by Puff Daddy and Ma$e. This "jiggy" period of rap used samples in a way that was based on instant gratification and easy recognition, rather than creativity. The Shiny Suit Era's musical ethos was made plain by Puffy's rap on Ma$e's "Feel So Good": "Take hits from the '80s (yeah, yeah!) / But do it sound so crazy? (yeah, yeah!)" These fluffy, glossy retreads of well-worn pop hits made rap more palatable to an anxious white audience who no longer wished to be reminded of the struggle behind other rap songs, something that was becoming harder and harder to ignore.

The horror movie violence, the political conscience, the vulnerability, the weirdness, and the spirit of innovation were all pushed further underground while the party raged on in the mainstream. Calling it conscious rap suggests that mainstream rap is somehow unconscious, which is partly true in that pop rap is often physical music that relies on the body. The other implication is that mainstream rap doesn't stimulate the mind, which isn't always correct. Hip-hop culture seems to oscillate: conscious or gangsta becomes the dominant mode every few years.

One of the main aspects of underground rap is that it defines itself in direct contrast to the mainstream. Lyrics in underground rap are often about the ills of commercial rap, as it was once called. The mainstream functions as a bogeyman for the underground rapper to direct their aggression at. Groups like the Roots defined themselves by how unlike the commercial rappers they were. Their video for "What They Do" lampooned the sexism and conspicuous consumption of the Shiny Suit Era. It drew the ire of Biggie before he died.

Around the turn of the century, the duelling sides of hip-hop became more rigid and hostile towards each other, shifting the battle within hip-hop from regional to ideological lines. Using the D&D alignment chart, most underground rappers would fall firmly under the chaotic good banner: individualist, anti-authority, living by a moral compass of their own design. If you were a headwrap-wearing Rawkus fan, you wouldn't be caught dead listening to a Ruff Ryders album. This attitude primarily appealed to nerdy, self-righteous teenage boys like myself. The separation between conscious and commercial rap was initially a way for labels to market rap to different people. But as the years went on, it felt like a tangible philosophical dividing line.

The underground rap of the '00s took the lyrical intensity, social conscience, and introspection of "The Message" to its logical extreme. Words became the primary focus while danceability and entertainment were only distractions. Underground rap was sometimes criticized for being a bunch of guys rapping about rapping. This was not rap that translated well to a live audience. You would never play it at a party. And if you did, you'd be met with blank stares or harried requests for you to play something, *anything* else. What is the point of rap music that doesn't rock a party? Underground rap probably had more in common with progressive rock than the funk and disco that had birthed rap in the first place: a somewhat pretentious subgenre that operated with a racially tinged sense of intellectual and moral superiority.

◆

For my sixteenth birthday, my mom took me to Listen Records in Edmonton and bought me two CDs of my choosing. The albums I chose were ones I'd read about on Hip Hop Infinity and had only heard tinny RealAudio Player snippets of online: Cannibal Ox's *The Cold Vein* and Buck 65's *Vertex*. Both of these albums are emblematic of underground rap at its best and of the two contrasting styles that define it. Hailing from a small Nova Scotian town called Mount Uniacke, Buck 65 became a major inspiration to me. We later toured Canada together and collaborated on my song "(You Can't Stop) The Machine" and his track "Benz."

To the average Canadian, he might be better known as Rich Terfry, host of CBC Radio One's *Drive* show. If you are familiar with his music from when he was briefly in the mainstream, it would likely be from his offbeat 2003 single "Wicked and Weird" and the country-rap Canucklehead vibes of the high-rotation music video. But by that point, he'd already been putting out records since the early '90s. *Vertex* originally came out in 1997 on a smaller than small label called Metaforensics, but the album was given wider exposure when it was rereleased in 2002 by Warner. Snagging a copy of the original release with the gas mask on the cover, I was blown away that such foreign-sounding, impossibly alien rap music came from Canada.

This was rap as I had never quite heard it before. It was true to the spirit of hip-hop's roots, founded in a virtuosity forged through Buck's deep study of the original masters as a radio DJ on CKDU. But it also subverted expectations and did something truly unique. It was art rap yet decidedly unpretentious. He seemed to be equally influenced by the abstract rhymes of Kool Keith and the bizarro films of David Lynch. He's probably the first person to apply Dadaist ideas to rap music.

It was as if he had intently memorized the rulebook of hip-hop, only to rip up the entire thing in front of us all. And amazingly, Buck did everything on his records: the raps, the beats, and the scratches. At the time of *Vertex*, he had not yet adopted the grizzled Tom Waits voice of his later albums and was still rapping with a squeaky-sounding hoser accent. He wasn't trying to "sound like a rapper" by faking a New York accent like so many Canadian emcees before him. Buck showed that you could have interesting rap lyrics without being confrontational. There was a thread of vulnerability throughout this album that wasn't common in rap at the time. The songs on *Vertex* were less straightforward and more conceptual than contemporary mainstream hip-hop. He made unlikely declarations and had the oddest cultural references:

> *I love little babies and I cry at award shows*
> *It's nice to hear sad songs played on the piano*
> *I'm a fan of the fine arts and John Galliano*

Songs on the album come and go seemingly at random. There is a three-song suite about a baseball game. He wrote a track from the perspective of a misunderstood centaur. He rapped about hunting for samples and hiding records from rival producers and DJs, but he'd follow it up with atonal noise, snatches of beat poetry and obscure films, sandwiched between twisted answering machine messages. He even does a creepy cover of Roxy Music's "In Every Dream Home a Heartache" featuring a breakbeat, creaking doors, and a squealing saxophone in the background. *Vertex* was the first time I heard someone speaking my creative language who came from a similar background. Buck 65 pointed the way towards a world of possibility for me.

My response to Cannibal Ox's *The Cold Vein* was completely different. I believe that listening to great music can inspire only one of two responses in a musician: it either makes you want to make something yourself or it's so good that it makes you want to quit. For me, *The Cold Vein* was the latter. I had no illusions that I could possibly make an album like this. Discovering Cannibal Ox was like hearing Wu-Tang Clan for the first time all over again. Hailing from Harlem, they were gritty and streetwise but poignant and poetic in a way that felt both contemporary and timeless.

The two emcees were a perfect match for each other. Vordul Mega rapped in long continuous bursts of unflinchingly potent imagery, weaving a tapestry of Black poverty and urban disillusion that felt as rich, confounding, and detailed as any Basquiat painting. Vast Aire's rhymes were more immediate and felt like ancient aphorisms that you'd known for your entire life but needed reminding of. He pulled you in and Vordul kept you there.

There's a sense of spontaneity and improvisation to the making of this album that you can still hear in the recordings. Vordul yelling "I don't have an end piece!" when the beat cuts off after finishing his stream of consciousness verse on "Ox Out the Cage" felt like the inverse of Nas claiming not to know how to start "N.Y. State of Mind." One of the album's best moments is on the absolutely ravenous and harrowing "Raspberry Fields" where Vast Aire opens the track up with "If first you don't succeed, try, try again," proceeds to mess up by repeating a word, and then starts his verse over again, thus exemplifying the proverb.

Expertly produced by El-P, *The Cold Vein* is dense, electronic, and positively subarctic, sounding like the cybernetic bridge between rap's golden age and an uncompromising dystopian future. At times, it feels like he's reimagining hip-hop as industrial music, his beats brimming with anarchic weirdness as he flips unplaceable sounds into a postmodern pastiche of sample sorcery that could make RZA turn green with envy. This vision of prog rap is reflected in his choices of unlikely source material: high-minded songsmiths like Brian Eno and Philip Glass whose relatively unfunky compositions had largely been ignored by other hip-hop producers during the '90s.

Most of all, you must not ignore the coldness! This album *sounds* the way being cold feels. It opens with a snatch of conversation from the movie *The Big Chill*. Playing this record helps ease me into the mood of winter after the first snowfall. Listening to this album feels like floating across the galaxy with a rip in your spacesuit. The atmosphere is stifling and suffocating, evoking Han Solo frozen in carbonite, gripped with a hopeless ambience. It almost singlehandedly led underground rap into its most fruitful period, as one of the first full-length albums on Definitive Jux.

After I discovered these records, my obsession with underground rap grew exponentially during the early half of the '00s. I listened to every new release from the notable labels of the time and discovered a broad spectrum of styles and perspectives: Rhymesayers, Quannum Projects, Anticon, Old Maid, Def Jux, Stones Throw. I mail-ordered CDs from online retailers like Sandbox Automatic, Hip Hop Infinity, Turntable Lab, Fat Beats, and UndergroundHipHop.com. It felt like every day I was discovering a new artist who blew my mind: politically minded emcees like Sage Francis and Brother Ali; rapper/producers like Madlib, MF DOOM, and Count Bass D; oddballs like Antipop Consortium and Andre Nickatina. So much of the music felt like art for art's sake, wilfully obtuse and indifferent to whether they would make the charts or not.

I listened to all the significant underground releases from the late '90s. It felt like I'd uncovered a hidden world where people rapped about whatever they wanted to. It was liberating. I was most surprised to realize that some of the underground rap featured online was coming out of Canada. Noah 23 and Epic who were prominently featured on Hip Hop Infinity turned out to be from north of the border. This led me to search for my local rap community.

Unbeknownst to teenaged me, there were several active rap crews with different sounds and styles around the city. Dangerous Goods Collective were true school purists, featuring Touch, a gruff-voiced rapper who is one of the pioneers of Edmonton rap. Tuffhouse and Politic Live were Black groups with a sound similar to what was happening in Toronto. There were a few notable Indigenous rappers like War Party and Advokit, who was a member of the group Non Status. Five years after *Breaking Kayfabe* came out, the label Old Ugly started releasing idiosyncratic nerdy rap that seemed to be directly influenced by me.

But the crew I was most familiar with when I was first starting out was the Low Budget Affiliates, a rowdy group of hard-partying hosers who made dark, brooding underground rap that was heavily inspired by the battle scene and horrorcore. I would say rappers like Swollen Members, Cage, Non Phixion, and Necro were probably the most influential artists to the Edmonton underground rap scene in the '00s. Ill Bill's label Uncle Howie even signed a rapper from the city named E-Dot. Back in 2001, only 1.5 percent of Edmonton's population was Black. It wasn't a very diverse place. It seemed like all these white people who liked hip-hop were inspired by these rappers' post-Eminem cartoon violence and juvenile crudeness.

Non Phixion were like a twisted update on Beastie Boys, three deranged conspiracy theorists from Brooklyn who mixed pseudo-political jibber jabber with virulent homophobia, casual sexism, and action-movie violence on paranoid screeds like "The C.I.A. Is Trying to Kill Me" and "Black Helicopters." They were given instant credibility through their association with white rap pioneer MC Serch and the unbelievable production lineup of New York mainstream luminaries on their debut album *The Future Is Now*: DJ Premier, Pete Rock, Large Professor, and Juju from the Beatnuts. And the beats by Necro stood out impressively alongside them.

Necro was a good example of a rapper who only could've blown up during the underground rap era. A Jewish Brooklynite with Israeli parents, he built an independent empire off shock rap with his label Psycho+Logical-Records. He merged death metal iconography and content with self-produced beats and made abhorrently violent, misogynistic songs with titles like "Dead Body Disposal," "I Degrade You," and "I Need Drugs." I went to Necro's show in Edmonton. He easily packed the Starlite Room, and if you were to see that same crowd today, you might think you were looking at an alt-right rally.

I never quite fit in with any of the local crews. Certainly none of them ever formally asked me to join, though different members collaborated with me at different points. I was by far the youngest person on the scene and I came in with a different set of influences and a proto-hipster fashion style that was a little bit ahead of the curve for hip-hop at the time. And though I could appreciate some aspects of their music, I could never fully commit to the down-and-dirty hyper-offensive style that was popular back then. I once entered a rap battle at the Butterdome that doubled as a car show. Tucked in the corner of the large marigold arena, beyond the candy painted speedsters, was a stage where we got to send our finest punchlines at each other in front of a small crowd. I ended up in second place because I refused to match my opponent's homophobic disses.

As outrageous as some of the rapping was at the time, there always seemed to be a streak of conservatism lurking beneath the outwardly radical image of the battle scene. That highlights one of the main contradictions of underground rap. The artists "deserve to be more popular" and their lack of success is supposedly because they're too groundbreaking and visionary for a mainstream audience. But more often than not, underground rap is firmly rooted in the past, stubbornly adhering to a retrograde form of hip-hop orthodoxy that's devoted to keeping things the way they once were.

Many of the Canadian underground rappers wanted to Make Hip-Hop Great Again. They were imitating music that was once innovative, similar to the garage rock revivalists in New York and London of that time. If you weren't doing something that was already accepted somewhere in the States, there wasn't really context for you in my country. You could be weird or you could be Black, but you couldn't be both and be successful rapping in Canada.

One person that I did vibe with was a local eccentric who called himself DJ Weez-L. Born Erik Stendie, Weez-L was a farm boy from near Edson, Alberta. His family didn't really have an address: it just said "Rural Road" next to their mailbox in the middle of nowhere. He somehow managed to procure some turntables and spent all of his free moments mastering the art of scratching. He was completely obsessed with Kool Keith and even booked him to perform in Edmonton with his janky promotions company, Superstars of Rap.

The first time I saw him perform was during a local qualifying round for the Pioneer DMC World DJ Championships at the Sidetrack Café. He put on an impressively dramatic six-minute set where he rapidly rifled through different scratch routines, played a Jimi Hendrix record, picked it up, and then set it on fire. I went up to him afterwards and asked him to be my DJ. He told me he would think about it.

This made sense because I was just some random teenager walking up to him and he was already *DJ Weez-L*. Erik was one of my major gateways into the Edmonton rap scene. He was an established figure in the underground, known for his eccentricity and unbelievable DJ skills, and working with him gave me instant credibility. He had a big bushy beard and a wild mane that he would occasionally cover with a coon skin cap, making him resemble an old-timey fur trader. He looked insanely Albertan and would become the Flavor Flav to my Chuck D for years to come.

Before I recorded my first album, I used to hang out at this hip-hop clothing and graffiti paint store called the Layup that was run by a rapper from Victoria named Ben.e Elim. He had a tightly trimmed goatee that made him look like a white Fat Joe. Years later, he became infamous as one of an endless cavalcade of openers for Nas at his Edmonton show. The impatient audience started throwing chairs on stage from the balcony at some hapless support act in an embarrassingly performative imitation of what they thought a rap crowd was supposed to act like. For many years, Edmonton rap shows were known either for pitiful attendance or mortifying behaviour, like the time some white kid touched Questlove's afro during a post-show autograph-signing session the night that I opened for him at Starlite Room.

The Layup briefly served as a creative hub for the Edmonton rap scene. Weez-L worked there for a bit and I would hang out after hours and record random demos there with Benny. One night there was a Peanuts & Corn show happening at New City Likwid Lounge, an early incarnation of the freaky downtown music venue that booked bands like the Vibrators. An underground rap label based in Winnipeg, I had initially read about Peanuts & Corn on Hip Hop Infinity and was curious to check them out in person. Benny said he would help sneak me in, as I was still maddeningly underage. Thanks to my oversized military green LRG winter jacket and my most imposing screwface, the door person let me in.

The main artists on the bill were John Smith and Pip Skid who had just released the collaborative album *All Beef, No Chicken* under the name Hip-Hop Wieners. Pip was lanky and somewhat feral-looking, rocking an amazing Scarface (the rapper, not the movie) hockey jersey. John was shorter with a newsboy cap on, his face like an old school gangster's; think Al Capone. They furiously rocked the house but also exuded a light-spirited and goofy attitude at times. There was some Beastie Boys energy to their performance: they had loose, spontaneous interplay together that made them seem like literal brothers. It wasn't a massive turnout and it seemed like everyone there was a local rapper. After they performed, it turned into an open mic night and I got to jump on stage and kick some verses. It felt like my formal initiation into the local scene.

The mysterious Low Budget Affiliates rapper Conspiracy also jumped on the mic that night. He looked like a mystical Rastafarian cartoon character with massive dreads and a huge nose ring. He rapped excruciatingly slowly with his eyes darting around the room aimlessly, and everything that came out of his mouth was completely random and nonsensical. In retrospect, he was a bit like Lil B without marketing or Viper without music videos. In an interview with *UGSMAG*, he once claimed to have done "like two grams of crystal meth" and subsequently "wrote three albums over a seven-day period, perfectly written, sequenced, edited, everything."

Turns out there was an entire constellation of offbeat rap coming from this Manitoba outpost. Peanuts & Corn was started by Rod "mcenroe" Bailey in the ridiculously small town of Brandon before relocating to Winnipeg. Sprouting out of the rap crew Break Bread, P&C included weird-sounding rappers with names like Gumshoe Strut, Yy, Gruf the Druid, and Fermented Reptile. Rod's lush, orchestral beats were the backdrop for nearly every song that was released on the label, making him something like the RZA of the prairies.

The Hip-Hop Wieners album from 2002 blew me away. John Smith and Pip Skid's downtrodden, introspective songs like "Poor Folk," where they rapped about being broke in Canada, spoke to me with a specificity that no rap ever had before: "Thinkin' 'bout Money Mart and their half-assed security / dreamin' 'bout an inside job, it's all absurdity." Later I dug into John Smith's solo albums. 2001's *John Smith's Blunderbus (Or, In Transit)* is a dark, strange narrative exercise where he raps about things no one else would ever consider: his disdain for pretentious urbanites on roller skates ("I'm Rollerblading!") and douchebags with gas-guzzling trucks ("Fucking Gas Prices Are Killing Me!"), his contempt for rude American tourists coming to the great white north to hunt wildlife ("One Sided Trees").

His album *Pinky's Laundromat* from 2004 is probably the masterpiece of the label, a hyper-local concept album on which Smith shouts out Winnipeg street names and details a seedy "Bible Belt Babylon" of grow-ops and drug fronts. John Smith spun intricate character studies about the drug dealers, "the man at the bar you don't know," and neighbourhood misanthropes that no one outside of Canada knew existed but I recognized immediately.

I reviewed Pip Skid's *Funny Farm* for *Pitchfork*, and mcenroe emailed me to say thanks. I mentioned that I rapped as well, sent him a SoundClick link with some of my rough demos on it, and asked him to sign me (a totally normal thing for a respectable journalist to do). He gave me some much-needed constructive criticism on my tracks. He inspired me a lot. We had a lot in common as prairie rapper/producers; we even have the same birthday. He asked me to contribute some verses to his song "Centrifuge." I also ended up dropping a verse on a Peanuts & Corn posse cut, "Eight Bars Each" by Park-Like Setting. Being on the same track as Pip Skid and Birdapres made me feel as if I'd made it onto the prairie version of A Tribe Called Quest's "Scenario." All of this was happening before I'd signed a record deal or was asked to record by any rappers in Edmonton.

mcenroe had me open for him when the *Nothing Is Cool* tour came to Edmonton in 2005. It was a collaborative album with Birdapres, a gentle giant from Vancouver who is still one of my all-time favourite Canadian emcees. He was disarmingly friendly in person, but on the mic, he was positively brutal, sporting a stone-cold multisyllabic flow and a cutting literary mind (I make a guest appearance on the song "Rays and Beams" from his 2011 masterpiece *Catch an L*). The title track from *Nothing Is Cool* might be the high watermark for the entire Peanuts & Corn discography, a withering takedown of the transient nature of coolness over a mesmerizingly filtered sample and rolling drum break.

During the summer of 2005, I was asked to open for Skratch Bastid, John Smith, and Pip Skid for the Saskatoon show promoting their album *Taking Care of Business*. Skratch was fresh off winning the Scribble Jam DJ Battle two years in a row and had built a reputation for himself as a rising underground star. Playing with these three was a big opportunity. A five-hour drive from Edmonton, Saskatoon is a town with a surprisingly rich underground rap scene. Their community was fostered by CFCR radio host and hip-hop obsessive Chaps, as well as labels like Soso's Clothes Horse Records and Factor's Side Road Records.

I was driven there by a rapper named Epic, who was based in Edmonton but originally hailed from Saskatoon. Epic was a local scene legend who had become popular on underground rap sites for his singularly bizarre music and atypical appearance. He was a tall, skinny white man in his early thirties named Erin who wore glasses and had completely grey hair. His 2001 album *8:30 in Newfoundland* featured an underground anthem called "Thought Process" with plaintive Spanish guitar samples and a chorus that went "These are my thoughts . . . yo!"

He looked completely unassuming and later went on to work a government job. He had an awkward, stilted flow (he made Buck 65 sound like Kool G Rap), but he gained some respect on the battle scene for his surprisingly funny one-liners. He later immortalized our trip to Saskatchewan on his 2008 hockey tribute "Ah Hemsky": "I was famous for a second / Went to Saskatoon with Cadence Weapon."

The show with Skratch Bastid, John Smith, and Pip Skid was at the Odeon on July 21, 2005, and it was the first time I ever played outside Edmonton. I was struck by how refined the Winnipeg and Saskatoon rap scenes were. Peanuts & Corn albums were impeccably produced and could easily stand beside what was coming out in the States. They had international distribution. Everything on P&C sounded professional and their business arrangements were so well organized. There was no such infrastructure in Edmonton.

To the outside observer, the prairie rap scene might sound like cultural appropriation. To me, it never felt like they were exploiting the culture. The white rappers did their homework and were reverent of the Black forefathers of the genre. They never tried to act, look, or sound Black. The prairies weren't very diverse back then, but even if they were, these rappers were never popular enough to be taking space from anyone else. Plus, the local scenes were often more diverse than the general population in their provinces at the time.

More than anything, it didn't feel like they were trying to be like anybody but themselves. So much of Canadian rap up to that point was stuck in this stubborn pursuit to try to sound American. Even some of the best Canadian stuff that would hit the mainstream airwaves sounded like it could've come from New York. The Toronto and Vancouver rappers on "Northern Touch" showed me Canadian rap's growth potential, but I actually saw and heard myself in the rap I found in the prairies. You could be from the middle of nowhere, as long as you were dope! It felt like prairie rappers were free of expectations so they were able to absorb rap from everywhere else, synthesize it, and then make something weird of their own out of the wreckage.

It wasn't long before I became disenchanted with the underground rap scene. The American releases were becoming spottier and less consistent. Musically, the sample-based sound felt like it wasn't being pushed into a more innovative space. There was a staid blandness to many of the releases in the second half of the '00s. From 2003 on, I became more and more obsessed with UK grime, a futuristic form of British rap that paired energetic lyricism from artists like Dizzee Rascal and Wiley with groundbreaking alien beats made using cheap computer programs. It was another side of the underground where artists made music that sounded like what I was making in my mom's attic.

Locally, the underground rap scene felt like it was stuck in neutral. The more popular my music got outside of town, the less people in the scene wanted to support what I was doing. I would get angry emails from people dissing me. The scene was painfully male, with just a handful of women, like promoter Melissa L.A. Bishop and visual artist Pearl Rachinsky, in ancillary roles. I often wonder what it was like for Manjito Singh, the sister of local rapper Corvid Lorax. She rapped too and was probably the most supportive fan in all of Edmonton rap, but I wish she was encouraged by the scene to release more of her own music.

On a larger scale, this era of alternative rap fell victim to its own pretensions. The holier-than-thou moralistic attitude that permeated many artists' lyrics was also reflected in how they presented themselves to the audience. Like progressive rock and intelligent dance music before it, underground rap marketed itself as being more intellectually valuable than the mostly Black form of the music that was saturating the airwaves at the time. This is exemplified by whiter-than-white Bay Area label Anticon sardonically titling their debut compilation *Music for the Advancement of Hip Hop*. But the irony is that while you never hear anyone talking about that album or Warp's IDM showcase *Artificial Intelligence* anymore, Chicago house and gangsta rap have managed to stand the test of time.

It's hard to determine how much of an impact this era of underground rap even made. Rap moves quickly; it's been that way since the beginning. What's hot in January might not be popping in March. The pace was slower in the early 2000s than it is today, but from year to year, you could see the mainstream slowly tilting towards more groundbreaking sonic ideas and subject matter. Kanye West hit the scene as a rapper/producer with both a Benz and a backpack, self-consciously merging the commercial and the conscious in 2004 with his debut album, *The College Dropout*. He exploited this dichotomy more and more with each of his releases, reshaping the entire hip-hop landscape in his image by pushing the ever-swinging pendulum back towards the sociopolitical, permanently scuttling the old binary of mainstream versus underground for good.

The underground rap from the '00s didn't sell millions of records. We were happy when they put an Atmosphere video on mtvU. The Canadian stuff likely didn't sell in the tens of thousands.

People in the prairies had to be part of a tiny subculture to even know about it at the time, and the rappers aren't exactly household names in their cities today. The music itself also didn't particularly age well. I put together an underground rap special for my show on ISO Radio a couple years ago and struggled to find songs that were safe to play. Ableism, misogyny, homophobia, painfully pretentious pseudo-intellectual verses—it was like a minefield.

The influence of the underground has grown more apparent in recent years though. You can see the echoes of it in the contemporary hip-hop world. The Roots wear suits every night as the house band for *The Tonight Show Starring Jimmy Fallon*. Madlib went on to produce for Kanye, which felt like a torch-passing ceremony of sorts. El-P hit the tenth spot on the *Billboard* charts in 2020 with the fourth Run the Jewels album, *RTJ4*. Even Necro has had a second life as an actor with parts in two Safdie brothers films, *Heaven Knows What* and *Good Time*.

The underground ethos lives on in artists like Kendrick Lamar; Danny Brown; Noname; Earl Sweatshirt; Tierra Whack; Griselda Records; and Tyler, the Creator but all on a much larger scale. The internet has hopelessly splintered rap beyond tidy categorization, making a moment like the prairie rap movement—a self-sufficient, isolated local niche music scene—a thing of the past. But there are still independent Canadian rappers, like Merkules, who are doing big numbers with the help of YouTube and social media.

In what might've been perceived as an underground rap scene of hardcore rappers if it happened back in the early 2000s, the Toronto drill scene has major labels scoping out Regent Park,

Rexdale, and Jane and Finch in search of the next big viral artist, someone like Lil Berete or NorthSideBenji, who already streams massively and has developed a huge following without the help of any mainstream TV or radio play in Canada. To paraphrase the lyrics of Ras Kass, for those with skills who don't need a record deal: remain anonymous.

3

CRITICAL BEATDOWN

I can still picture it in my mind's eye. Running through the halls of Velma E. Baker, I was the most excited ten-year-old in all of Edmonton. Waving a bent copy of the latest issue of *GamePro* magazine, I exclaimed to no one and everyone at the same time, "They published my letter to the editor!" I had written and mailed a physical letter to this publication enquiring about the identity of one of their writers. They all used aliases like Dan Elektro and Dr. Zombie, which made them seem like comic book characters, and I was writing to say that I had figured out who one of them really was.

Despite the fact that no one cared or understood what I was talk-ing about, it was thrilling for me to see my name in print for the first time in my favourite magazine. As a kid, I was heavily into video games. So much so that I regularly badgered my mom into buying me magazines like *GamePro* and *Electronic Gaming*

Monthly that featured snarky reviews and the most up-to-date news on upcoming systems and titles. Even though they didn't have much in the way of disposable income, my parents somehow managed to get me whatever game or system was coming out for Christmas on any given year.

The conventional wisdom at the time was that video games were a mindless exercise, sapping the life out of a generation of sedentary kids. In actuality, these games became an extension of my creativity. The adventures in games like *Chrono Trigger* and *Final Fantasy III* were beyond anything I could've conjured myself at the time. They also encouraged me to go beyond the source material and imagine worlds of my own. I dreamed of creating my own games one day until I realized how much math would be involved (not my strong suit). But the music in games like *Mega Man IV* and *Donkey Kong Country 2: Diddy's Kong Quest* directly inspired my beats. I couldn't understand why people didn't rap over music like this. I was also interested in the world around the games: how they were made, the hype leading up to them, and which games were good or bad and why.

That's what drew me to the magazines in the first place. It wasn't as easy to reach consensus back then. There was nothing like Rotten Tomatoes or Metacritic. When the internet came along, I was on IGN all the time looking for updates about the highly anticipated Nintendo 64. I'd stay up all night to see the slowly loading first images of *Super Mario 64* coming from the E3 conference in Japan over dial-up, no longer having to wait a month to learn already dated information about the world of gaming. I started my own fledgling GeoCities site called Sharp Gaming with a couple friends. I found a site/message board community hilariously called Nintendorks and eventually ended up writing some Game Boy Color reviews for them.

Not long after getting into video game magazines, I also started collecting music magazines like *The Source*, *XXL*, *VIBE*, *Spin*, and *Rolling Stone*. I'd pick them up at the Mac's convenience store near Mill Woods Town Centre where I used to play *Tekken 2*. *The Source* was considered the hip-hop bible at the time. I'd pore through the Hip-Hop Quotable section to analyze the verse that had been deemed the best of the month. The writers for that publication almost single-handedly created hip-hop's critical canon with their five-mic rating system. Any album that got an elusive five-mic score from these famously tough critics was deemed an instant classic, permanently added to the pantheon of rap. The reviews and interviews I read in these magazines revealed new complexity to the music, adding much needed context to what I was listening to that I couldn't find anywhere else.

When *Almost Famous* came out in theatres in 2000, I was particularly susceptible to its charms. It was a major motion picture about becoming a music journalist that made it look glamorous yet somehow attainable to a fourteen-year-old music nerd like myself. In the film, pint-sized wannabe music writer William Miller is mentored by the legendary rock critic Lester Bangs as played by Philip Seymour Hoffman. His spot-on portrayal of Bangs as an effusive rock crusader with a devil-may-care attitude piqued my interest, so I bought a copy of *Psychotic Reactions and Carburetor Dung*, the 1987 posthumous collection of his essays. It totally blew my mind.

Bangs put so much of himself into his reviews. I'd never read anyone write so conceptually about the experience of physically putting on a record before, never considering such ephemera would even be worth thinking or talking about in the first place. It was the first time that I realized that writing about music could be an art form in and of itself. While he was often painfully self-indulgent, morally repugnant, and willfully contrarian, his work opened up a new galaxy of thinking for me about what it meant to write about music.

Dovetailing with my discovery of underground rap, I became an avid reader of RapReviews.com and Hip Hop Infinity. The former was a no-frills website with all manner of hip-hop reviews on a blank background with no images. Albums were scored based on both music and lyric "vibes" criteria, each on a ten-point scale, culminating in a "total vibes" score. Hip Hop Infinity was one of the only places you could find detailed writing about underground rap albums. It had a message board, and it was also a mail-order store and a record label. The site was run by a mysterious man named Jay Seagraves who was known for his reportedly unscrupulous business practices. He later ran for office in Michigan.

In order to afford the type of expensive, obscure import rap CDs that I read about on Hip Hop Infinity, I landed my dream job at HMV West Edmonton Mall in 2002. After a couple years of working at places like McDonald's, Canadian Tire, and Athlete's World hoping to build up a substantial enough CV to secure a coveted record store job, it finally happened when I was in the twelfth grade.

West Edmonton Mall already figured heavily in my teenage life. Edmonton's most well-known landmark, it was the largest mall in the world until 2004. Featuring an ice-skating rink, an indoor waterpark, Galaxyland theme park, several arcades, a novelty hotel with garishly decorated theme rooms, a mini-golf course, and a shooting range, it also had a couple music venues (Rum Jungle and Red's) and regional replica "neighbourhoods" as well (Chinatown, Bourbon Street, Europa Boulevard). The massive SilverCity movie theatre had a fully functioning animatronic dragon suspended in the air that blew fire every fifteen minutes.

I've always felt that West Edmonton Mall carried a sordid, haunted energy, like a cursed roadside tourist trap that spanned 5.3 million square feet. Three people were killed while riding the Mindbender rollercoaster at the theme park in 1986. Two suicidal people shot themselves at the Wild West Shooting Centre in July 2007, and one of them died. Another man snuck under the barrier and was shot and killed five years later.

Four dolphins were captured and kept in the mall for over a decade, forced to entertain shoppers until three of them died in the early '00s. After years of complaints from animal rights activists, the fourth dolphin, Howard, was removed and surreptitiously flown to Theater of the Sea marine mammal park in the Florida Keys at two in the morning by private jet in 2004. Howard died the following year. The dolphins were replaced by three sea lions. The mall also used to have flamingos, but they were removed after inappropriate feeding caused them to gradually lose their pink colour.

Rumour had it that crust punks secretly lived in the service hallways. By night, the mall was a point of convergence for kids from the city's different schools and neighbourhoods. Galaxyland transformed into an all-ages alcohol-free nightclub once a month under the promotional banner Rock 'n' Ride until a fourteen-year-old girl overdosed on ecstasy and died. The mall has always had this undertone of dark energy, but it was also the same building that housed places I loved, like the Playdium arcade where I'd play *Dance Dance Revolution* with my friend Dan after school.

The HMV in particular was hallowed ground for me. My mom would drive me there on release days to buy albums like *Amnesiac* by Radiohead. The prime benefit of working there was that I could buy CDs at cost. I would regularly spend my entire paycheque on albums. Back then, I used to walk around school with a completely full one-hundred-disc CD wallet, swapping out albums between (and sometimes during) classes. This record store job was the ultimate music education, a paid internship in a vast library of music, an audiovisual cornucopia where art and commerce coexisted in perfect harmony . . . okay, maybe I'm exaggerating a little. Truthfully, it was just a really big record store in a really big mall and I loved working there.

My co-workers were alternative-leaning music nerds of different stripes. It was like *Empire Records* in real life. One guy there left on his last day of work with dozens of CDs taped to his arms and legs underneath his clothes. Our boss was a clean-cut, anally retentive white man named Ian who resembled Boomhauer from *King of the Hill*. I worked in the Dance Room, a cave-like annex tucked on the side of the main floor where they kept all the hip-hop and electronic music.

Only now do I realize what a strange form of musical segregation this was, especially considering rap music was one of the biggest selling mainstream genres at that time. The racial implications of siloing all of the "urban" genres into a literal cave was also lost on my employers. It wasn't a particularly diverse workplace. A supervisor named Dave once mixed me up with the only other

Black employee, Travis, and then frantically assured me that he "wasn't like that." Nonetheless, the Dance Room was a perfect cross-section of my musical interests and I thrived there.

My supervisor was Vanid. He wasn't particularly effective as a superior but his mellow, easy-going nature made it a pretty chill place to work. Plus, after work he would record me rapping sometimes. DJ Weez-L and other people from the local rap scene would come by occasionally to drop off flyers. I'd daydream about releasing my own album, using the label machine to create a plastic divider with CADENCE WEAPON on it to one day put in the rap section.

I worked as much as I possibly could. We'd get in trouble for playing random underground rap albums over the loudspeakers, instead of the corporately mandated CDs that we were supposed to be promoting. I was a human version of Pandora Radio, developing a local reputation for giving customers ridiculously personalized album recommendations. People would see me on the street and be like, "You're the guy from HMV that told me about *A Book of Human Language* by Aceyalone!" We mostly sold a staggering quantity of 2Pac and Insane Clown Posse CDs. Despite their music not being played on the radio or getting spun on MuchMusic, Edmontonians were absolutely down with the clowns.

The nights before release days were the most exciting because we'd get to play whatever new album was coming out over the speakers while cleaning up and setting up the displays for the next day. I remember first listening to Common's *Electric Circus* and Jay-Z's *The Black Album* that way. One of the lasting memories of my time at HMV was the listening booth. This might sound like the weirdest thing ever to the younger people reading this, but there was a time when folks would go to a record store, they'd let you open up a CD, and you'd sit on a stool next to other people at a circular desk wearing headphones while you all tried out albums before you bought them.

This was a rare opportunity at the time. The internet was still pretty slow and filesharing programs like Kazaa and LimeWire were active but didn't have the broadest inventory. Streamed audio was low quality. Album leaks weren't spreading that consistently yet and penalties for pirating music were becoming increasingly harsh. The best way to listen to a new release was still to pop over to the listening booth at your local record shop. I used to spend hours absorbing every new rap album this way. Today's streaming apps are obviously faster, more efficient, and much easier to use. But there's something I miss about the physical act of unwrapping a CD and committing single-minded focus to an album. The process of concentrating and discerning what was worth spending your money on helped me forge a more intimate relationship with the music I bought.

During my gap semester in 2003, I continued working at the record store to save money before going to university. When I wasn't there, I'd be making music at home, playing video games, or hanging out at Listen Records. Owned by a curmudgeonly man named Kris Burwash, Listen was the antithesis of HMV. A small shop that focused on independent electronic, rap, and rock music, it was a community hub for the local indie scene. I lived three blocks away so I used to hang out there nearly every day, fruitlessly trying to convince Kris to hire me, even though he already had a dedicated group of very capable employees.

I used to pester the clerks Drew and Jordan all the time. Drew was nerdy and rail-thin and dressed like Ian Curtis. He looked like a midwestern child from a '50s car advertisement and played drums in a really cool minimalist rock band called the Bummers. Jordan was bright-eyed and trippy with great taste in electronic music. I was a nerdy seventeen-year-old Black kid who rarely bought anything but would loiter around to argue with them about records all day. The first time I heard Dizzee Rascal was at Listen Records. It was where I first met Nik Kozub, who recorded and mixed my first album.

In August, I made a decision on a whim that permanently altered the trajectory of my life. I wrote an album review and sent it into Pitchfork Media. Founded by Ryan Schreiber in 1995, the music site was known for its abstract and acerbic assessments of contemporary albums with a focus on left-of-centre rock music. While I enjoyed reading their detailed, creative reviews of obscure records, I noticed that they had a blind spot when it came to hip-hop. In 2001, a banner year for great rap releases, their year-end album list only featured one rap record, *The Cold Vein* by Cannibal Ox.

The album I reviewed was 2003's *Shadows on the Sun* by Brother Ali, the fierce Minnesota rapper signed to Rhymesayers. I didn't understand why the site hadn't already covered this album, which was a highly anticipated underground rap release produced by Ant from Atmosphere. It had been out for three months with no review! So, I decided to take a crack at it:

A Molotov cocktail of Nas's chipped-toothed storyteller,
Slug's introspective emo-thug, and Common Sense's

*wordplay aficionado, Brother Ali has clearly studied the
album structures of mid-'90s masters. From the urine-
soaked authenticity of his portrayal of inner city Minneapolis
life ("Room with a View") to the staggering detail of a
conflict with his wife-beating neighbor ("Dorian") to a bass
monster spiritual alloy of The Legion's "Jingle Jangle" and
Atmosphere's "Flesh," where he claims to be "a cross between
John Gotti and Mahatma Gandhi" ("Bitchslap"), Ali focuses
his powerful delivery equally on reality-based depth charges
and classic rap braggadocio.*

Pitchfork published my review (an overly laudatory 8.7) and
highlighted it as one of the year's best as part of their year-end
retrospective book *Thesaurus Musicarum, the Pitchfork Year in
Music, 2003* (yes, they once published and sold a book made out
of articles from their website). A quote from the review was featured on a sticker on every copy of *Champion EP*, Brother Ali's
next release. At the age of seventeen, I quickly became *Pitchfork*'s
authority on hip-hop. Back in 2003, the site wasn't yet a household name. But plugged-in music nerds around the world were
familiar with it. This was before anyone talked about "the *Pitchfork*
effect," the term used by journalists to describe the stratospheric
sales boost that a positive *Pitchfork* review could have for previously unknown bands like Arcade Fire and Broken Social Scene.

I was a young Black rapper with a solid grasp of classic and underground hip-hop, which imbued my writing about rap with a level
of credibility that no reviewer there had before me. If you look
at the write-ups for *Pitchfork*'s top fifty singles of 2003, when
some of the other writers wrote about rap, it seemed as if it was
done begrudgingly, like they had been forced to acknowledge the
greatness of a track but wished that they didn't have to. It felt

disrespectful. Some writers wrote about rap music like they were detailing the movements of a newly discovered tribe in *National Geographic*. Mainstream rap and R&B singles were solely treated as guilty pleasures by white critics back then. This was before the poptimism movement took root in critical circles in 2004, where writers eschewed rockist perspectives and attributed more artistic relevance to mainstream pop, rap, and R&B music.

I enjoyed deep listening, living with a new album and taking the time to break down what was special about it. When I was covering a record that was firmly in my lane, like Ghostface's *The Pretty Toney Album* or Aesop Rock's *Bazooka Tooth*, I was proud to have the opportunity to review it. All those years of accumulating music knowledge that seemed to nearly everyone else to be a complete waste of time finally had a useful application. Writing for *Pitchfork* connected me to an international network of fellow music nerds that went far beyond my pals in Edmonton. I felt like I was doing a public service by spreading the gospel of underground rap to a wider audience.

Getting published by a professional website quickly gave me an overinflated sense of critical superiority. I'd tell anyone who would listen that I wrote for *Pitchfork*, whether they knew what that was or not. My conversations at Listen Records changed in tenor, as I approached every musical debate with more swagger and an unearned confidence in the veracity of my opinions. I was competitive with the other writers. I was already a bit of a smart aleck but getting this gig pushed me over into arrogant asshole territory.

I soon gained a reputation for being a tough, vengeful reviewer. Promo CDs started filling my mom's mailbox (getting discs for free was a dream come true) and I wrote reviews like I was on a mission. Great albums inspired me, but mediocre ones filled me with anger. And to make something that truly sucked? That was unforgivable. I would crush bands with harsh reviews and punitive scores, never stopping to consider what impact a negative review from *Pitchfork* might have on their careers. I reviewed albums with the fervour of a crusader converting pagans to Catholicism.

I usually stuck to the conscious side of the hip-hop divide when I chose what to review, and when I covered something more commercial, I didn't pull any punches. My most publicly maligned piece by far was the 3.2 review I wrote for Juelz Santana's *From Me to U*. It occasionally resurfaces on Twitter. People believe that what I wrote was sacrilege. At the time, I was actually a card-carrying Diplomats fan. I even used to rock an XXXL Dipset promo shirt that I picked up for free in Harlem on a trip to New York to visit my dad. But I perceived the Juelz album as a prototypically undercooked solo effort from a member of a strong group. I still agree with my opinion from back then, but my approach leaves a lot to be desired:

> "Dipset (Santana's Town)" is—and this is no exaggeration—
> the worst song of the year. A stuttering abomination, the
> beat by Self sounds like what might happen if "Flight of the
> Bumblebee" got mixed with the theme from Psycho and
> random female utterances. The lyrics don't help, with Santana
> screaming, "The whole bird gang's in here / Like Kurt Cobain
> was here, YEAH YEAH YEAH YEAH!!!," subsequently setting off
> the nonsensical rhyme of "They the paparazzi, they the livest
> posse/ Kamikaze, Nazi, Nazi, copy, papi?" and ending it with
> "I'm a baller baller / You're not at all a baller / That's why
> I squashed your daughter / Left her home, call her, call her."
> The song ends and you just sit. You think. You wonder. The

*song has a place in your heart now. Your arteries close. Your
heart explodes. The song has taken another life. Fin.*

What I didn't understand back then was that rap that was meant
to be hype or for the club shouldn't be assessed with the same
criteria as rap that was meant to be lyrical. I found Juelz's lyrics to
be repetitive, misogynistic, and generic. But if lyrics aren't the
point in his music, did he succeed in generating the vibe that he set
out to create with the song? Clearly he did, because people are still
passionately angry with me about the review decades later and
folks likely still go crazy when the song comes on in the club or on
the radio in New York, whether I like it or not.

There are many things that I'm proud of from my time writing for
Pitchfork though. I was happy that I could bring more American
attention to Canadian rappers like Buck 65 and Pip Skid by covering their albums. My review of Viktor Vaughn's *Vaudeville Villain*
and the collaborative review with Nick Sylvester of *Madvillainy*
helped to solidify MF DOOM's rightful place in the pantheon of
great emcees. I reviewed *The Grey Album* by Danger Mouse,
assisting in the definition of that album's cultural significance.
Most importantly, my writing pushed the editorial compass of
Pitchfork towards hip-hop, a direction that the site has progressively shifted to more and more ever since.

The nadir of my time at *Pitchfork* involved an email interaction
I had with El-P. I had recently reviewed 2004's *Definitive Jux
Presents III*, a compilation album from the preeminent underground
rap label. My 4.0 review was by far the most self-indulgent thing
I've ever written: a concept review (these are never good) in which
I wrote a script that satirized the label's rappers as a bunch of
sex-crazed, drug-addled losers who were purposefully trying to

make bad music, riding high on the success of their earlier work. It was sophomoric and petty, but it accurately represented the feeling of disappointment I had about the direction the label seemed to be going in.

I received an email from El-P telling me that the review hurt a bit but it was also funny. I took this as an invitation to unload a torrent of constructive criticism on the state of Def Jux to him. Maybe I saw it as my Lester Bangs versus Lou Reed moment. Kill your idols and all that. I said that he should sign Breezly Brewin from Juggaknots to the label, and he needed to get Vast Aire to smoke less weed so his music would improve. El-P was not happy about receiving unsolicited career advice from some random eighteen-year-old from Canada. He found a link to my early demos and battle raps where I had listed him as an influence. He made fun of them on a Def Jux message board. When I confronted him about it, he told me I needed to grow up, to only contact him through his publicist, and to never email him directly again. This whole situation was ridiculously unprofessional and I'm still mortified by how I conducted myself. But I'm at least thankful that I made these mistakes when I was young and had a chance to grow and learn from them.

By the summer of 2004, things at *Pitchfork* were becoming less rewarding. I had a quota of reviews I needed to deliver within a given time frame and I was getting saddled with more and more generic, uninspiring promo albums to fill it. I became disillusioned with the expectation that I should pass lasting judgments on albums primarily based on first impressions. I was studying at Hampton by then and had to contend with my job at a professional publication at the same time. I started missing deadlines, burnt out from reviewing an unending stream of dull releases.

There was also the issue of my payment, which seemed to be getting slower and slower. Obviously, this was pre–Condé Nast. I regularly had to beg Ryan for what I was owed after long stretches of waiting. There was no *Pitchfork* union at the time. I had no contract. So my only recourse was to do petty things like naming the email attachments that held my reviews in them stuff like pay_me.doc.

I also started to bristle at Ryan's editing style, which was more and more intrusive. He occasionally added in his own passages, including his own references without consulting me. He added a bunch of stuff about KISS and Hall and Oates to my year-end write-up about OutKast's *Speakerboxxx/The Love Below*. He started changing the scores I assigned to my reviews. I would've appreciated a more collaborative editing process and more communication about the quality of my writing if it was such a serious issue. After he claimed that my writing "lacked clarity" and was "too unclear to edit," I was fired from *Pitchfork* after only eleven months.

I proceeded to have an internet meltdown. I posted about getting fired on both the Hipinion and I Love Music/ILX message boards, including some of the personal email correspondence I had had with Ryan. The Hipinion board was initially the official *Pitchfork* message board (called Pitchfork Media Smackdown originally) but it eventually branched off and became its own independent web community that still frequently criticized the site's reviews. "*Pitchfork* fired me so you guys can stop hating me if you want," I glumly posted. I could dish it out but I couldn't take criticism myself.

Ryan is a true music lover and I was honoured to be part of what he built. But I felt a bit like I was a problem that he needed to get

rid of, *Pitchfork*'s only Black contributor dropped unceremoni-
ously in the middle of a pay dispute. I recorded my song "Sharks"
not long after, where I make a reference to my firing:

> *Used to write for a site but I didn't spark smart*
> *Or write right, who could think it? My first pink slip.*

I got the money that they owed me a few months later. In October
2004, I started writing for a similar website, *Stylus Magazine*, that
was created by Todd Burns. It had a smaller readership but I had
a great rapport with Todd. We later worked together at Red
Bull Music Academy. Around the same time, I tried my hand at
writing for a local publication. Armed with a suddenly renewed
well of irrational confidence, I reached out to *See Magazine*'s
music editor Zoltan Varadi, an effortlessly cool guy who resembled a slightly more vampiric Ric Ocasek.

I dove headfirst into contributing at *See* after dropping out of
university at the beginning of 2005. It was the place where I truly
learned how to write. It was the first time that I got to work with
an editor in person. I got the chance to write my own columns
and features. I felt like I had more creative control than ever
before. I really enjoyed the ecosystem of the paper as well, this
motley crew of strange hipsters writing articles about sex and
rock and art and civil disobedience. It was a side of Edmonton
that I hadn't known existed.

See Magazine was where I first encountered Juliann Wilding.
Originally from British Columbia, she was the coolest person
I'd ever seen. A little older than me, she was a brilliant, self-
assured fashionista who seemed to be skilled in every artistic
discipline she tried. She stuck out like a sore thumb in Edmonton.

Her house parties were epic. After we met, she invited me to take part in a fashion shoot she was doing for *See*, introducing me to a local scene of weirdos and outcasts that I'd never come across before.

See didn't have the same level of prestige as *Pitchfork* but I loved it nonetheless. I'd come by the office to hang out with Juliann and see what promo CDs were lying around. I would bang out hundred-word CD reviews for fifteen dollars a pop. It gave me an opportunity to develop my voice and make mistakes without any danger of upsetting a multinational corporation.

See was one of two fiercely competitive alternative weekly news-papers in Edmonton at the time. After Zoltan left *See*, I moved over to their competitor, *Vue Weekly*, in 2007. I wrote several columns there, including one on TV called He Watch Channel Zero and a music column called Backlash Blues. I loved working with the editor, Eden Munro.

It was hard to tell whether or not anyone in town actually read anything I wrote but it still felt tangible. I saw my role as a local journalist as being an archivist of our city's music history, which had felt fleeting and ephemeral up to that point. I wrote about iconic local moments that might have otherwise been forgotten, like the time that Jeremy Nischuk threw squids at his former band the Wet Secrets during one of their shows. I'd also write tour diaries and review shows that I saw abroad. It allowed me to get my reps up as a writer while I tried to make it as a rapper. I wanted to help turn *Vue* into Edmonton's *Village Voice*.

See Magazine and *Vue Weekly* were bought by B.C. businessman Bob Doull and merged into one paper in 2011. *Vue Weekly* was shuttered in 2018 after being sold to Great West Newspapers. Edmonton went from having two alt weeklies to none in just a few short years.

I probably wouldn't be writing this book if it weren't for my local alt weekly newspapers giving me the opportunity to write. And when it comes to my music career, nearly all of the cover stories that raised my public profile were published by alternative papers: *Vue, See, Montreal Mirror, Eye Weekly,* and *Exclaim!*. Other than *Exclaim!*, those papers have all folded. To get that level of media attention is a pipe dream for emerging artists today, even if they have an expensive PR firm behind them. When I had an album coming out in the '00s, an interview with me might be featured on the front page of the *Globe and Mail*. Now most major Canadian newspapers don't have a dedicated music writer and barely have a culture section. In 2017, it was estimated by Statistics Canada that culture (music, art, film, TV, writing, live performance, libraries) contributed $58.9 billion to Canada's GDP. That's more than utilities ($46 billion); accommodation and food services ($46 billion); agriculture, forestry, fishing, and hunting ($39 billion); or sports ($7.3 billion). But culture is the first thing to go when a publication needs to make cuts. What does this say about how we value music and art in our society?

And what opportunities are left for young BIPOC journalists in Canada who want to write about music? Music journalism is a profession that doesn't pay well at its highest levels and typically requires you to be a hobbyist for quite some time before you ever see remuneration. I was able to do it because I was a teenager who lived at home with his mom, and even then I had to work other jobs at the same time. It's an occupation with a dwindling number of available jobs and a high barrier to entry. Coming from a privileged background can be the difference between making it or not. This fact tends to disproportionately affect BIPOC writers.

Without alt weeklies, there are even fewer potential entry-level opportunities for people to start their careers in the industry. Cities with active alt weeklies, strong culture sections, and local arts reporting—like New York, Los Angeles, and London—are often the places that maintain vibrant arts communities over long periods of time. But in Toronto, despite having the largest number of artists in the country (27,000 people or 17 percent of all Canadian artists) and briefly being home to the hottest rap scene in the world, there's currently only one local alt weekly (*NOW Magazine*, which was bought by Media Central Corporation in 2019) and arts coverage in local papers and on TV is shrinking more and more every day, with stories on real estate often taking their place.

Picking up the local alternative paper was always the first thing I did when I got to a town on tour. They gave you a clear idea of the vibe and flavour of a city. The alt weeklies were the lifeblood of local scenes. The internet certainly accelerated their demise. Message boards like Indecline and Stillepost took their place as digital representations of local Canadian scenes for a short few years before MySpace and Facebook rendered them both obsolete. But the local exposure in the form of a physical publication distributed all over town can't be replaced. These are the places where bands get their first press and their first reviews, where fans get in on the ground level, where writers find their voices. The scene gets to build something together and the local press helps to legitimize what's happening. Posting on a blog or on Reddit isn't quite the same experience.

I returned to music journalism after moving to Toronto in 2015, freelancing for several publications. But I never had the urge to get back into reviewing albums. After years of going through the ringer as a musician, I had no interest in attributing negative value to someone's art. And the whole enterprise felt more and more pointless with the advent of streaming. People didn't need to read what I thought about an album; they could easily hear the music at home and decide for themselves.

When today's music press tries to push an album, it often feels forced and artificial, like an extension of PR spin. Today, consensus is manufactured through publicity teams using fake accounts to post tweets and comments about a new TV show, or labels paying to have their singles play in the background of an influencer's Instagram story. It rarely seems to happen organically anymore. Streaming playlist editors and TikTok stars are today's biggest gate-keepers and arbiters of taste. They dictate what gets heard more than any review or profile that gets written. A weird album spon-taneously taking the world by storm has never felt more unlikely.

Back in the early 2000s, *Pitchfork* was a daily destination for music nerds and a career obsession for the musicians I knew. Now you don't really hear anyone talk about the site unless it's given an album a 10.0 or the year-end lists are out. In 2015, *Pitchfork* was sold to Condé Nast for an undisclosed amount. However much money it was, it wasn't for the value of the website, the reviews, or any of the content. It was the value of the readership (tone-deafly referred to as "millennial males" by Condé Nast's chief digital officer) to advertisers.

But is there still much value in written music criticism anymore? The most influential music critic today isn't a writer: it's YouTuber

Anthony Fantano from the *Needle Drop*. Fans on Twitter debate their top five rappers, dead or alive, and their picks feel more stratified and personal than ever. There are human beings who consider J. Cole to be the greatest living rapper. Others would rather die than listen to him. Some people think Playboi Carti is horrible, while many others think he's the second coming. Does it matter if we can't all agree?

◆

In early 2019, I was tagged on Instagram by someone I didn't recognize called DJ Design. The image was a screenshot of an old review I had written with the following caption:

> *Foreign Legion gets a 2.1 out of ten on Pitchfork in 2004.*
> *I wonder what the point one was for?* 🤢 😆 *This reviewer*
> *guy ended up becoming a rapper himself.*

I felt a tinge of sickness when I read it. I didn't remember writing the review at all. I didn't remember the group or the album. It was just another review to me. It made me think back to all the times when I felt I'd been unfairly judged for my own music. I went back, read what I wrote, and listened to the record, Foreign Legion's *Playtight*, again. It was average, not particularly compelling or groundbreaking but not the absolute worst thing ever. The score I gave was way too low and the review was brutally mean-spirited.

I responded in the comments with a mea culpa:

> *I wish I hadn't gone so hard in my reviews back then. I was*
> *eighteen with a chip on my shoulder and an extremely myopic*

view of what I considered good rap. Anything I wasn't
personally into felt like a direct affront to me. I got way
too personal in how I critiqued your music and I'm sorry for
that. Today I believe music writing should be about amplifying
the music you love, not taking down the things you're not into.
I'd like to apologize to you for being so unnecessarily cruel.

DJ Design accepted my apology and said it helped to give him closure after all these years. But our interaction made me reflect on why I ever wanted to be a critic to begin with. Why did I even think I had good taste in the first place? I grew up with a hip-hop DJ for a father. I learned the canon. Worked at a record store. Taught myself how to rap. Knew more about the culture than anyone in my city or anyone that I talked to online. People often told me that I had good taste. It became part of my personality and I defined myself by it.

Reading *Why You Like It* by Nolan Gasser made me think about how my taste in music has been shaped by my personal background. My taste profile was based on being a young, urban-dwelling, working-class Black man who gravitated towards off-kilter, gritty sounds as a reaction to growing up in a city where rock, pop, and country were the dominant genres. All of this dictated my perspective as a critic. Being hired by *Pitchfork* was a validation and reinforcement of all the assumptions I had about my own taste. I've also come to believe that becoming a critic was partly rooted in a subconscious desire for the social mobility that such a role could potentially provide me. And it wasn't often that someone with my particular cultural background even got the opportunity to become a critic at all, especially in Canada.

When I first started writing about music, it was an extension of my long-time desire to share my unbridled enthusiasm about the songs I loved. I wanted to add another dimension to what people listened to, just like my journalist heroes did for me when I was growing up. But somewhere along the line, hubris got in my way. Becoming an authority about a subject as a teenager who had never held any form of power in society had a corrupting effect on me.

In the philosopher David Hume's 1757 essay "Of the Standard of Taste," he describes the "true standard" for being a good critic as a combination of "strong sense" and "delicate sentiment, improved by practice, perfected by comparison and cleared of all prejudice." I ticked off most of those boxes but I let my personal bias and prejudice get in the way of fairly assessing some albums. I was punishing artists for making imperfect art. I took it personally. And yet my own approach was inconsistent. In some cases, I'd take an assignment deathly serious; for other reviews, I would be carelessly flippant.

For a long time, I felt shame and embarrassment when people discovered my past as a music reviewer. I would talk about my time at *Pitchfork* like another bad job I had as a teenager, like when I worked at the garden centre at Canadian Tire. But I realize now that this feeling was related to how my tenure there ended. I was also concerned that my past as a critic would somehow make my music seem as if it came from a less authentic place. Only now have I grown comfortable imagining another foray into the world of music criticism, one where I can explore the constantly shifting galaxy of hip-hop with curiosity, with compassion, and without malice.

4

THE DONUTMOBILE

After working with me for months to get my album finished, Upper Class Recordings faxed me three contracts on September 30, 2005: one for publishing, one for recording, and one for management. My mom worked at a law firm and had a lawyer there (whose specialty was not music law) look at the contracts. I asked the label to also fax the contracts to Nik Kozub who had recorded the album, but Upper Class was adamant about only my immediate family and my lawyer being allowed to see the agreements.

The management contract gave them "20% of all of the gross proceeds earned by Artist from the exploitation of their recordings, compositions, live engagements, image and sponsorship rights, and any other negotiable rights to Artist that are now known or created hereafter." The publishing contract gave them "50% of the copyright in and to the publisher's share of the publishing in respect of all musical compositions written by the Artist" for anything I released on the label "in perpetuity." The record contract was for one album with four options on it (essentially a five-album deal), making the masters for those albums "the property of UCR in perpetuity." The record and publishing contracts required the label to account to me semi-annually.

Combined together, these contracts essentially amounted to what is now called a 360 deal. A 360 deal is when the label gets a cut of everything you do, instead of just record sales. They were invented to make up for the loss of record sales that resulted from illegal downloading. At the time, the contracts I was given would've been considered industry standard for a major label but a little out of step with what a small indie label would put together.

The label told me they'd spent at least five thousand dollars on my career. They had already pressed and released the album. It didn't feel like I could possibly back out. I didn't want to miss out on what could be my one chance at stardom. Plus, everything they were doing seemed to be working. I was on the cover of *Exclaim!* that February. Connecting with Upper Class helped to put me on the map in Canada.

After a few months of back and forth that didn't amount to significant changes, I signed the deals. The executed contracts were sent by the lawyer my mom worked with to Upper Class on February 24, 2006, almost three months after *Breaking Kayfabe* was released.

Things escalated quickly. I was getting more local opening spots, getting the rare opportunity to perform with mainstream artists whose records I used to stock at HMV, like Questlove. A booking agent from Paquin Entertainment named Steven Himmelfarb offered to work with me after seeing me perform with reckless abandon at Sneaky Dee's for a secret Wavelength show that attracted five attendees. I played as if there were five thousand people there and it paid off. His roster was mostly white indie bands, but he was excited about my music so we ended up working together. I went to Toronto again for Canadian Music Week where I performed at a showcase with Raekwon and played a show at the Silver Dollar that was profiled on CBC Television. I wore a white tee with Mike Jones's phone number on it in gold foil print that night.

I played all around Ontario that March, making my first stops in Kingston, Hamilton, Guelph, and Brantford. I opened for Hot Chip in Montreal and Toronto. My music manager drove Weez-L, now my official DJ, and me around on these dates and we played *Donuts* by J Dilla so much that we called our vehicle the Donutmobile. *Donuts* hit us all like a lightning bolt, a restless pastiche of sounds and references that totally changed the way I thought about music. It was completely unprecedented, the sample generation's answer to *The White Album*. *Donuts* was designed to end the same way that it began, functioning as an endless loop. It was cyclical and so was driving around on wheels and so was life and so was the process of touring that would start in one place and inevitably bring us back there when it had concluded. We felt like the name fit perfectly.

Travelling to new towns felt like when you uncover new sections of an unexplored world map in a role-playing game. I went to Austin, Texas, for SXSW and it was a revolutionary experience for me. It was a music fan's greatest fantasy. Every up-and-coming band you could think of was there, and free drinks were flowing like water from a fire hydrant. All the people who wrote the blogs I read were there in person. I received a free package of guitar strings and some headphones. I had never been happier. I was living the dream.

While at the festival, a photographer who did some work for *The Fader* took some shots of me and told me he was supposed to be photographing Ghostface that day, but the rapper had missed his flight. Later that afternoon, I heard that Jay-Z had put Ghost on a private jet to make sure he didn't miss the festival. Ghost's show was at the same time as mine and I went to his first, making myself a few minutes late for my own ill-attended performance. But the photographer arrived at my venue at the end of my set with a copy of the issue of *The Fader* with Ghost on the cover featuring a personalized autograph from him to me! Unbelievable! The man with the camera seemed a little wobbly. Sounding inebriated, he asked if I wanted to come for dinner with Ghostface. Not totally believing him, I was like, "Hell yeah!" I grew up idolizing Ghost; he was my favourite member of Wu-Tang Clan. His album *Supreme Clientele* was a major influence on me.

I followed the photographer into a nearby P.F. Chang's and lo and behold, seated at a table with several Def Jam execs was the man himself: Ghost Deini, Ironman, Tony Starks. Someone quickly ushered the visibly drunk photographer to the bar away from the label people and I took the only available seat at the table, which placed me directly next to Ghostface Killah. I was wearing a striped polo shirt—free swag from a VICE event I performed at earlier that day—and someone at the table asked me if I was a rep for Original Penguin clothing. I murmured that I was a journalist and tried to keep as low a profile as possible so I wouldn't be ejected from my fortuitous circumstances.

Ghostface was promoting *Fishscale* at the time, a real return to form after a couple years in the wilderness. Def Jam's senior director of media and artist relations Gabe Tesoriero was there hyping him up about it (this is the same Gabe that Kanye calls at the end of "30 Hours"). Gabe was working up a sweat talking about how great "Shakey Dog" was and I had to agree. During a lull in conversation, I mentioned to Ghost that it was great to hear him on those beats that J Dilla used on *Donuts*. He was like, "What do you mean?" He seemed unaware that some of the instrumentals on his record had previously appeared on J Dilla's posthumous album. I kept my mouth shut for the rest of the dinner.

A starving artist who had subsisted primarily on free tacos and drinks for several days, I was quite happy to be eating on Def Jam's dime. Ghostface made his order with authority and it was something I will never forget: "I want fried rice with MAD eggs in it!" After a sizable dent had been put into the heaping plates of Chinese food, the label people sent for the leftovers to be disposed of. Ghost shouted, "No! We're gonna pack this food up and hand it out to homeless people tonight!"

SXSW 2006 was also when I first met the guys from Islands in person. I was booked to support them on their tour that coming spring, performing with them, Why?, and Busdriver across North America. Islands was the new project from Nick Thorburn and Jamie Thompson who had been two-thirds of the Unicorns. 2003's *Who Will Cut Our Hair When We're Gone?* turned the Unicorns into a Montréal success story before Arcade Fire took over the world. I saw them play at Red's at West Edmonton Mall. They performed a moribund, ironic cover of "P.I.M.P." by 50 Cent and they all looked like they were suffering from a bad case of the flu. The Unicorns broke up in 2004 before they could truly benefit from the hype around them, and Islands sprang forth a couple years later.

Islands was a seven-piece band, so they travelled in a tour bus by necessity. I was paid one hundred dollars a show, all of which went into paying for my spot on the tour bus. I basically got paid in exposure, but in this case, it was actually quite valuable. Despite me being a rapper and them being an indie rock band, touring with Islands helped to build my profile. Many of the shows were at midsized venues in cities I'd never been to before. It was a baptism by fire, my first real tour. I was only twenty so I was underage for most of the American dates. The venue would put Xs on the backs of my hands in permanent marker so I wouldn't be served alcohol. I wasn't allowed to leave the green room area on certain nights. Sometimes I had to play my set and then go back and sit in the tour bus. This never prevented me from getting totally hammered with the band after the show.

The Islands crew were a nerdy group of really nice guys. I was on the bus with the aforementioned ex-Unicorns, Jim Guthrie, Patrick Gregoire, Patrice Agbokou, Alexander and Sebastian Chow, and tour manager Mark Lawson. They were like a band class on steroids. They would often wear all white outfits on stage, making them look like a cult or the Polyphonic Spree. I usually wore vintage blue jeans, a graphic tee, maybe an American Apparel hoodie. I had long stopped getting my hair cut. What I looked like on stage was not something I thought about at all.

I admired how much Islands' fans cared for them. The band repaid that support by doing unconventional things like ending shows by playing a snare drum and leading the entire audience of hundreds outside onto the street. Their performances felt magical. Islands would have me jump on during their set whenever they played "Where There's a Will, There's a Whalebone." I've always loved rapping with live bands because it reminds me of my days playing with Uncle Brett and Magilla Funk Conduit. Depending on who was in the building on the Islands tour, I might be joined by someone like Despot or the original rappers from the recorded version of "Whalebone," Busdriver and Subtitle.

There wasn't enough room in the budget for Weez-L to join me for this tour so I performed alone almost every night, using only a large CD turntable my managers rented me to play my beats. What could've been a major setback actually helped me develop my skills as a performer. I whipped myself into a frenzy and bounced from wall to wall on a nightly basis to make up for the lack of musicians on stage. Inspired by the punk and hardcore bands I saw growing up in Edmonton and watching Naeem from Spank Rock climb on top of a stack of speakers at SXSW, I started performing with more of a physical presence. I opened for Spank Rock in Toronto and Hamilton right before the Islands tour and I played with a fury; Naeem seemed visibly shocked when I came off stage. I might not have the biggest show but I was gonna be unlike anything anyone had ever seen before.

On the Islands tour, I was playing for white indie rock crowds who had probably never been to a rap show before. I had to explain myself to every audience I played for. I would start the show by saying, "I make rap music but just give me a chance." I would jump off the stage into the crowd and do full laps around the venue, high-fiving fans during instrumental breaks. I'd rap full verses on the floor, eye to eye with the people. We played at First Unitarian Church in Philly and I chipped a tooth while screaming into the mic during my set, causing a stream of blood to spurt out of my mouth onto my chin. My sister Gena was in town for that show and she helped me find a pharmacy so I could get Anbesol to numb the pain. I was willing to do myself physical harm to earn the audience's approval, and usually by the end of the show, they were on my side. I gave maximum effort every time I hit the stage, but I also sensed that I could forge an even closer connection with the audience with more practice.

I quickly learned that touring puts you into weird situations you'd never experience otherwise. One night we were playing at the El Rey in Los Angeles. Weez-L had been flown in solely for this performance because people from Epitaph were going to be there and they were considering signing me in the U.S. The venue was packed with hundreds of fans. We crushed it that night. After my set, I struck up a conversation with two women in the audience. They were working on a screenplay. Amazing, I'd never met anyone who was making a movie before! I thought this was the coolest, most unique thing ever so I hung out with them for the rest of the show. They invited me back to their house so naturally I was thinking it was about to go down. But when one of the ladies opened the door, there were a handful of people passionately rolling around on the carpet. They were literally rolling on ecstasy, wriggling back and forth on the ground like centipedes. I laughed and took a cab back to the tour bus.

Despite having fun with the bands, making new friends, and playing for some big crowds, I also learned that touring can take a toll on you. We played twenty-eight shows in thirty-two days, which in retrospect was a completely inhumane schedule. Travelling on a tour bus sounds romantic and luxurious, but in reality it was cramped and stressful. We all slept in these stacked sleeping chambers that made me feel as if I was resting inside a coffin in the back of a moving hearse. I survived solely on the meagre per diem I received on show days.

My diet was horrible. I ate fast food or whatever was backstage and drank excessively every evening. I often performed drunk, thinking that it loosened me up and improved my performance. I've got friends who claimed they couldn't play unless they were high and they used that as a crutch, thinking it was the drugs that made them sound good. I eventually realized that, for me, it wasn't true. Those shows were just sloppy if you look back at the tape. It's like when you think you are being really funny and loquacious when you're drunk at a party but you're actually just being obnoxious.

I was untrained and performed with bad technique, screaming like a hardcore singer in a way that would leave my head ringing painfully after holding longer notes. After weeks of treating my vocal cords with disrespect and screaming my raps with no warm-up, I woke up one day unable to make a sound for the first time in my life. It was horrifying to lose my voice to that extent. I managed to rest enough to perform later that night, but it shocked me how far this tour was pushing me.

The road will test your mettle. It exposes a person's true nature. It destroys relationships. It breaks people. Watching your tour mates play the same set nightly for a month gets repetitive and exhausting. When you're stuck in the same van with the same folks day in and day out, sometimes the mix of personalities can clash. But touring can also bond you together. I still feel an unusual closeness to those I've toured with. There's a certain understanding that tour mates have with each other that is unlike any other kind of relationship. It's like having a temporary roommate that you perform with every night.

One of the weirdest things about going on tour is how time stays the same on the road while things change back home. After being gone for a couple months of your own personal Groundhog Day, you get back home and everyone has different haircuts, a bunch of your friends have broken up with each other, and your favourite restaurant went out of business.

◆

Burnt out after the Islands tour and a string of festival dates that summer, I was feeling anxiety about not having any money, despite having toured almost ceaselessly for the first half of the year. I wasn't getting paid much for the Islands tour but I was selling a decent quantity of CDs every night. I would go deposit that money into the record label's bank account. I needed a job but I was touring so frequently that I couldn't possibly keep one. The label wired an advance of one thousand dollars into my mom's bank account in May following the tour, but other than that and the fifteen dollars a review I was getting at *See Magazine*, I didn't have much in the way of income. I was already starting to resent the vagueness of my business arrangement with the label. While I was navigating all of this, my managers hired their friend Laila to shepherd Weez-L and me on the drive to our nation's capital to perform at Ottawa Bluesfest, one of the biggest festivals in the country.

Arriving at Bluesfest on July 14, I was excited to share the stage with the Fiery Furnaces, a quirky indie rock band that I was obsessed with at the time. Unfortunately for me, they were performing on the more intimate side stage. For some reason, I was booked on the main stage. Ottawa Bluesfest attracts hundreds of thousands of people and runs for almost two weeks every year. Van

Morrison played for over thirty thousand people there in 2007. Booking me on the main stage turned out to have some consequences.

I looked at the itinerary for the day and I was scheduled to go on right before Rihanna. Back then, she was a relatively new Caribbean pop star that I recognized from her Diwali Riddim–sampling hit single "Pon de Replay." It was pretty catchy but I preferred the Lumidee track that used the same riddim. A couple months before Bluesfest, Rihanna had scored her first number one single with "sos" and was quickly becoming a household name. A bus emblazoned with her face was parked backstage. Rihanna was walking from place to place with a small army of dancers and hangers-on surrounding her. I had developed a certain level of underground buzz for an abstract rap album I put out seven months before the festival. My debut video for "Black Hand" was uploaded to YouTube two weeks before Bluesfest. It hit MuchMusic the week after the Ottawa show. Your average person would have no idea who I was.

Already tired of playing the same old tunes, I thought this might be a great opportunity to try out some unreleased, more club-oriented songs that I had written for my sophomore album. The performance couldn't have gone worse. It was probably the most terrible show I played in my entire life. I tried my best but the stage was simply too big for just a DJ and an emcee with no other visuals. I was woefully unprepared to play a show like this. I had no idea how to engage with an audience of that magnitude. I probably looked like someone who stumbled on stage by acci-dent. It was a nightmare unfolding in real time. I'd play a song and the audience wouldn't even clap when it finished. Just silence and thousands of staring eyeballs. At a certain point, they started chanting, "Rihanna! Rihanna!"

A foppish young white boy who looked somewhat like James Corden in a sparkly tracksuit locked eyes with me from the crowd during a song and mouthed, "Move along!" This was the last straw. I screamed into the mic at him, "Fuck you, cunt!"

When you scream anything into a mic while you're on stage, it seems as if you're saying it to the entire audience. In this case, that included several thousand people. The show ended soon after, putting myself and the audience out of our misery. Laila looked nervous at side stage.

Weez and I DJed an afterparty that night at the Clocktower Brew Pub where some audience members assured me that they tried to cheer as loudly as possible and they had enjoyed the show. I also received some supportive emails from fans who were there. But there was immediate fallout. I was informed that my music would be banned on 106.9 FM the Bear, a Bluesfest sponsor and rock radio station that had never played my music before and probably hasn't done so since. I called them to apologize for my language and the ban was lifted. My managers subsequently signed me up for media training from a woman who normally worked with Toronto Argonauts players.

It wasn't an appropriate way to react to a heckler and it was a tasteless thing to say in the heat of the moment. But who in their right mind would put me in that situation in the first place? Why did the festival just lump the Black acts together and assume it would work out? Why didn't my managers ask them to move me to a smaller stage? It was like having Bad Brains play before Whitney Houston. This was a time when rap music wasn't really played on the radio in Canada, let alone the weird stuff I was making.

Your average Canadian didn't have much appreciation for the genre back then. Drake was still a main character on *Degrassi: The Next Generation*. He didn't have a record deal yet; he self-released his first mixtape that February. I was usually the only Black person and the only hip-hop act performing at any festival I played. At the Arts County Fair at UBC that spring, I was the sole Black artist on a bill where the other acts were the New Pornographers, the Weakerthans, and Corb Lund, playing for a primarily white audience.

◆

Despite the setback in Ottawa, the Islands tour in the spring had put me on the map in the North American indie scene. An audience for my left-leaning electro rap might actually be out there. After cutting my teeth on the Canadian festival circuit over the summer, I learned that I had been shortlisted for the inaugural Polaris Music Prize. Inspired by the U.K.'s Mercury Prize, the Polaris Music Prize represented an alternative to the Junos. The award appeared to have been created in response to the Canadian indie rock explosion that had been making waves in the States after the success of albums like *You Forgot It in People* and *Funeral*. It was adjudicated by Canadian music critics and there was a twenty-thousand-dollar prize for the winner. I was nominated alongside more established bands like Broken Social Scene, Metric, Wolf Parade, and the New Pornographers. There were only two nominated records that were created primarily by artists of colour: my album, and K'naan's *The Dusty Foot Philosopher*.

The Polaris nomination boosted me out of obscurity into the national conversation as a notable Canadian musician. My weird little record went from being a local buzzy curiosity to a national subject of interest overnight. I was interviewed by *Eye Weekly* in Toronto and put on the cover with Final Fantasy, a.k.a. Owen Pallett, an Arcade Fire member and fellow Polaris nominee. We made a mock confrontational boxing pose opposite each other, standing in for the clashing interests of indie rock and underground rap. As an indication of the level of seriousness I gave the proceedings, I told *Eye Weekly* that if I won the $20,000 prize money, I would "buy a house made of Big Macs—that's food and shelter." In the interview, I also spoke with great excitement about potentially being able to pay my ballooning Rogers phone bill with an award sponsored by their company.

The ceremony happened on September 18, 2006. Going into it, I didn't think I had a chance of winning against these more well-known bands. I have to give my label and management credit for getting my record in front of enough people that I could be considered for an award like that in the first place. Our table had a two six of vodka and a bowl full of candy and I partook in both liberally. The event was thankfully the only time the awards were not televised or streamed live. I wore a brown graphic tee with a deer on it, vintage blue jeans with ripped knees, and an army-green military cap.

As the night went on, journalists from the jury kept coming up to me to assure me that I had a real chance of winning. When Final Fantasy's *He Poos Clouds* ended up taking the prize, I was devastated. I drank the lion's share of the vodka. When I got to the afterparty at the Drake Hotel, I ended up throwing a beer at one of the Constantines (or was it a member of the Weakerthans?) for no reason. My friend Alex took me up to my hotel room; I puked and passed out. I felt like I had been rejected by all of Canada.

Indie rock was the music of the day. I didn't really stand a chance. I felt like I would need to make an undeniable classic record to break through and win an award like that one day. Or maybe I needed to make music that appealed more to an indie audience to be further accepted. It was discouraging but I dusted myself off and got back on the road. I got to open for Lady Sovereign on her dates in Toronto and Montreal. She had the most elaborate rider I've ever seen: a full Thanksgiving dinner with all the trimmings. I came backstage after the show was over and nothing had been touched. (What's on an artist's rider says a lot about them. When I played a show with Fatlip from the Pharcyde at the Knitting Factory in New York, he told me he kept a bottle of Hennessy on his rider that he always left unopened as a monument to his sobriety.)

In November, I got the chance to open up for Jurassic 5 on their Canadian dates. I couldn't have been more excited. I listened to *Quality Control* extensively when I was in high school and had majored in kickflips at university while playing *Tony Hawk's Underground* in my dorm room listening to "A Day at the Races" on the soundtrack. Chali 2na was like a rap deity to me at the time. Jurassic 5 turned out to be a great group of guys who were very health-oriented and businesslike. I never saw them party at all. Their rider had organic food I'd never seen before on it. Backstage at our show at Red's in West Edmonton Mall, my mom braided my hair into cornrows. I couldn't believe that I was about to see these West Coast underground icons do their thing! I peered down from the balcony above the stage and watched them work with unmatched synchronicity and precision, leaning against the railing with my eyes wide.

J5 had really elaborate routines and a defined structure to their show. They worked as a unit and were incredibly well rehearsed.

They were also adept at coming up with lyrics and ideas on the fly, a skill likely forged during the iconic open mic nights at the legendary Good Life Café where they originally became a group. They had school desks on stage with MPCs built into them and they all did a routine playing a beat together live.

On the final date of the tour at the Spectrum in Montreal, they invited me on stage to rap with them at the end of their set. Cut Chemist and DJ Nu-Mark threw on some breakbeats and I got to kick a verse along with the rest of J5. It was like something out of a movie! Just a year before, I was making tracks in my mom's attic and suddenly I was rocking the mic with some of my heroes. I pulled out a speedy verse from my days of rapping with my uncle's funk band and heard the roar of approval from the crowd. It was such a gracious, encouraging gesture and I've always been thankful to Jurassic 5 for doing that for me.

5

WOT DO U CALL IT?

Surfing the web always felt like an apt description for the act of using the internet. An endless morass of options and directions, one might feel themselves pushed by invisible forces when online. It's as if the keys at your fingertips are a rectangular Ouija board, complete with unseen voices beckoning you to click your way into a vortex that might change the trajectory of your entire life. I used to forage for sound every day on the web, digging through Tumblr pages and mp3 blogs in search of the random detritus of the early '00s: electro clash remixes, Baltimore club bootlegs, obscure Italo disco cuts. This was the Hollertronix era when everything was fair game and kids around the world were forming distinctive transatlantic taste profiles from the comfort of their own homes for the first time.

That's how I initially stumbled across a new genre bubbling up from England called UK grime. The first recordings I heard were freestyles taped off pirate radio that I downloaded on Soulseek. These London DJs and emcees would break into a tower block, plant a radio antenna, and set up shop for as long as they could evade Scotland Yard. The crusty low-fidelity recordings I had of these sets made their music sound like alien transmissions from a faraway planet. The people on the mic were certainly rapping, that much I could understand. But what they were rapping about? What were *creps*? What was *armshouse*? I had no idea. It felt like I was eavesdropping on a detailed story about an event that happened in a foreign city and I didn't know any of the parties involved.

Some of the emcees rapped in Jamaican patois that made them sound like dancehall DJs, but mostly they had heavy English accents. I already had an appreciation for British rap from listening to Tricky, Massive Attack, and other trip-hop artists, but these grime rappers were much more technically robust. The flows they favoured were off-kilter and serpentine. They would go back and forth, straining to one-up each other with more inventive patterns and verses as their pals from the neighbourhood hooted in the background. It was an alternate reality version of the freestyles I heard on SMACK DVD, *The Wake Up Show* with Sway and King Tech, or BET's *Rap City: Tha Basement*. The grime emcees had names that sounded like adjectives: Dizzee, Wiley, Footsie, Shystie, Tinchy.

At radio sets and during their live shows, DJs would wheel up and rewind instrumentals whenever the audience responded enthusiastically to a rapper dropping a particularly sick set of lines. Inspired by Jamaican soundclash culture, this action is called a rewind or a reload. Every grime rapper has a set of reload bars that they know will get an instant reaction wherever they perform. North American freestylers were expected to come up with spontaneous, original rhymes at a moment's notice. Crowds in the U.K. encourage and anticipate the repetition of certain classic verses. For instance, Jammer pulls up to grime raves and almost exclusively raps the chorus from his 2005 anthem "Murkle Man" and no one seems to tire of it. Several of Dizzee Rascal's verses on *Boy in da Corner* were originally reload bars that he used to repeat on pirate radio.

Downloading rips of Rinse FM and Sidewinder sets was like uncovering a distant world where sonic invention and pure rapping ability were paramount. It was exactly what I needed in the early '00s when I was largely disenchanted with North American hip-hop. Mainstream rap that fixated on remaking '80s pop singles and was obsessed with consumerism and misogyny didn't speak to me. The underground rap scene was becoming incrementally blander as the years went by, the staid beats and pretentious lyrics growing tiresome.

Grime provided an unending supply of wild new talent bursting out of my computer speakers from across the pond. I felt a kinship with the jagged DIY approach of artists like Skepta and Jme. The producers made beats using a video game called *Music 2000* on their PlayStations. Either that or they were making instrumentals with the same computer program that I used, Fruity Loops. I felt emboldened by the fact that somewhere thousands of kilometres from my hometown, there were kids who understood music the same way that I did and made it on their own terms.

Any music that features rapping and comes from outside of the U.S.A. will inevitably be judged on how it stacks up against what's happening stateside. Grime in 2004 afforded itself well when placed in direct opposition with American hip-hop from the same year. In fact, I would argue that grime creatively surpassed U.S. hip-hop in the early '00s. Grime was certainly influenced by American rap. Both scenes shared a similar aesthetic proclivity for sports apparel and U.S. urban clothing brands like Akademiks and Avirex. Dizzee was quick to shout out Three 6 Mafia, Ludacris, and Nas in interviews. But what really inspired me about U.K. grime was how they showed appreciation for what came before them without directly imitating it. Their wayward attempts at making their own version of American rap ended up cultivating something even more innovative and progressive than the source material that inspired it.

Grime was the first rapping I ever heard that was intensely regional and uncompromising about where it came from that hadn't originated in America. In Canada, there was always this thing where rappers tried to sound like they were from New York or they used the same sounds and samples that were trendy in the States in order to make more exportable music. U.K. grime artists were proudly shouting out their postcodes and neighbour-hoods ("Bow E3") while sonically pushing boundaries by rapping over the nastiest beats possible. What was happening in England represented a different path forward that I hoped might be possible for Canadian hip-hop at the time: local rappers having a platform and succeeding by being themselves. The more I got into grime, the more I felt like I should've been born in Edmonton, U.K., instead of Edmonton, Alberta.

Grime also originally sprouted out of another genre called U.K. garage. Like a faster hybrid of American R&B and garage house, U.K. garage occasionally featured emcees kicking verses about the champagne-soaked high life that were homologous to Diddy's jiggy raps from the late '90s. Somewhere down the line, a more minimal strain of this music that harkened back to darkside hardcore from the early '90s appeared. It was largely instrumental, perfect for rapping over. Shunned by the shiny happy people that populated the clubbier U.K. garage scene, the denizens of this then-unnamed genre scuttled off to the underground where they proliferated their music through pirate radio, 12-inch vinyl singles, and DVD series like *Risky Roadz* and *Lord of the Mics*.

What is grime music anyway? The name itself was in question in those early years, referred to variously as sublow, two-step, garage, eskibeat, and 8-bar as evidenced by Wiley's genre-defining single "Wot Do U Call It?" I was a hip-hop head who instinctively appreciated rap and electronic music equally: grime was the music of my dreams. Grime music is gritty, dark, hard, heavy, cold. A melting pot that combines ragga chatting with a more skeletal take on hardcore rave beats, this music was the first I heard in my lifetime that truly sounded like the future. The focus on clashing between emcees also made sense to me coming from a battle rap background.

Though grime was once a purely local concern, the internet presented a distribution system ripe for its proliferation across international boundaries. Watching YouTube clips taken from the DVDs added some much needed context to the proceedings for me. There was a thrilling rawness to watching Kano and Wiley go for broke in Jammer's dingy basement stairwell or seeing Ghetts rapping endlessly in broad daylight in front of a terrace house with his MySpace URL superimposed over the screen. I loved the characters of the grime universe. D Double E, the quintessential yard man with a high top fade who could shut down an entire club night with just a few wordless utterances.

Jme, an impossibly clever lyricist with a singular style who plays with language like pretty much no one else. As futuristic as the music sounded, there was something retro about the artists' dedication to lyricism. These videos were just rhymes and beats with no commercial aspirations getting in the way, no industry to water it down. Pure, unadulterated bars and I couldn't get enough of it.

I still turn back to early grime tracks for inspiration today. When I was making my 2021 album *Parallel World*, I wanted songs like "Play No Games" and "SENNA" to have the spontaneous feeling of a pirate radio grime freestyle. There's something alluring about the ambiguity of form: the music hasn't yet formulated into a specific sonic template. The artists haven't decided what kind of music they're making yet, which means their creations are unclassifiable and impervious to cliché. You get to feel the push and pull between existing genres and witness the real-time discovery as it happens over the course of a particular song. I love when music exists in that liminal space between different genres (wot do you call it?), and early grime is that in a nutshell.

Mondie's "Straight" with God's Gift on the vocal from 2004 is a great example. Over a beat that isn't much more than a massive distorted kick drum and jittery hi-hats, God's Gift issues a gruff warning with heavy delay on his voice about his earth-shattering fearsomeness. My mp3 still has "U.K. Garage" tagged as the genre and the song title as "Unknown." That exemplifies the elusive nature of classic grime. Danny Weed's twisted undulating beat for "Roll Deep Regular" by Roll Deep uses uncommon sound effects, like camera flashes, and has a snare that is barely noticeable, only a hint of a drum sound. Wiley's beat for "Freeze" is almost unbearably dark, akin to being trapped in a frozen cave, likely owing to an obsession with coldness that has led him to produce songs with titles like "Avalanche," "Blizzard," "Ice Rink," and "Igloo."

Straddling the lines between genres without even being aware of it, "Oi!" by More Fire Crew came out in 2002 but wouldn't sound out of place if it dropped in 2022. After the group dissolved, Lethal Bizzle went solo and two years later made one of the first anthems of a genre that he helped standardize with "Pow! (Forward)." It's a ridiculously aggressive record with blistering 8-bar verses from a variety of emcees that was banned from certain clubs in the U.K. because it routinely ignited conflicts. On "Pow!," Napper threatens to crack your skull open. Hotshot names sixteen different guns and commands you to shoot all of them during his verse, which was so violent that his section was completely removed from the music video and the official release of the single. This was not music for vibing in the club with a bottle of champagne. This was grime.

Grime was heavily policed and regulated from the outset, a victim of moral panic just like gangsta rap in the '90s. Grime events have been cancelled due to fears of violence. In 2008, the London Metropolitan Police came out with a "risk assessment" document called Form 696 that licensees and promoters had to fill out if they were putting on an event that featured any music performed alongside a backing track. Live bands were curiously not required to fill it out; it directly targeted DJs and grime artists. The form asked for the government name, artist name, home address, and phone number of everyone scheduled to perform at an event; the police would decide if the show could be a risk to public safety and potentially force a venue to shut it down. The form also asked for the ethnicity of the likely attendees and what music genres would be played. Those questions were removed in 2009 after journalists and activists described them as clear-cut examples of racial profiling.

In 2010, "Pow!" was blasted out in Parliament Square as an unofficial anthem during the U.K.'s student protests against tuition increases. Grime music is made by disenfranchised Black youth who rap about the inequality of their environments with unflinching honesty. This makes it quintessential protest music. But as a result of the increased police scrutiny connected to Form 696, there was a shift towards radio-friendly, dance-oriented singles by grime artists, such as Wiley's "Wearing My Rolex," Boy Better Know's "Too Many Man," and Dizzee Rascal's "Dance wiv Me" and "Bonkers." Dizzee made it to number one on the U.K. charts by making clubby electro pop, not for making the grime that put him on the map in the first place.

The success of those songs inspired other grime rappers to follow suit in the late '00s with diminishing returns, marking a fallow period for grime. After a few years underground, the genre experienced a resurgence in 2013 with the video for "German Whip" by Meridian Dan, Big H, and Jme as well as the release of "That's Not Me" by Skepta and Jme in 2014. The latter song showed that grime had finally been around long enough to have nostalgia for itself. It featured bleepy classic grime production that eschewed the pop instincts of the forgettable electro grime from the end of the previous decade. The "That's Not Me" video features projections of clips from the old school DVDs in the background as Jme and Skepta perform.

A song about staying true to the roots of grime turned out to be exactly what the scene needed. "That's Not Me" won the

MOBO Award for Best Video in 2014 and the single was featured on Skepta's *Konnichiwa*, an album that won the 2016 Mercury Prize. A new wave of emcees appeared, including Stormzy, whose *Gang Signs & Prayer* became the first grime album to top the U.K. charts in 2017. Form 696 was scrapped that same year.

One of my biggest influences in recent years is a rapper who returned to prominence during grime's second wave: North London's President T. A founding member of Meridian Crew—the Tottenham-based grime collective featuring Skepta, Jme, Big H, and Bossman Birdie—President T's flow feels counterintuitive, herky-jerky, and full of pauses. It's an anti-flow. I find it invigorating. He punctuates his lines with internal conversations, using unpredictable rhyme schemes and emphasizing unexpected words. There's a sense of delayed gratification to his delivery. He's almost like a comedian setting up punchlines.

His track "Ending Careers" was a big inspiration for my song "On Me," which featured Roll Deep member Manga Saint Hilare. Getting a legit grime emcee on one of my tracks for the first time was a major moment for me.

Throughout my career, I've found myself relating more with U.K. grime culture than I do with Canadian rap. Dizzee Rascal won England's Mercury Prize for his 2003 debut *Boy in da Corner*. They were inviting grime emcees onto Tim Westwood's BBC show to freestyle during prime time. In Canada, you'd barely hear any rap from our country on mainstream radio. There were a couple crossover artists, like k-os and Swollen Members, until Drake blew things open and forced the powers that be to properly acknowledge homegrown talent.

Why don't we have a radio show on CBC with Canadian rappers performing live like they do on BBC 1Xtra? The video of #SixtyMinutesLive with Dizzee, Boy Better Know, Lethal Bizzle, Tempa T, and General Levy from 2014 is one of the most exciting clips on YouTube because you can see the connection between generations of artists in one room, a warm synchronicity between the grime rappers and the jungle emcee that turns into a celebration of the fondness that they have for each other. Imagine doing that here with Kardinal, Maestro, Shad, Haviah Mighty, Backxwash, and myself! What's stopping us from doing this in Canada?

Maybe our lack of this kind of history and infrastructure in Canada is what inspired Drake to share a similar kinship to the U.K. that I have. He posted a still from the infamous Skepta versus Devilman *Lord of the Mics* battle to his Instagram. He has a Boy Better Know tattoo. He bought the rights to British hood drama *Top Boy* and brought it back on Netflix in 2019 after it had been cancelled. He's freestyled on Link Up TV and Fire in the Booth, featured Giggs on 2017's "KMT," and dabbled in U.K. drill on "War" and "Only You Freestyle" with Headie One.

Just like grime's rise signalled U.K. garage's fall, grime's popularity has declined in the face of genres like U.K. drill and Afrobeats. British music genres in the hardcore continuum aren't built for long-term dominance. These offshoots reflect the temperature of the streets at a particular time and recede into the tapestry of U.K. club music as a vibe for future generations to occasionally draw from. I can't wait for whatever is destined to come next and the outsized impact that this unknown genre is sure to command.

6

AFTERPARTY BABIES

In December 2006, while I was recovering from the Jurassic 5 tour and gearing up to record my second album, I met a woman named Kathryn at a house party through our mutual friend Steph. Kathryn lived in Calgary and was inscrutably strange with an unflappable bubbly attitude. She was incredibly hard to read and uncannily positive. I had never met anyone like her. After hanging out a few more times, we started dating.

She studied French in Quebec City one summer and I went and stayed with her for a week. While we were there, we saw a rap group from France called TTC perform. We wore neon shirts with crazy patterns on them. Kathryn was incredibly hyper and made bird sounds at random. She was a really joyful person and I adored her. She worked as a flight attendant, setting up her shifts to land in Edmonton so we could hang out. She gave me buddy passes which helped immeasurably with navigating our long-distance relationship and for travelling within Canada to play shows or meet with my label.

But even with the airfare largely taken care of and almost a hundred shows in the bag by 2007, I still had no money to show for it. My noise rap album didn't exactly take the charts by storm, only selling a couple thousand copies. The label implied that I hadn't broken even for the expenses incurred over the previous year, which meant I wouldn't yet start receiving show fees. Not breaking even made sense with what I imagined the total cost of travel, hotels, and other expenses were. But that didn't make it any easier for me to survive. I had received my first SOCAN publishing royalty payment in November and it was for only $219.49, which was what I was left with after Upper Class took their 50% cut of my publishing earnings.

I was still freelancing for *See Magazine* occasionally. Through some friends in the local indie rock scene, I started working under the table as a temp in the shipping department at Holt Renfrew over the holidays. It was seasonal work so it was unstable and hard to rely on, but it afforded me flexibility for touring, I made ten dollars per hour, and I was paid cash at the end of every shift.

I mostly lugged boxes around and put security tags on high-end clothing items like fur coats and designer purses. The irony of a grubby group of Edmonton hipsters preparing luxury goods for wealthy oil magnates and their wives was not lost on me. We worked in a windowless basement. We were treated like subterranean sewer creatures by both the management and the other employees, who traipsed around the aboveground retail floor swathed in designer clothes.

I'd eat whatever fried garbage I could find at the food court and write lyrics in my rhyme book during my lunch break, fantasizing about a future when I could focus solely on making music. One nice by-product of this job was that it allowed for ample time to listen to music that I wasn't familiar with. I developed a deeper appreciation for the back catalogues of Bob Dylan, David Bowie, and Neil Young during my time there on account of my flannel-covered friends in the shipping department.

At the same time, I was in negotiations with Upper Class about signing a licensing deal with American record label Anti, a subsidiary of the legendary punk label Epitaph Records. The company was flirting with releasing rap music back then. Upper Class faxed the contract over to the lawyer from my mom's firm and we discussed the terms over speakerphone. The inducement letter that came with the contract had been negotiated by lawyers for both labels and said that I would solely be liable for damages if Upper Class didn't follow through with the obligations of the licensing deal. If they fell off the face of the Earth, I would be responsible for anything that had been left unsettled. My lawyer had an issue with that. My business manager from the label said I should get a proper entertainment lawyer to look at it but in the same email also mentioned that the contract was "Anti's standard deal" and that "we could jeopardize the deal" if we didn't "act fast." I assumed the sense of urgency was related to the fact that the contract gave Upper Class a thirty-thousand-dollar advance for my first album and Anti promised an advance for my sophomore album of between fifty and eighty thousand dollars. It also included a three-thousand-dollar artwork budget for both albums, twenty thousand dollars in tour support, and a fifty-thousand-dollar marketing budget for each album. I assumed that this money would go toward the debt I owed to

Upper Class and would help pay for expenses around my sophomore album.

I had no idea where I could find or how I could possibly afford
to hire an entertainment lawyer. Orly suggested that I had to
sign or we would have to move on from the Anti deal. I signed
the contract. The deal was announced publicly soon after that
and *Breaking Kayfabe* received a proper American release on
March 13, 2007. A similar deal was struck with Big Dada in the
U.K. and my album received a proper release in Europe on
September 24.

The video for "Sharks," a song from my first album, was released
around this time. Directed by Cosmonaut, it was shot in downtown Toronto and featured me as a real-life video game character.
There were homages to *Donkey Kong, Frogger*, and *Mortal Kombat*
in a nod to the retro synth sounds I used in the track. The video
got played frequently on Much, even getting nominated for the
MuchMusic Video Award for Best Post-Production. The success
of the "Sharks" video turned out to be a blessing and a curse.
Having a video in rotation on TV brought me a certain measure of
fame, which some people equated with wealth. This led to awkward moments when I would get recognized while pushing a cart
full of perfume boxes around Holt Renfrew.

In my mind, I had already moved beyond songs like "Sharks,"
which I had written several years before. Most of my free time
was spent composing and recording my sophomore album. I
had spent my first years of adulthood deeply immersed in the
hipster milieu. My friends worked at American Apparel and
VICE. I wanted to synthesize what I had heard, seen, and experienced in bars and nightclubs at home and on tour. The album

had the working title *Scenery* but I eventually decided to call it *Afterparty Babies*.

The name came from my dad. He used to joke about us, saying, "These kids? Oh, they were afterparty babies!" In retrospect, it seems a little cruel. But it also made me think about my entire generation: a bunch of accidents dragged into life against their will at random, forced to make do with a world that didn't have room for them in the first place. I envisioned a lost generation of kids like me who were the product of a Really Good Time.

I thought about the art freaks hanging out at Juliann's loft, my retail celebrity friends who worked at High Grade in West Edmonton Mall, the displaced ravers who shuffled from shuttered venue to soon-to-be-shuttered venue like rats escaping a sinking ship. I wanted to capture the neon-flecked energy of gritty nights at Hifi Club with Kathryn where DJs like Noah York would play indie rock jams, as well as the sleeker house vibes of Halo where dancers would be dressed to the nines in Diesel jeans and A.P.C. shirts. I wanted these clubs and late-night locations to be the settings in the songs on my new album, with each track representing a different side of the nightlife.

Recording with DJ Nato at his home studio, I packed the album with weird ideas. It opens up with "Do I Miss My Friends?"—the whole beat is made up of me humming and beatboxing. I included a recording of my friend Sheri Barclay interviewing her mother about how Sheri's childhood friend named Rollie used to play with Barbie dolls. It wasn't actually about me but I put it in there just to mess with people's expectations. My lyrics had become ridiculously dense to the point of being impenetrable, a mélange of inside jokes, convoluted wordplay, and pop culture references. I even wrote a song called "Juliann Wilding" that was my version of Bowie's "Queen Bitch," a tribute to an ineffable character who opened up an alternative side of the city to me:

My old guard fears your face
Based on the space of our embrace, give chase
In the race for respect from a female elder
I hold heat like a welder or Prometheus in you

Instead of the noisy, clattering underground synth rap I had become known for, I started making 4/4 beats inspired by house music. I had always been attracted to electronic music but it had usually been more on the IDM side of things before Shout Out Out Out Out and DVAS came on the scene in Edmonton and shook up my world. My appreciation for dance music increased as I travelled more. I had been spending more and more time in Toronto where I would shop for vinyl singles at Play de Record and watch DJs like Rory Them Finest and MSTRKRFT spin at bars.

I wanted to escape the prison of classification. I rapped about subjects that no one else had considered rapping about: gentrification, texting, celebrity obsession, vintage clothing, the dumbing down of society. Weez-L had a knack for finding the perfect thing to scratch in to emphasize my points, and Nato's mixing helped make the whole production sound more professional. I wanted to translate the excitement of discovery I was experiencing as an amateur DJ and neophyte house fan into my music.

The music itself was full of happy accidents. There was a lot of trial and error. The results were probably more inventive than they would've been if I had actually known what I was doing. It felt like a natural progression for me. The last thing I wanted to be was one of those artists who plays it safe by just making a new version of the same old album year after year. I never wanted to repeat myself. I've always had the impulse to go left. There was still a ramshackle edge that kept my music from sounding anything like the pristine club tunes you might hear out at Rum Jungle at West Edmonton Mall.

My production was becoming more sonically detailed with a wider spectrum of musical influences, ping-ponging between French house, electro, techno, Baltimore club, and nu-rave— sometimes all within the same song. I was enamoured with electronic artists who defied genre: Daft Punk, Basement Jaxx, M.I.A., Maurice Fulton, Switch, and Mr. Oizo. Lyrically, I was inspired by the narrative skill of Mike Skinner from the Streets. I wanted to examine the characters in my life like Dylan and Bowie did before me.

As a rapper, my flow became more dexterous, my lyrics some- how obtuse and personal at the same time. I'd rhyme way offbeat on purpose for long stretches and frenetically stuff my verses with words, as if I was trying to sonically represent my increasingly frantic lifestyle and emotional state. Grappling with becoming a minor celebrity in a small city, I performed with a more defiant attitude on this record. I had also somehow developed a weirdly strong sense of nostalgia for a twenty-one-year-old, rhapsodizing about clubs that had only closed a year prior and friends who had moved away only months before.

After years of sitting in the corner of the bar drinking a rye and ginger and watching closely, *Afterparty Babies* was my attempt to deconstruct the scene. We finished the album in April 2007.

I was pointing a magnifying glass at the hipster generation, burning what I didn't like and expanding on everything else. The *Afterparty Babies* album cover photo was taken in the Black Dog basement by Aaron Pedersen on May 5, 2007. I wanted it to be like a class photo that featured friends, roommates, lovers, local rappers, cool kids, and DJs—the exact kind of people populating the stories I told in the songs. It was like Edmonton's answer to *Sgt. Pepper*. The cover had a weird effect on people. Some thought it was meant to be satirical, a send-up of the typical hip-hop posse. A notable American underground rapper told Weez-L that he was going to listen to the album until he saw how many white people were on the front. The inner photos were from a party I threw with Nik at kHz. I wanted the shots to be done in the style of party photographers like Bronques from LastNightsParty and the Cobrasnake. I wanted to create the ultimate scenester time capsule.

◆

After finishing the album, it was time to get back on the road. Before hitting the summer festival circuit, I had my first local headline performance in Edmonton at the Starlite Room. We booked a mysterious rapper from Oakland that I'd met at SXSW called Kirby Dominant. He was portly with long dreads and a legendary aura. Weez-L and I become obsessed with a CDR he gave us of an album he'd made with his group Assistant Green, which never received a proper release. It was a hazy, self-assured hybrid of rap, R&B, and electronic music that was really ahead of its time and had a big impact on me. It was like underground trip-hop. His song "Everything's Happening" became our catchphrase for the year and we were stoked that he had a track called "Canadian Ice Wine." Touch and Nato also played the show, which felt like a homecoming and a farewell.

At the urging of my management, we rehearsed extensively, working on different sets of songs for different audiences: rap, hipster, and U.S.A. We were ready for anything. We played the Sasktel Saskatchewan Jazz Festival, Jazz Winnipeg, and the Beats, Breaks & Culture festival as well as dates in Guelph, St. Catharines, Brantford, London, and Ottawa. All of this culminated in my biggest show up to that point: a spot at the Pitchfork Music Festival at Grant Park in Chicago. I took great satisfaction in being booked by my former employer. I ran into Prince Paul, the legendary producer for De La Soul, and showed him my *Stakes Is High* tattoo. I think it creeped him out. He was probably wondering why I was showing him a tattoo of an album he didn't really work on. On stage, I wore a purple Charles Barkley Phoenix Suns jersey, pale blue jean shorts, and a pair of Nike Vandals designed to look like playing cards with the king and queen of hearts on them.

I crowd-surfed across a sea of appreciative fans. I performed a ghettotech cover of "Pink Triangle" by Weezer. I was probably the only rapper who played covers like that back then. People thought I was being ironic but I just liked the song and wanted to make my own version of it. When I first started playing live in Edmonton, I often covered Joy Division's "Isolation." Over the next few years, I performed my own fractured electronic versions of songs like "I Need Somebody" by the Stooges, Chad VanGaalen's "Mini TVs," "Summer Goth" by Wavves, and "Dancing Choose" by TV on the Radio. I guess this was my way of trying to speak the audience's language. I was a big fan of Tricky, who covered songs on his records in unconventional ways. I really enjoyed subverting the form of these rock songs and reinterpreting them through my own lens.

We followed Pitchfork Music Festival with a short East Coast run before returning to Canada to play Wakestock on Toronto Island. I performed right before Lupe Fiasco and saw him pacing around backstage while holding his laptop in his hands with headphones on. Then I had a month of downtime. Strapped for cash despite having played a run of shows and festivals over the summer, I had to ask my business manager to wire me an advance of four hundred dollars to cover rent for November. This kept me going long enough to get through my most substantial excursion of the year: a journey with Final Fantasy in the fall for what was marketed as a dual headline tour of North America.

Owen Pallett had learned to create fantastically elaborate solo orchestras on stage, with just a violin and a loop pedal, performing with the visual artist Stephanie Comilang who did live projections featuring silhouettes of puppet-like human shapes and abstract buildings during Final Fantasy shows. Stephanie also directed music videos for groups like Junior Boys and made stirring documentary films. Owen and Stephanie were effortlessly cool and inspiring. I really enjoyed getting to know them both better on the road.

For the tour, the label found Weez-L and me a tour manager: a rocker dude called Keebler. Keebler did resemble a cartoon elf but he did not have a magical, playful persona. He was a straightedge hardcore guy with a militaristic streak. There was no fun to be had with him at the helm. In the rental car, he'd blast Foo Fighters, air-drumming on the steering wheel. He'd crank up grating pop punk at obscene volumes, never letting us pick the music while he was driving. Weez-L and I put our headphones on. I listened to my iPod in the car for a month straight.

Ultimately, Keebler didn't seem to respect us or our music, saying our merch sales were paltry compared to other bands he had tour-managed before, like the Bouncing Souls. If we didn't pack up our turntables fast enough, he would say, "This wouldn't fly at Warped Tour!" He wouldn't advocate for us with the sound techs who had likely never done sound for a rap act before. Keebler and Weez-L in particular did not get along at all. Weez-L was a well-meaning oddball but he didn't respond well to authority. Keebler was not charmed by Weez-L's free-spirited rural energy. It was a total mismatch.

At the show in Los Angeles, I met with the folks from Anti and I went for dinner with my American publicist, Judy Miller Silverman. She asked me questions about the release plan for *Afterparty Babies* that I didn't have the answers for. I didn't know that the press run for the album was days away from starting. I emailed my business manager looking for clarity and she responded by saying, "I love that you don't know what's going on in the boardroom or rather bored room . . . It keeps your mind on music, love, the scene, hot chicks, performing." This was an incredibly disturbing thing to read. It was such a rock 'n' roll cliché. This was the first time that someone from my management team said something like that.

Spending time on the tour with Owen also made it clear to me that not making money from shows was abnormal for a touring musician. In 2006 and 2007, I played around 140 shows and never made a dime from merch or performances. I understood that I had to pay off previous expenses but the label never explained what those were or what it would take to balance the ledger. When I asked my business manager for transparency during this email exchange, she said I needed to sell two thousand dollars in shirts to pay for the cost of making my merch but didn't specify any other expenses. After we finished playing all the shows, Keebler sent us a document that said we made $1,956.65 on the Final Fantasy tour before paying his fee. This didn't include the merch we sold on top of that. I needed to get to the bottom of what was happening with the money, but I was in the middle of a tour and there were shows that needed to be played.

Touring with Final Fantasy was interesting because Owen was significantly more established and connected in the entertainment industry than I was. Gus Van Sant came to our Portland show (Owen was in talks to score his film *Milk* at the time). In New York, I tagged along with Owen and Ed Droste from Grizzly Bear as they went shopping at Opening Ceremony and ate lobster rolls. While in town, we were asked to take part in this Pitchfork.tv comedy sketch with Fred Armisen and a bunch of white indie rock guys at the Pitchfork office. It was supposed to be improv; I don't think it was ever released. My inability to be spontaneously funny seemed to cause Fred to lose his patience; he looked furious.

The fanbase for Final Fantasy were passionate nerds who devoured the mystical world that Owen had created, bringing gifts like Russian literature to many of the shows. I was jealous of the dedication of Owen's fans. Though it was somewhat implied that we were on equal footing, I was really just along for the ride. My performances were mostly greeted with confusion. These shy chamber pop devotees didn't seem to have the bandwidth for super-charged electro rap, but I tried to adapt to the situation as much as I possibly could. On certain nights, I would come on during Owen's set to perform a cover of "She Cracked" by the Modern Lovers.

In Austin at Fun Fun Fun Fest, I ran into Dan Bejar from Destroyer in the beer tent while Owen was on stage. I was a big-time Destroyer fan, heavily influenced by his lyrical approach on the albums *Your Blues* and *Destroyer's Rubies*. Knowing that Owen occasionally performed a cover of Destroyer's "An Actor's Revenge," I asked Dan if he would come with me so they could perform it together. He said, "Can I get a beer first?" and then I dragged him on stage. Owen had already played the cover during that set, but we all did it again together and I geeked out to an embarrassing degree, flapping my arms and jumping around to the point that I was forgetting lyrics.

I left North America for the first time three days after the last gig with Final Fantasy to play some U.K. shows in support of *Breaking Kayfabe* being released there. After seventeen straight dates of playing for indifferent, bewildered audiences, I was finally making a trip to the place that I considered my spiritual home musically: London. Big Dada was a label that specialized in futuristic electronic rap and I was their lone Canadian signing at the time. It was the perfect place for me to be. On November 16, I played their tenth anniversary party alongside Roots Manuva, Jammer, and others in a huge multiroom venue called Electrowerkz.

I played back to back with Diplo and the response from the crowd was unlike any show I'd ever played up to that point. I felt a wave of relief pass over me as I performed for this audience that intuitively understood what I was doing. I didn't feel like a sideshow for once. I played with aplomb, going all out. A promoter in the audience came up to me after my set and asked me if I wanted to open for Mos Def the following week at Shepherd's Bush Empire. Between those shows, I played with the Go! Team at Tripod in Dublin.

The day before the Mos Def show, I went to *VICE* magazine's fifth anniversary party at Heaven in Charing Cross with my friend Alex from Toronto who worked there. I was thrilled because T2 was playing. He had recently released a single called "Heartbroken" that I had fallen in love with. It was the flagship song for a new genre of music originating in Sheffield that people called niche or bassline house. It was a faster take on U.K. garage, somewhat reminiscent of speed garage, that functioned as an R&B response to grime. Big Dada commissioned a remix in this style for my song "House Music" by the producer A1 Bassline. Dubstep was everywhere in London at the time and *Untrue* by Burial had just come out. So much seemed to be happening in the U.K. and it was utterly intoxicating to be immersed in such newness.

After an incredibly busy week in the U.K., I flew back to Canada for three final West Coast dates to close out the year. These shows were all poorly attended, a bit of a comedown after the European stretch. On my final show at Sugar in Victoria, I performed to basically no one during a rare snowstorm while suffering from debilitatingly tooth pain that had been getting incrementally worse over the course of the year. I tried to numb the pain with

Jameson. I hadn't seen a dentist or a doctor for years. My health was not something I thought about at this time in my life. Self-care wasn't the buzzword it is today. I got a very expensive root canal when I returned to Alberta and spent the winter licking my wounds, hanging with Kathryn at her place in Calgary and preparing for what would be the busiest year of my life.

◆

My first show of 2008 was Tomorrow Never Knows Festival in Chicago. Weez-L missed his flight, and I ended up having to perform alone. Erik could be elusive. He was often difficult to get a hold of. He wouldn't respond to emails. People all over town would call and email me looking for him. You used to have to ring his mom's landline to talk to him. He could be unreliable, sometimes forgetting to bring his equipment from his family's farm when travelling to shows. Worst of all, we had been operating on a handshake agreement that we made back in 2005 that he would get 25 percent of any show fees I got and it was creating issues for me.

That agreement made sense when I was making one hundred dollars a night opening at the Sidetrack Café, but it was becoming untenable after playing almost two hundred shows together around the world. All of our flights, hotels, food, travel expenses, merch costs, the booking agent cut, and the management cut came out of my show fees while he didn't have to pay for anything. This caused tension between us. He got paid by my managers quarterly and I wasn't making any money at all. He would get a cheque from Upper Class after sending them a list of shows that he had played. But being ridiculously disorganized and busy touring with me, Erik would forget to send them the list or write it in illegible scribbles and he wouldn't receive anything from them for months at a time. The thing was that Weez-L was so incredible on stage that it made it all worth it. He could barely keep his life organized off stage, but behind the decks, he was a savant. Erik had a strange charisma about him that worked well for our live show, which just kept getting better and better.

In early 2008, he still hadn't been paid for any of the shows we'd played in 2007. The whole situation was unnecessarily complicated. I was reluctant to renege on our agreement, even though I wrote all the songs and our current arrangement was heavily lopsided in his favour. I wanted to make sure Weez-L was always fairly compensated. My managers and I had discussed the situation once or twice over the previous years but it lingered on. I just wanted to focus on music and hoped that my management would figure it out for me. My inexperience with the music industry had made me vulnerable.

The label finally explained how much money we were making from shows in invoices they sent to Weez-L and me. In 2006, we grossed $24,400 from live shows. After my management deducted 20 percent and my booking agent deducted 10 percent, we were left with $17,080. Weez-L got $4,270 of that for his 25 percent of net, and that left me with $12,810. I never saw it. It went towards what I can assume were expenses, leaving me with nothing. What those expenses were specifically was never explained to me. I felt as if I was facing insurmountable debt that I would never be able to pay off, a mysterious number that the label held hostage. My career seemed to be taking off, but my finances were a mess. I wish I had hired an independent accountant to figure it all out.

Going into *Afterparty Babies*, my managers discussed developing a more equitable structure with Weez-L, where he would be paid a set amount incrementally as my fees increased, but it never went into effect. My management did eventually decide that Weez would be responsible for repaying missed flights and handling his own gear repair.

I was developing some name recognition in the electronic world after signing with Big Dada. Simian Mobile Disco reached out and I recorded a demo for them. I recorded vocals at U.K. DJ and producer Hervé's flat in London for what became a collaboration with legendary Canadian turntablist A-Trak called "Roll with the Winners."

2008 was a unique time to be releasing a new album: the music industry was experiencing a significant contraction right as my career was building momentum. The artists who were active back when labels could use television and radio to sell CDs in significant numbers went on to have a lifelong advantage over those of us who came in at the tail end of this time. Now that I was releasing internationally on bigger labels like Anti and Big Dada, my music became more susceptible to intellectual property theft. On January 21, my sophomore album leaked and was posted to torrent sites What.cd and Waffles, six weeks before it was scheduled to be released. This didn't stress me out too much. Since I had benefited greatly from internet piracy by using cracked programs to produce both of my albums, it felt appropriate in a karmic way. But Upper Class was freaked out and tried to get it taken down to no avail.

In February, I returned to London to do press for the album. We had all of our work permits and necessary documents but

Weez-L's lack of seriousness upon arriving in the U.K. almost got him deported back to Canada by border patrol. The border guard made me spit some bars for him to prove that I was a rapper. This was the first but not the last time that I've been forced to do this. I wonder if they ask guitar players in white rock bands crossing the border to plug in their amps and play "Freebird." We hung out at the Big Dada office all day, doing interviews and scooping up vinyl from their back catalogue.

Grime icon Jammer invited me over to his mom's house in Leytonstone where I was interviewed by him on camera in the dank, claustrophobic basement that has become a significant location in grime history. Jammer filmed me rapping in the very same stairwell that Kano and Wiley had once battled in. I wrote my name in permanent marker on the graffiti-covered wall next to many of my favourite artists, feeling like I had been welcomed into the fraternity of grime.

That night at my show at Bardens Boudoir in Dalston, Jammer and some members of Neckle Camp showed up, jumping on stage with me to rap over the beat for "House Music." I celebrated turning twenty-two at midnight with my Canadian friends Jahmal and Julia in my tiny hotel room.

I spent most of my birthday conducting interviews with the European press at Hotel Johann in Berlin. A publicist named Soeren took me out that night, and my Edmontonian friend Stephanie, who had been going to school in Munich, joined us. We all went to see Justice at a massive venue called Huxley's and then we hit a mysterious warehouse and raved into the early hazy morning before Stephanie caught her train back. This turned out to be one of my best birthdays ever, a transcendent evening where I learned to appreciate the rave on a higher level. From there, Weez and I flew to Dublin where I was happy to return and visit our pals in the band Super Extra Bonus Party. They were like the Irish version of Shout Out Out Out Out. Erik and I would hang at their house when we were in town and drink Buckfast with them.

But our performance in Dublin couldn't have gone worse. Back then, Weez-L played my beats off a Numark CDX he owned. This device was a very large, front-loading CD turntable that came out in 2005 and was already archaic in 2008. You could put a CD inside and it had a platter with a fake vinyl record on top of it that you could manipulate. This allowed us to play my beats live and for Weez-L to scratch and mix them with his other records.

There weren't Pioneer CDJs in every bar on Earth like there are today. DJing with your computer was not yet very common either. Released in 2004, Serato Scratch Live allowed you to use your computer, an audio interface box, two signal records, and a Rane mixer to DJ and scratch using digital files but we didn't have it yet. Weez-L travelled with a box of real vinyl records that featured breaks, samples, and sound effects that he would scratch over my beats. This led to hundreds of dollars of overage charges from airlines in Europe.

Unfortunately, we were having problems with the Numark CDX. The fake record on top came off and we had to crazy glue it back on. The machine had a tendency to overheat, which would make the CD inside skip, putting a complete stop to our show. This happened during our performance in Dublin. Then Weez-L's headphones exploded and died. I was also losing my voice. Everything stopped cooperating at the worst possible time. The final date of this European sojourn was in Paris where we played at La Flèche D'or with borrowed records and gear sourced by Big Dada.

That's when I first learned about European hospitality. Before the show, we were served braised chicken and a beautiful bottle of red wine as we overlooked the graffiti-covered walls lining the train tracks outside the venue, which was inside the former Gare de Charonne. In North America, you were lucky if you got a fruit tray and a drink ticket. There was much more of an appreciation for artists and art in Europe. In London, they played cutting-edge electronic music and grime during prime time on BBC Radio. They have real music culture. In Berlin, the entire society seemed to be based around art and club culture, instead of it being an afterthought like it was back in Canada. Despite our tech issues, I came away feeling creatively nourished and thrilled to return soon with a new album to share.

Afterparty Babies was released on March 4, 2008. The critical response was mixed. It got crushed with a one N review in Toronto's NOW *Magazine* by Tim Perlich: "The boring beats and throwback rhyme flow (circa '92)—which is weak even by Edmontonian standards—put *Afterparty Babies* somewhere beneath Don Cash's home demos and the outtakes from Organized Rhyme's *Huh? Stiffenin' Against the Wall*." Damn. *Pitchfork* suggested my motives were unclear: "Most of the songs here are critiques of the same fast, slick youth culture in which Pemberton is an avid participant, and this paradox is what gives *Afterparty Babies* its self-contradicting aura."

The album was better received in the U.K. where they had the backdrop of garage and grime to understand where I was coming from. "Subscribers to the 'hip hop is dead' school of thought are dealt a crushing blow by the release of this talented Canadian wordsmith's second album," wrote *The Observer*'s Bharat Azad. *The Guardian* gave it four stars, saying, "Pemberton's second album owes much of its charm to his confidence to be exactly who he is" and that "Pemberton doesn't strain to impress. He doesn't need to. His darting intelligence and racing imagination are evident in every line."

To promote the album, we went on a North American tour with Born Ruffians, an upbeat Toronto-based indie rock trio who were also booked by Steven Himmelfarb. The legendary electronic label Warp Records released their album *Red, Yellow & Blue* on the same day that *Afterparty Babies* came out. This was during a strange period when Warp was regularly signing rock bands. Born Ruffians appeared to be primed for meteoric success. Their lead singer Luke Lalonde looked like a young Bob Dylan. This tour was another dual headline arrangement where I usually played first and the lion's share of the audience was coming to see the buzzy rock band. Born Ruffians were lovely guys, a band of nerdy brothers who were a joy to share a rental van with. But my patience for being an opener for rock bands and playing for unreceptive white audiences who didn't understand rap without even getting paid for it was wearing thin.

Right at the beginning of the tour, we noticed our show dates lined up with another band with a similar sound to Born Ruffians. We ended up playing in some of the same cities on or around their show dates. They were called Vampire Weekend and they became one of the biggest bands in the world that month, siphoning a like-minded audience away from our tour.

But we made the most of it and had a decent time on the road. The shows actually turned out to be better than I expected with a hundred or more people attending most of the shows and many fans coming out to see both of us.

Born Ruffians had a film crew from IFC making a documentary about them. It had a reality TV show feel to it: the directors tried to manufacture screen-worthy moments. In New Orleans, they suggested our touring party should go take a look at the aftermath of Hurricane Katrina. The IFC team insisted I walk alongside this white Canadian rock band in a storm-ravaged Black American neighbourhood, still filled with boarded-up windows and derelict houses years after the initial disaster.

Their local contact was a jazzy white woman who explained to us that the symbols spray-painted on the doors of houses signified how many bodies were found after the flooding. It looked like a war-torn country. It was like we were on an American ruin porn field trip. A small Black boy yelled at us to go away. I agreed with him. On camera, you can hear me say, "I wanna bounce, I don't like this." It was exploitative and the other guys didn't want to be there either. The IFC team interviewed Born Ruffians afterwards to get their take on what happened. Even though I was the only Black person in the touring party, no one from the film crew asked me how I felt about it.

During the tour, our gear issues continued. The CDX overheated and literally melted during an in-store performance at Waterloo Records in Austin because of the boiling temperature in the city. We had test presses of the *Afterparty Babies* instrumentals on vinyl, but the borrowed turntables were skipping and wouldn't cooperate. Our tracks would stop at random and I would have to rap acapella. We tried to use instrumentals from random 12-inch records we had with us instead of my beats. It was a disaster and we looked woefully unprepared. I recorded a live Daytrotter session with Weez-L scratching, my music manager on drums, and his friend Paul on bass because of our malfunctioning gear.

Thankfully, we didn't have too many shows left on the tour. It ended at the Pike Room in Pontiac, Michigan. We were all so sick with the flu that only I ended up performing. During an instrumental break on "House Music," I ran to the bathroom, puked, and then jumped back on stage to finish the song.

I didn't have long to get better. Six days later, Weez-L and I would be joining forces with one of my musical heroes, Buck 65, and turntable wizard Skratch Bastid in Moncton. Buck was touring Canada in support of his album *Situation*, which featured a verse by me on the song "Benz."

It would be my first opportunity to perform in front of consistently packed Canadian audiences that had an appreciation for off-kilter rap music. Weez-L finally bought Serato and we joined the rest of the twenty-first century. There were no more technical mishaps. Buck had hired lighting and effects people to build a stage set-up at every venue. Starting on the East Coast, we played primarily in theatres. Director Christopher Mills made a documentary with footage from the tour called *The Lost Tapes*.

The shows were some of the best of my life. I felt like I had finally found an audience in my own country that appreciated what I was doing. I performed to engaged rooms at nineteen shows from coast to coast and sold almost eight thousand dollars' worth of merch.

Six days later, at the beginning of May, we were already packing our bags for Europe again. Borrowing a DJ mixer from legendary group Coldcut, we played for ravenous hordes across the U.K.: London, Brighton, Leeds, Newcastle, Liverpool, Edinburgh, Glasgow. These audiences were rowdier and drunker than any I'd experienced before. Leaving the Tube on the way to a show in Hoxton, I saw a young man with a gaping, gushing head wound sharing a bottle of wine with an older homeless man. I asked if he was okay and he exclaimed, "Cadence Weapon! I'm coming to your show tonight!"

But unlike on that first European leg, as I travelled in trains rattling across the lush English countryside to share my music with the world, I didn't really appreciate it in the moment. All I wanted to do was get back to Edmonton to see my friends and to get back to Kathryn. In the face of my touring schedule, maintaining our relationship had proven to be incredibly difficult. I didn't have a smartphone. The first iPhone had come out less than a year before. My laptop was ancient and the keys didn't work so I had to attach a USB keyboard to use it. Wi-Fi was not prevalent. Video chat wasn't possible. I would buy calling cards to reach her back home from the occasional payphone, struggling to navigate our different time zones. I was pushed to the edge of exhaustion by my ceaseless touring schedule and still dealing with anxiety about not being able to afford expenses back home. My focus wasn't on our relationship and it was probably incredibly frustrating for her.

Weez-L and I went to Barcelona to perform at a huge multi-room club called Razzmatazz. The promoter took us for a fancy dinner and I ate a strange dish that had strawberries inside of a piece of fish. It was almost eleven o'clock; I was somewhat alarmed by how late we were dining on the night of a show but I was told not to worry about it. Eventually, we headed to the venue and stepped onto the stage with a curtain in front of us. "Smells Like Teen Spirit" was playing on the PA. The curtain fell, our beats dropped, and the crowd roared. We performed at 3:15 a.m., which is apparently a normal time to play in Spain. We left the venue a couple hours later, surrounded by sleepy Spanish ravers, all of us misted by a warm summer rain under a rapidly brightening sepia sky.

Our next show was in Dublin opening for Public Enemy at Tripod. Known for his hard-edged political rhymes, Chuck D was one of my biggest influences. It was funny how I gravitated to Chuck while Weez-L chopped it up with Flavor Flav because I always felt like we had a similar dynamic between us. Before their show, Chuck D was stretching, running up and down stairs, working up his heart rate. I had never seen anyone do that before but it made sense, considering they performed for over an hour. After the show, Chuck took a photo with me, gave me his auto-graph and his email address, and hooked me up with a free Public Enemy shirt.

I always show love to younger artists now because of how respectfully and openly Chuck treated me. After performing with Public Enemy, I realized that I had shared the stage with nearly all of my stylistic forebears in alternative hip-hop in just a few short years: De La Soul, Mos Def, Kool Keith, Busdriver, Fatlip from the Pharcyde, Jurassic 5, Questlove from the Roots, and Del tha Funkee Homosapien. I felt like I was solidly becom-ing part of that lineage.

On a short trip back to Edmonton before heading back to England to play one of the biggest festivals in the world, Glastonbury, Kathryn and I broke up and I found out I was once again nominated for the Polaris Music Prize. These experiences encapsulated the duality of my life at the time. It felt like for every great opportunity I had, there was some drawback that brought me back down to earth. I felt like I was on one of those airport moving walkways that stretched on into infinity with no emergency brake, leaving me trying helplessly to grab onto whatever moments I could along the way.

Jay-Z was the headliner at Glastonbury that year, a controversial decision at the time that now seems completely inoffensive. Meeting up with my managers at a hotel just outside of the farm where they held the festival, I was shocked to look out the front window of the lobby and see rapper Memphis Bleek, one of Jay-Z's proteges, standing there. Acknowledging that he had been recognized, Bleek moved to come inside and say hello and accidentally walked face first into a glass window instead of through the front door of the hotel.

The vibe at Glastonbury was decidedly not my thing. Camping outdoors and clomping around acres of fresh mud in galoshes isn't my idea of a good time. My shows were all poorly attended but especially the one I played just before Jay-Z's set. I was able to stumble away from the tent I had played in to join the crushing throng of humanity assembled to see this American hip-hop star take the stage. I had never been around so many people at the same time; there were faces as far as the eye could see going on forever. Noel Gallagher had said that having hip-hop at Glastonbury was "wrong," so Jay-Z opened the show by pulling out an electric guitar and singing along to Oasis's "Wonderwall" before transitioning into the rock-inflected tones of "99 Problems." This was one of the most subversive, defiant, provocative performance moments I'd ever seen. It was incredibly inspiring to see how he fought back.

A couple days later, I played in Birmingham and London with the Cool Kids, a Chicago rap duo with minimal, hard-hitting beats that felt both fresh and rooted in old school hip-hop at the same time. In between shows, I asked what they had been up to and they said they had been hanging at the club with Pharrell the night before. I think Weez-L and I had gotten some KFC. After that, we went on a whirlwind festival run performing at Eurockéennes, Roskilde, Splash!, Slottsfjell, Summercase, and Lounge on the Farm as well as dates in Glasgow, Dublin, Belfast, and Manchester.

All of this led up to our biggest show ever, Lollapalooza in Chicago. The lineup was absolutely jaw-dropping. The headliners that weekend were Kanye West, Radiohead, and Rage Against The Machine. The first day we arrived, I received a free Dell Inspiron laptop after doing a short interview with VICE. This was life-changing. There was a gift lounge where they were giving away free tattoos. We stayed with my friend Sasha at her spacious loft. We were about to play for a huge audience at one of the biggest festivals in the world. It felt like we were really building some tangible momentum. But I was also feeling angst about the instability of my personal life in the wake of my breakup with Kathryn. Would I be choosing between being a successful artist and having healthy relationships for the rest of my days?

Unfortunately, the grind of constant touring was also starting to get to Weez-L. His girlfriend had recently broken up with him and it was hitting him hard. He saw a photo of his ex with another guy on Facebook and had a meltdown. He started stomping around the loft, threatening to harm himself. It felt like losing control of his relationship made him try to gain it in other parts of his life. At our show, he climbed up the stage's scaffolding and dangled from it to draw attention to himself during our set. He appeared to be getting sick of being my sidekick, asking for us to start being billed as DJ Weez-L and Cadence Weapon.

We had another show the following week at Wolfe Island Music Festival where we were asked to DJ the afterparty. Weez-L moped around the whole time we were there. He had fried his Rane mixer on tour in the U.K. by not using the right voltage converter and was trying to get me and the label to pay for the repair. He wanted to spend the Wolfe Island party playing only his own music: dinosaur-inspired underground rap instrumentals. Weez-L was always trying to hustle his dino rap mix CDs at our tour dates. He had his own clothing brand called Rural Wear featuring hoodies with dinosaur fossils on them that he had mass produced. I tried to explain that this probably wouldn't be the best time to play his stuff. We had to rock the party right and we were responsible for painting people's final impression of the festival. He decided to not perform at all and threw a sealed plastic water bottle at my head. We played a couple university gigs in Ontario and he put in the bare minimum of effort. Those were our final shows together.

I returned to Europe with Skratch Bastid for a few dates in the fall. We rocked huge festivals in Lyon and Tilburg. My sister

Gena came to our show in Zurich. It was a remarkably low stress series of dates after the increasingly chaotic gigs with Weez-L. After we played Fri-Son in Fribourg, Switzerland, in typical respectful European style, the venue treated us to a delicious homemade dinner. I remember walking around the empty club and seeing a giant poster of the band Tad from when they had played there back in the '90s. Who opened for them? Nirvana. I wondered if one day people would see old posters of me supporting Born Ruffians or someone else and be surprised that I'd ever opened for anyone.

I ended off the year with a bang: a headlining thirteen-date Canadian tour featuring Woodhands as my opening act. They were two synth nerds from Toronto whom I got along with really well. Disc jockey duties were shared by DJ Cosmo in the Maritimes and DJ Co-op for the rest of Canada. Co-op and I knew each other vaguely through his connections to Peanuts & Corn and the Winnipeg rap scene. He was a bit older than me and had major dad vibes. But his indie rock sensibility, mature attitude, and good-natured sense of humour made him the perfect tour mate for me. Once we linked up, we had instant chemistry.

The dates were all well attended and there was a sense of excitement surrounding the tour. For the Edmonton show, I wanted to do something special. I put on an event at the Starlite Room called the Cadence Weapon Variety Show. I wanted it to be similar to the public access show *TV Party* from the '80s. I wore a suit, we put a couch on stage, and between songs, I interviewed guests like a late-night host. I had some of my friends sitting on stage the whole time and my uncle Brett and some members of his band joined me for the performance.

It was my big homecoming show. The house was packed and it ended up being one of my most memorable performances ever. I had played Halifax Pop Explosion on that tour and got a stick and poke tattoo on my left arm from my friend Laura with some lyrics from "New York Telephone Conversation" by Lou Reed: "Who has touched and who has dabbled here in the city of shows?" It felt like such a succinct encapsulation of the essence behind *Afterparty Babies*, this external analysis of the social scene, Page Six in lyric form.

By the end of October, I was completely tapped out after playing over a hundred shows with very little rest between them. Despite still being strapped for cash, physically depleted, and emotionally frayed from losing both my relationship and my DJ, I was feeling pretty accomplished. I started working on remixes and compiling features and outtakes for a mixtape I was calling *Separation Anxiety*. I thought of it as a palette cleanser, a stop-gap measure before delving into work on my next full-length album. But an unlikely opportunity would soon emerge that would completely change the direction of my career and place my words under more scrutiny than they had ever been before.

7

POET LAUREATE

In March 2009, on a typically blustery winter day, I was at the house I rented with my friends Nicki, Adam and Jessica off Whyte Avenue practising beatmatching with vinyl on my rickety turntables in my bedroom while watching the wisps of snow fall outside the C&E Railway Museum across the street when the doorbell rang. Local musician and filmmaker Trevor Anderson said he wanted to run something by me. I knew Trevor from playing shows with his band the Vertical Struts and doing a remix for his other group, the Wet Secrets. I invited Trevor upstairs and he told me that he wanted to nominate me for the position of poet laureate of Edmonton.

The first thing I said was "What is that?" I'd never heard of a poet laureate before. Having a poet laureate seemed like one of those things that certain cities did to prove their metropolitan status. It was like building an angular-looking Frank Gehry-inspired art museum or having an annual film festival. Trevor told me that I would be asked to write some poems and be the literary ambassador of the city. I'd represent Edmonton in my travels, similar to how I already did with my music. I was having trouble understanding how I could possibly be qualified for something like this. I looked up the outgoing poet laureate online and he was a seventy-four-year-old white man named E.D. Blodgett.

I'd performed at the occasional open mic night here and there and published poems in my high school newspaper, but I never thought of myself as a traditional poet. I idolized Leonard Cohen and appreciated how he oscillated between the artistic disciplines of poetry and music. I marvelled at the wildness of Bob Dylan's book *Tarantula* and dreamed of making an experimental poetry collection like that one day. I suppose Trevor saw my lyrics as poetry before I thought of them that way. (In his nomination letter, he called me a "poet of the people.") It was true that my songs were unabashedly Edmontonian. Maybe I could become a great artistic representative of the city.

But Upper Class was reluctant for me to apply. They thought it would distract me from my music. I had built up a strong infrastructure with international label distribution and booking agents. I had a lot of momentum following the release of *Afterparty Babies* and they were worried about squandering it. Like Kanye West once said, "Don't leave while you're hot, that's how Ma$e screwed up." Still, this seemed like a once-in-a-lifetime opportunity. The two-year appointment came with a ten-thousand-dollar honorarium that I would receive directly.

I prepared a few poems for my application and sent it in. They were called "Water, Alberta," "Windy Cities," and "Valley

Girls." The latter served as a tribute to the summers I'd spent hanging out in the city's river valley, Edmonton's most underrated landmark:

> *Our tall progeny may relocate*
> *But their souls will never leave this place*
> *Permission slips to whiskeyed alleys*
> *My heart belongs to the girls in the valley*

Soon after, I was invited for an interview in front of a six-person committee that included members of the Edmonton Arts Council; they asked me questions and had me perform. In the end, they picked me.

Selecting a young Black rapper to be Edmonton's third poet laureate was a radical choice that went against the public perception of the city as a staid government capital in a conservative cultural backwater. It signalled an aspirational progressivism that might hopefully seep into other parts of the city's future. It was as much about choosing me as choosing what I represented. It was a bombastic, controversial choice.

At twenty-three years old, I was the youngest poet laureate in the world at the time. Receiving this distinction drastically altered the trajectory of my career. It instantly boosted me from being an Albertan curiosity known primarily to music nerds to being a nationally recognized multidisciplinary artist.

The press largely perceived my appointment as something of a novelty, if not an outright insult to the world of traditional poetry. The *Edmonton Sun* made fun of me for saying that I was going to "do some poems" at my inauguration and called the position a waste of tax dollars. Peter Mansbridge smirked as he introduced the segment about the rapping poet on CBC's *The National*. The *Globe and Mail*'s Brad Wheeler made a head-to-head comparison between me and Shakespeare, including my most unpoetic lyrics and describing me as "a nice young man with little taste for gaudy medallions" while helpfully informing readers that "rappers are more often men than women, with lyrics not infrequently referring to 'bitches' and 'hoes.'" This was especially ironic because my song "Sharks" actually directly references *Hamlet*: "Sharking up lines from lawless resolutes."

My predecessor E.D. Blodgett did not attend my inauguration and was quoted by the *Globe and Mail* as saying he "didn't think that this was how a poet laureate was to be defined." I bristled at being criticized this way by a fellow artist. I received a great deal of support from Edmonton's first poet laureate, Alice Major, but my appointment must have been threatening to the city's literary establishment.

There were definitely some established poets in the city who were more qualified and experienced in the field. But as an artistic representative of the city, I had already proven myself a worthy ambassador. My live shows could've been sponsored by Tourism Alberta. Everywhere I went, I educated hundreds of people about the city and the province.

Over the years, people have told me that they moved to Edmonton because of my music. A guy from Russia wrote a blog post in which he said that he visited Oliver Square because of my song and was disappointed to arrive at a generic strip mall. I may have been an unconventional choice to many but I felt ready for the challenge, especially after Canada's Governor

General Michaëlle Jean gave Edmonton props at the 2009 Global Youth Assembly for selecting me:

> *I saw how this year, you stole the heavyweight title of*
> *Canada's hip-hop capital by appointing Cadence Weapon*
> *as your poet laureate! Mayor Mandel, you and the residents*
> *of Edmonton are to be commended for the leadership you are*
> *displaying in this regard. And I encourage others to follow suit.*

◆

My whole career is predicated on research. I pride myself on being able to dig harder than anyone else and find more specific references to draw from. So after I became poet laureate, I started studying. I read Amiri Baraka and John Berryman. Anticipating criticism of the technical structure of my poems, I examined different traditional forms. I found myself attracted to the visual, impactful writing of imagist poets like H.D. and William Carlos Williams.

I've always been passionate about lyrics but I started to think differently about them after I became poet laureate. When I first became a rapper, I wasn't writing with an audience in mind at all. I was trying to say the most radical thing I possibly could. I just wanted to write some fly lines. After my rhymes were belittled by the media, I told myself that you'd be able to print my future songs in book form and they would be unassailable on the page. I wanted to write myself into a protective cocoon that couldn't be breached.

Lyrics were one of the things that made me want to devour songs as a child but I didn't quite know what it was about them that I liked at first. Back in high school, my drama teacher Mr. Huot asked our class to share something that meant a lot to us. I showed him André 3000's blistering verse from OutKast's 1998 song "Y'all Scared" where he concisely deconstructs several decades of American drug policy in less than a minute.

I've obsessively analyzed lyrics for as long as I can remember. In the early internet era, I was a frequent user of OHHLA.com, the Original Hip-Hop Lyrics Archive. This was just masses of unverified text posted on some webpages, nothing like Genius and the crowd-sourced, meticulously annotated lyrics database and social network they've cultivated, but it was like a reference library to me.

One of the things that attracted me to lyricism was that it was a form of expression that was an equal playing ground. Just as basketball is a more accessible sport than hockey because the only equipment you need is a ball, some sneakers, and a hoop, rap was a game that anyone with a pad and a pen could play. And like basketball, the skills were scalable. You could easily try out techniques that you saw on TV at your local street court. At home, I would try to rap fast like Myka 9. Writing was incredibly empowering. As a shy nerdy Black kid growing up in the Canadian prairies, it felt like the only place where my words held weight was on the page.

Lyrics can be playful, powerful, painful. Listening to the legends and fables of the hip-hop stars I idolized, it seemed like you could really change the world with some well-placed words. Or at least change some minds, change some lives. That's what happened to me when I first heard Pharoahe Monch, Posdnous, Too Poetic from Gravediggaz, Ghostface, and Aesop Rock when

I was a kid. I appreciated how all the rappers had different ways of expressing themselves. The way you rapped was just as distinctive as your penmanship and just as difficult to copy.

Rhymes over a beat can be like an incantation, an electric burst of magic with limitless potential. But ultimately, lyrics are a form of communication, a vehicle for sharing ideas, memories, and emotions. It's about both grasping for the intangible and tapping into the collective consciousness. It's oral storytelling and it's also a way of making sense of your experiences and the world around you. Lyricism is the synthesis of life. Even mainstream pop songs have ideologies and perspectives that inform them.

Lyrics can be impactful. Rap verses are often used in criminal trials, as if they were incontrovertible evidence of real-world wrongdoing and not examples of artistic licence. I've seen careers ended with one line. I've seen lyrical beefs escalate into real-world conflicts. But I've also seen lyrics lead to outrageous wealth and fame. Part of what makes songwriting feel magical is the fact that even if you repeat the methodology behind making a hit, it might never feel quite the same when you try again. Despite what the pros in Nashville and L.A might tell you, it isn't an exact science.

For example, I remember a period of my life when I was writing really strong choruses for one particular month. I haven't gotten back to that place ever since. That was around when I wrote "Sunrise" with Alice Ivy. Anyone who tells you they can turn on the faucet and it pours out a torrent of hit songs is lying. No one can truly harness the intangible spirit of creativity. A big part of it is putting yourself in the right state of mind to write something. For me, that often means drinking lots of water, being well rested, being physically active, and having a clean environment at home.

You also need to be aware of when something magical is happening and how to properly capture it when it does. A songwriter is a composite of their influences and their experiences. The better you get at translating your experiences, the less you'll need to rely on your influences. When an artist puts more of themselves into the music, I find that it sounds better and resonates more with the listener. If you write about something that isn't true to your experience, you can hear it.

Personally, I think lyrics should be beautiful. The subject matter can be strange, dark, or disturbing, of course, but I think the construction, craft, and technique should be something you can marvel at. I love when lyrics feel *right*, like you couldn't possibly swap out a single word for something different. I appreciate when lyrics are skilful and artful but the technique doesn't needlessly bring attention to itself. You'd never see a great architect waving blueprints at passersby outside their completed skyscraper. Recently, I've marvelled at the vividly dense imagery in Frank Ocean's "Chanel," the playful battle wizardry of Tierra Whack on "Unemployed," and Jay-Z's nostalgic lyrical mastery on "Marcy Me."

My writing process has evolved throughout my career. My songs used to always be three verses, as was the rap custom back then. Now I sometimes write songs as if they were one long continuous verse like I'm freestyling on pirate radio. On my first two albums, I came up with the song titles first and then based all the lyrics around different themes. I'd write my verses before making the beats. Then I would create music that fit the topic of the song I'd already written. I never used to write along to a beat back then, which probably explains the disjointed nature of my early work. Now I always write along to the music, recording voice notes with nonsense words and flows and then editing the lyrics into something logical over time.

I like to get into a trance, listening to a looped beat for hours until the words and flows come to me. It's as if the beat is telling me what to say. By the time a song is finished, I feel like I've been living inside the music. Most of my best ideas have come while on a jog, washing the dishes, standing in front of the mirror in the bathroom, or doing anything where my creative mind is able to churn along in the background.

Artists are really just conduits for energy. I'm reluctant to ever take too much credit for anything that I write because I was just the person who caught the idea at that time. I believe that there's a pool of the same creative ideas that we all have access to, a well that we all draw from. The more often you write, the more you exercise that muscle, the easier it gets for you to draw from the well. We are the chosen vessels for these concepts and we have a responsibility to make the most of the gifts we are given.

In January 2020, I was invited to the Banff Centre, an arts and culture institution nestled in the Albertan mountains where musicians and artists from around the world of all disciplines go to learn, collaborate, and create. I was asked there by creative producer Rio Mitchell and audio engineer Tyler Fitzmaurice to work on a project for Fort Edmonton Park, a former trading post that was turned into a heritage site that recreates what Edmonton was like in the late 1800s and early 1900s. I got to collaborate with an incredible group of Indigenous musicians for a project called Mâmawapihk (the meeting place). During those sessions, I met a Cree elder named Ekti Cardinal who talked about listening to "the little people"—these small spectral beings who are always around us, whispering ideas to those who are open enough to hear them. I'd previously suspected that there were external spiritual forces behind creativity so it was really encouraging to hear her speak about this.

◆

Regionalism has been a recurring theme in my music since the very start. This tendency in my writing led to a turning point in the way I thought about my subject matter, inspired by a transcendent young Oilers player named Connor McDavid.

Edmonton had a proud hockey history going back to Wayne Gretzky's 1980s Oilers championship dynasty that put the city on the map internationally, but the team hadn't found much success in recent years. With the arrival of the incredibly skilled McDavid, fans in Edmonton were feeling optimistic again. Trucks drove by with orange-and-blue flags, radio jocks were discussing the team, the energy was palpable. Pride for the Oilers hadn't been at this level since the 2005–06 team made it to the Stanley Cup Final. I felt the urge to make an anthem for this kid, something for fans to blast in their trucks on the way to the game, a song that would encourage local pride. Co-produced with Gibbs, "Connor McDavid" took on a life of its own. It was played for Connor live on television during *Hockey Night in Canada*.

Weirdly enough, the experience of writing for hockey fans inspired me to see how I could potentially create social change through my lyrics. I always appreciated the subversive potential of lyrics, which Samuel A. Floyd Jr. describes in *The Power of Black Music* as "a musical code decipherable by knowers of the culture but inaccessible to those outside it."

Struggling to find a place to rent after moving to Toronto in 2015, I wrote about the city's housing crisis and gentrification from the perspective of a demonic condo developer hellbent on destroying the social fabric of society. Inspired by the yuppie satire of David Byrne, I lampooned the NIMBYism of Toronto in my song "High Rise" and ended up getting interviewed by the *Toronto Star* and asked to speak on a panel about vertical living.

From that point on, I started using my personal experiences to write something more universal. On my most recent album, 2021's *Parallel World*, I was inspired to write more overtly political songs by the social effects of the COVID-19 pandemic. I had previously shown an inclination towards political commentary on older tracks like "30 Seconds" but had never done it with as much thought and research behind it. I wrote songs about racial profiling, the erasure of Black Canadian history, structural inequality, systemic racism, and how the surveillance state disproportionately impacts people of colour.

Inspired by my partner Sara's work as a labour reporter, I had become more plugged into the news and the world around me than ever before during the pandemic. The protests following the murder of George Floyd made me feel a responsibility to speak truth to power. I wanted to make a difference with my lyrics and try to make an impact like the socially conscious artists who came before me.

My song "Skyline" was inspired by a walk down Queen Street West in Toronto after the first COVID-19 pandemic lockdown ended. I saw closed stores pockmarked with For Rent signs, and the only new businesses were dozens of legal marijuana shops. They were a harbinger of gentrification, the new coffee shop.

I continued down the street and walked by the encampments at Trinity Bellwoods for the first time. This scale of poverty was something I was used to seeing in the Downtown Eastside in Vancouver and Skid Row in Los Angeles but never in Toronto. It seemed to be a direct result of the government's failure to provide affordable housing. The city was doing eviction blitzes over video chat during the pandemic, kicking people out of their homes at a rapid rate during a global health emergency.

These encampments were also a symbol of the human cost of structural inequality. Some of the displaced were artists and people of colour. My upstairs neighbours on Roncesvalles had just told me they were permanently moving to a different city to escape the pandemic. I thought about the privilege it takes to be able to just leave and get a house elsewhere if things aren't going your way. I thought about who is prioritized in our cities. I criticized both Mayor John Tory and Premier Doug Ford on the track.

On July 20, 2021, the City of Toronto cleared an encampment in Alexandra Park with the help of private security and police officers that numbered in the hundreds. Nine people were arrested as city workers in hazmat suits destroyed tents and rifled through personal belongings. I was invited to perform at a nearby protest by the Encampment Support Network, a volunteer organization that provides help and supplies for unhoused people in

Toronto. I was joined on stage by activists Desmond Cole and Diana Chan McNally. I performed "Skyline" live surrounded by people who had just been evicted from the park as well as people from other communities.

I felt like I'd come to an important turning point with my lyrics. Writing about the blues in her book *Lyrical Protest*, Mary Ellison describes the role of the blues singer as having a responsibility to "create empathetic channels of communication between the individual and society, and give potent public voice to shared grievances and complaints." I felt like I had made my most meaningful music yet by using my platform to shine a light on injustice.

◆

I took office as poet laureate on July 1, 2009. I immediately became inundated with press requests beyond anything I'd experienced before. I performed all over the city. Shania Twain interviewed me on CBC Radio. I was invited to speak at several schools and I talked to kids about my journey and the importance of art, music, and poetry. I was invited to be a panellist on CBC's *Canada Reads* in 2010 where I defended Douglas Coupland's *Generation X*. I felt a sentimental connection to his satirical send-up of youth culture, seeing it as a predecessor to *Afterparty Babies*.

My managers at Upper Class coordinated directly with Edmonton Arts Council on my behalf. When the contract came in, my managers told me not to sign it and that they would deal with it. The next time I saw the contract, it said, "The Edmonton Public Library, the Edmonton Arts Council, and the City of Edmonton agree to pay the Poet Laureate an honorarium in the amount of

$5,000 for each year of the two-year term for a total of $10,000 over two years. Payment will be made to Upper Class Recordings." When I asked them if they were taking money from this literary position and applying it to my music debt, they ignored me. Any time I brought it up, they didn't respond to my emails. I was earning pocket money from DJ gigs and freelance writing, which was barely enough to make ends meet, and I had earmarked that poet laureate money as a substantial amount that could help get me over the hump. Despite asking about it several times, I never got an answer.

As the poet laureate opportunities stacked up, I was working on demos for my third album with the basic home studio equipment that my music manager had bought and flown to Edmonton to help me set up at the end of 2008. By early 2010, I was spending more time in Montreal and Toronto, adapting my demos into live band arrangements at Rehearsal Factory with some session musicians that the label had connected me with. I flew back across the country to read an original piece called "Victory" while some medals were presented at the 2010 Vancouver Olympics. I had my afro mohawk and I wore a bright pink cowboy shirt.

I went to the Canadian Poet Laureate Summit as part of Halifax Jazz Festival that summer. The poets all discussed what kind of social impact they could have on their cities through their writing and we all performed on a boat and at a club. I was commissioned to write a poem that was posted on banners hung up throughout Edmonton's downtown core, featuring the work of local artists, whom I selected.

The poem I wrote was called "Monuments (The City in Three Parts)." It commented on the nature of Edmonton's urban self-perception as well as the value of natural and manufactured landmarks. I thought of the whole thing as a public meta-art project that would convince people to spend more time down-town while reading about the idea of the city simultaneously:

Have you been to The City?

When you read this
is it among colours?
The rush of infinity ants
passing gold and crimson

The founders,
their drinks on blueprint coaster
the wasted nights

Them of the bridge
bowing and swaying at the will of Aeolus
No shelter cushions the blow

Behind the unnatural tribute
a greening artifact is a gridiron play

If any of these places exist so must this thought
There is no City apart from the minds of those who live there
and a city is not a City until it believes it is one

So may I ask again
have you been to The City?

My term as poet laureate ended in June 30, 2011. I was suc-ceeded by Anna Marie Sewell, a local artist who founded the

Stroll of Poets Society and had been active as a poet for two decades, and I was there to pass the torch at her inauguration. I went on to release a book of poetry on Montreal's Metatron Press in 2014 called *Magnetic Days*. The whole experience of being poet laureate changed the trajectory of my career and made me completely rethink my role as an artist.

◆

In 2019, I was invited to speak to a group of young men at the Edmonton Young Offender Centre. Located in a bleak area on the far northwest edge of the city just beyond Anthony Henday Drive, the juvenile detention centre is a squat brutalist building with the outdated design characteristics seen in the plentiful mini-malls scattered around the city. I felt claustrophobic as soon as I stepped foot inside. I was led through the halls by a corrections officer to what looked like a typical school classroom with a television monitor for me to play my music videos on. There was a glass panel in the wall so the students could be observed from the hallway.

The majority of the kids were Black and Indigenous. Some were withdrawn, a couple were gregarious, a few seemed anxious. But they all had one thing in common: they loved rap. Most of them were emcees themselves. We went around the room and one by one, they kicked verses for me. The subject matter was drugs, sex, violence, and materialism. They wrote songs about "juuging and finessing" and buying red-bottom Louboutin shoes, their rhymes representing an aspirational escape from the oppressively grim setting they found themselves trapped in. They were heartened by the typical tropes of contemporary trap music. When it was Q&A time, they asked me what car I drove ("don't have one"), how much money I had ("I make a living and not much else"), and where my jewellery was ("I have some tiny gold chains at home but I wasn't allowed to bring them").

One of the Indigenous boys seriously impressed me with his lyrics. He had real poetic verve to his writing; it was soulful and contemplative. He had one line about how he watches the sun change into the moon from his cell. This particular image still comes to my mind from time to time. That's a powerful lyric. For these young men, writing was their primary form of expression, their release from a shackled existence. With the corrections officer, I walked out to look at their empty, cramped cells in the panopticon setting that makes up the hall where they spend most of their days. I thought it might be the most uninspiring environment possible. And yet that boy had come up with that line there. The power of an engaged mind is unstoppable. Before I left, I encouraged them to stay focused on rapping together, to get into a studio when they get released. Arrested bodies with free minds.

8

IT TAKES A VILLAGE

For many years, I was resistant to the idea of moving away from Edmonton. In 2008, I wrote a song called "We Move Away" that questioned why anyone would ever leave a great place like this. I felt a deep sense of loyalty to the city and the people in it which I brought with me everywhere I went. I wondered if I stayed put, if maybe I could become Canadian rap's answer to Bruce Springsteen in New Jersey. Plus, so much of what made my music great was predicated on the environment that I'd grown up in. What if I went elsewhere and failed? Then again, how many of the great artists that I looked up to lived in the same place for their whole lives? Would we still be talking about Bob Dylan today if he had never moved away from Duluth, Minnesota?

Even though I'd played all over the world, many of my fondest music memories happened in Edmonton. The first live local rock show that I can remember going to was a house party. The

Vertical Struts played on the roof of Hecla Block on Boyle Street on June 26, 2004. A two-piece featuring Raymond Biesinger and Trevor Anderson, they played blistering art punk and were signed to local label Pop Echo Records, which was run by Travis Dieterman a.k.a. Travy D, one of the DJs who put on the famed Mod Club parties at Halo. Everyone looked so cool and was smartly dressed, wearing either preppy designer garments or perfectly coordinated punk uniforms of black leather jackets and Vans. It was like being in a Strokes video or something. It was what I imagined shows must be like in Brooklyn. It was different from the house parties I'd gone to in high school where kids chugged a two six of Sour Puss and puked up neon bile.

After that night, I went to as many shows as possible and discovered a seemingly unending well of compelling local bands: Whitey Houston, 7 and 7 Is, Our Mercury, Bebop Cortez, Field + Stream, the Secretaries, Frosted Tipz, Junior Bloomsday, Mark Birtles Project, Faunts, All Purpose Voltage Heroes. The Wolfnote and the Floor were getting popular when I first hit the scene. The local bands often shared members. The punk energy of these groups started to influence my performance style. There was a sarcastic edge to many of the acts coming out of Edmonton in the mid-'00s and synthesizers were prevalent. I saw in them a reflection of the electronic rap I was making in my mom's attic, which I didn't see represented at all in the staid local hip-hop scene.

The Wet Secrets started as a drunken dare between friends and became a local supergroup featuring members of the Vertical Struts, Whitey Houston, and Faunts. The members all wore matching red-and-white marching band outfits, even breaking out some brass instruments. I made a Baltimore club remix of their song "The Chinball Wizard." They played sludgy, anthemic rock songs with titles like "I Teabagged Myself" and "Grow Your Own Fucking Moustache, Asshole."

There was D.B. Buxton, the notorious street busker known for his sharp mod wardrobe, dazzling talent, and mouth full of busted teeth. He was an absolutely incredible performer. He performed in front of the Army & Navy store on Whyte Avenue every weekend, sometimes in -20 degree Celsius weather, playing for disrespectful barhopping drunks. His records never did his talent as a live performer justice. If he lived in Los Angeles, he probably could've been like Ariel Pink without the fall from grace. He had a similarly prolific output, played multiple instruments, and seemed to know every style of music. Edmonton didn't know what to do with him.

One of the bands that influenced me the most was Dietzche V. and the Abominable Snowman. Helmed by Jered Stuffco, his band made live electro funk with vintage hardware. I remember seeing Jered plugging floppy disks into his ancient synthesizer at their shows. Their music had elements of French filter house and Belgian electronic body music. Nothing else in town sounded like them. There had never been electronic music with this level of sophistication coming from our city before. They were like Edmonton's version of Chromeo but with a darker, weirder edge, singing sarcastic songs about sex addiction. Their big local hit was "Bromance" with its shout-along chorus that went "We're gonna get so high tonight!" Jered played all the keyboard parts on my album *Hope in Dirt City*, signed to Upper Class Recordings after I did, and later found success in the electronic music world with his label Good Timin' under the name Jex Opolis.

But the biggest local inspiration for me was Shout Out Out Out
Out. Nik Kozub was the leader of this group and it featured
members of several existing local bands. They were Edmonton's
answer to !!! or the Juan Maclean. Nik recorded my first album
and organized my first proper live performance as a solo artist at
Victory Lounge. It functioned as my introduction to the scene
from one of the most well-known figures in it. There was a stadium rock flair to Shout Out Out Out Out's performances:
they'd connect an impossibly complex array of synths using MIDI
and jump in the air and do high kicks. They'd lead the crowd in
screaming "Shout! Out Out! Out Out!" as if it was a hockey
chant. They were electronic excess personified, the first band I'd
ever seen using modular synths on stage. They had six members,
including two drummers playing at the same time and multiple
bass players.

They regularly sold out the Starlite Room. Their 2005 single
"Nobody Calls Me Unless They Want Something" was a local hit
in the scene, a sardonic and snide track that was reminiscent of
LCD Soundsystem. Nik sang through a vocoder on every song,
making the band occasionally sound like Daft Punk with a social
conscience. Their song "They Tear Down Houses Don't They?"
was about the rapidly encroaching shadow of gentrification on
our city, a topic that resonated with me but was an unexpected
subject for a dance track. That spirit of unlikely juxtaposition
inspired me a lot. Like many of the other bands in town, they
also had a knack for comedic song titles, such as "Your Shitty
Record Won't Mix Itself" and "Chicken Soup for the Fuck You."

In a sea of aspiring local bands, Shout Out Out Out Out had the
most professional recordings, the best live show, and the most
complete artistic package. They were the standard that I aspired

to reach. They were often the only other act from Edmonton that I'd see when I played festivals in the States. I was featured on the song "Coming Home" from their sophomore album *Reintegration Time*. Nik and I became DJ partners, collaborating countless times in many different configurations. He was always encouraging and supportive of me and my music.

Though pretty diverse when it came to stylistic varieties of rock music, the Edmonton scene was almost completely male and 95 percent white. I was regularly the only Black kid at the rock show. Sometimes I felt like people didn't understand why I was there. They might walk by and shoot me a quizzical glance, as if I were some lost tourist. At first, I was just happy to be there, overjoyed to find out that my city had a music scene at all. But when I started playing live and releasing music, some of the older rockers didn't get it. I begged local labels like Pop Echo Records and Rectangle Records to sign me and they wouldn't give me the time of day.

It took labels from outside the city to see the value in what I was making, whereas for other people, all it took was being in a band or being interested in the music and they'd be easily integrated into the community. I tried as hard as I could to impress people in the scene, which was pretty laddish at times. I dressed the part and learned everything about the music that was coming out of our city. I drank beers at the same pubs and struggled to understand their inside jokes. Then I tried to make the best music I could possibly create, but it still felt like my presence was only begrudgingly accepted. I existed in a nebulous space, too indie for the rap scene, too rap for the indie scene.

When my music started taking off, it mostly happened outside of the city as a result of my internet savvy. I got press attention in the States from blogs and sites like *Pitchfork* before I received any in Edmonton. I played festivals in countries all around the world but I've still never been asked to play Edmonton Folk Music Fest, despite the fact that they regularly book local artists of all genres. I was excited and quite vocal about what I was making, which some people in the scene perceived as arrogance.

Back then, being ambitious wasn't cool. Many of the bands were perfectly happy just trying to meet women and drink beer. You were expected to have that Canadian attitude of false humility. Even if you thought what you were doing was good or interesting, you could never verbalize it. It wasn't that far removed from the '90s slacker era where the preferred pose was aloofness.

This encouraged me to spend my time at home, working on my craft. In Edmonton, the winters are long, which gives you plenty of time to stay inside and create. The isolation can make you get weird in a good way. We were not really on anyone's radar and that allowed for a further layer of strangeness to develop. We collectively indulged in our eccentricity, which stood in stark contrast to the stiff conservatism and brutish hockey hooliganism that were the mainstream attitudes in Edmonton.

Around the end of the '00s, I started to notice a new wave of younger local musicians who embodied a more lo-fi approach: the Bummers, Outdoor Miners, the Subatomics, Gobble Gobble, Happy Trendy, the Group Sound, Makeout Videotape, Michael Rault, Calvin Love, Jessica Jalbert, Brazilian Money, Matt Perri, Sean Nicholas Savage. They often recorded themselves and released their albums on cassette with hand-drawn covers. Despite musically sounding scrappier and more amateurish than the previous generation, there was also a wider embrace of the tunefulness of pop music among this group. This was radical in itself because pop had been considered a dirty word in the indie scene just a few years prior.

This new generation of local bands had their visibility boosted by Aaron Levin and Marie LeBlanc-Flanagan's music blog *Weird Canada*. Aaron, a fellow hip-hop nerd, collected vintage Club Monaco crewneck sweaters, and instead of saying he was buying albums, he would say he was "gripping records." Started in 2009, *Weird Canada* became a galvanizing force for the most unusual corners of the Canadian indie scene, quickly getting into promoting festival-style events under the Wyrd Fest banner. These shows, typically held at the ARTery when in Edmonton, were some of the most impressive, exciting bills I'd ever seen locally. There were also the Ramshackle Day Parade shows where artists like Zebra Pulse performed improvised experimental noise music. New venues to accommodate and foster these emerging musicians started to spring up like the Shark Tank, Avenue Skatepark, and Wunderbar.

As encouraging as these developments were for the growth of the scene, everything wasn't going perfectly for me in Edmonton. In the months following the release of *Afterparty Babies*, there were a few incidents in rapid succession that made me feel like I was wearing out my welcome. One night I was at the Black Dog and a woman I didn't know came up to me and asked, "Why are you here?" I said that I was just hanging out with my friends, and she responded, "No, I mean, why are you still living in Edmonton? Are you trying to be a big fish in a small pond or something?" Her words shook me. The suspicion that I wasn't welcome in the scene was no longer just an inkling I had. The last thing I wanted to do was become some aging local star who hogged all the gigs and press and refused to get out of the way for the next generation.

As my profile grew, it seemed like more and more people were irritated by my presence. At a show at the ARTery, I was blowing my nose in a bathroom stall when an older rocker guy came into the washroom. He spread around the untrue rumour that I was a cokehead. Rednecks in pickup trucks would yell homophobic slurs at me when I walked down the street, possibly because I was wearing "weird" hipster clothes, like white jeans. They represent a particular style of ugly Canadian that isn't specific to Alberta but is nonetheless worryingly prevalent there. There was a strange duality to life in Edmonton. The city is home to some of the friendliest, most open-hearted people I've ever met. But there was also occasionally an attitude of open hostility towards people who were different.

Toxic masculinity was rampant in Alberta. One night I was walking along 100th Avenue near Government Centre station with my friend Charlotte on the way to a backyard firepit. I briefly turned in her direction during our conversation, then looked ahead of me to see someone running full speed directly at me. He punched me right in the nose with full force. As I writhed on the ground, I screamed "Why?!" as a group of three muscle-bound jocks scuttled off laughing. It was the night of a UFC event and these guys were drunk, fired up, and looking for a fight. I wrote about the incident in my Shout Out Out Out collaboration "Coming Home" and became depressed for months afterwards. I couldn't help but feel like the city was turning against me.

In 2008, I saw my old friend David Carriere at a Christmas party at my friend Ted's family home. They were both back in town for the holidays from Montréal. David could've been a member of the Little Rascals: he looked like a human cartoon character. During an unusual period where my family stayed in one house for longer than a year, we had lived across the street from each other. We used to run around his room and listen to KoЯn. David had recently started a band called Silly Kissers with his partner Jane Penny. The two of them shared a childlike energy and often seemed more like brother and sister than boyfriend and girlfriend.

While we were all standing around the kitchen chatting, some incredible music came on. I stopped in mid-conversation to say, "What is this?" Ted said it was an album that he had recently recorded with David and Jane. I couldn't believe it. From that point on, I listened to the Silly Kissers album *Love Tsunami* ceaselessly. It blew me away. The songs were like previously undiscovered '80s new wave artifacts. There seemed to be five different vocalists and you never knew who was singing when. There was something theatrical about the vocal performances on the album; it was as if they were the lost children of Bowie. The music was brittle but extremely catchy. The project was totally uninhibited. Its feeling of freedom was intoxicating.

I'd see photos of the band performing at theatres in Montréal on Facebook and they were all dressed flamboyantly with dramatic stage makeup. They were all smiling and having fun. No one was yelling at them from a truck. It seemed like anything was possible in Montréal.

I had long held a romantic view of the city after watching *Ladies and Gentlemen . . . Mr. Leonard Cohen*. I played at Jupiter Room to an audience of about five people in 2005 at the POP Montréal Festival. The next year I played at Club Lambi and the building was at capacity with a line around the block of journalists and fans trying to get in. It was one of the first moments when I felt like I had arrived. My first time in town was when I shot the video for "Black Hand" in an old factory building in Verdun. It felt like each time I came to the city, I fell in love with it a little bit more. If my old neighbour David had moved there and reinvented himself, maybe I could too.

It was a risk to move across the country to a city where I didn't speak the language and barely knew anyone. But I knew that I'd kick myself if I never took the chance. I wanted a new challenge. I wanted to be in the heart of our country's artistic scene to really see how my music stacked up against the best of the best. I moved, staying on my friend Monique's couch at her house on Roy and de Mentana. She had come from Edmonton several months before I did.

The night after I arrived in Montréal, I went to see Micachu and the Shapes play at Il Motore. Based in London, they were the exact kind of band who would never make the trek to Edmonton. Most international touring acts avoided our city, opting to play in Calgary (since it's closer to the U.S. border) or skipping Alberta entirely. The show completely blew my mind. I bopped wildly, soaking in the group's unbridled intensity, and I talked to them after, about the handful of times I'd been to the U.K. I looked around the room with wild-eyed wonder, amazed by how many other people in this town were also interested in music like this.

Monique's place was where I first started to experience the lifestyle of the city. There was a local culture of dinner parties and park gatherings that was different from what I was used to back home. Our friend Nevine came to visit from Toronto and we all did mushrooms and hung out among the stately fountains of Parc La Fontaine. The branches on the trees looked like arms and the leaves moved like a hand's flexing fingers. The bucolic environment appeared muted and suspended in time like an eighteenth-century French landscape painting.

I eventually moved in with Ted, my pal who'd thrown the Christmas party back in Edmonton, and three others, including Jane Penny from Silly Kissers. Jane was bright-eyed and freckly with a one-of-a-kind laugh, an unmistakable series of bleating sounds made in rapid succession like a machine gun being fired. The apartment was in the heart of the Plateau on St. Laurent near Duluth. The roads nearby were narrow and paved with cobblestones like an ancient European hamlet. There were cafés and parkettes filled with people chatting at all hours of the day and night. A porn theatre called Cinéma L'Amour was just steps away from our building. So was the majestic Parc Jeanne-Mance, which felt like our backyard.

The walls in our apartment were painted algae blue and there was a door that led to a communal nearby rooftop that was lined with loose pebbles and surrounded by neighbouring apartments where we would drink under the stars. Our place was above a pet shop and the pub Barfly, whose noisy customers would smoke cigarettes outside and scream into the early morning hours. The apartment was filthy. There always seemed to be a mysterious new roommate rotating in. At night, we'd throw house parties or go to shows at neighbourhood venues like Le Divan Orange and Casa del Popolo. When POP Montréal would swing around, we'd attend each other's shows and perform together.

◆

I remember my first time venturing to the Mile End. It was a few months after I'd moved to the city. I was with Jane, Dave, and Sebastian Cowan. Seb was a skinny young man from Vancouver who reminded me of the protagonist of a Mark Twain adventure novel. He'd wear a uniform of white tank top and slacks while doing sound for shows at Divan Orange. Starting from Duluth, it felt like we were walking forever. When we got to several abandoned buildings on Beaubien in the dead of night, I honestly felt a little scared and wondered where exactly they were taking me. Walking up the stairs into the large open loft space, there was a projector and a bunch of people sitting on the floor. A guy named Jasper Baydala performed songs there between screenings of black-and-white art films, doing a hyperactive Bob Dylan impression on guitar.

Lab Synthèse was an arts space that Seb started with some friends in 2007. They lived there and threw afterparties and live music shows. It was the first loft I went to. Not long after that, I went to meet my friend Courtney at another loft called Silver Door. A guy named Jackson helped me find the place when I looked lost on the corner of Parc and Van Horne. A band called Angels in America were playing. It seemed more like an apartment than a music venue. By day, part of Silver Door functioned as a recording studio for bands like Pat Jordache, Karneef, and Sheer Agony. The show was representative of the experimental rock scene that I often associated with Montréal through labels like Constellation Records and bands like Godspeed You! Black Emperor and Silver Mt. Zion.

There was a lawless energy to these unofficial shows that added a tinge of excitement to the proceedings. I returned to Lab Synthèse for a show where Braids, Pop Winds, and Tonstartssbandht were performing. Between bands, I went outside, where a police car was engulfed in flames. The crowd gathered around the warm, rising blaze. People whispered that it might be mob-related, something that I would come to realize was a common factor in Montréal nightlife. It seemed like businesses were getting fire-bombed every week. Lab closed permanently soon after some undercover cops became aware of their lack of a liquor licence.

The loft scene in this area had a magnetizing effect on me. You no longer had to beg some bar owner who didn't actually care about music to let your band play. You could just do it yourself by renting or breaking into a disused building that had been left empty for years. I wanted to be closer to the action and get involved with this scene myself. Eager for a more stable and less populated living situation, Jane, David and I moved into a third-floor apartment at 1060 Avenue Van Horne near Durocher in Outremont. This was around the same time that an artistic community was coalescing around the record label that Seb had started called Arbutus Records. Originally from Vancouver, he lived across the street from us in a shabby-looking pale apartment that we nicknamed White Castle. Musicians like Phil Karneef, Matt Perri, Thom Gillies, Jasper Baydala, and Seb's brother Alex from Blue Hawaii all lived in the building at various times.

Around the corner from us on Avenue du Parc was Marilis Cardinal, who was a big part of the label, and her roommate Claire Boucher, a Vancouver expat who had recently started releasing music under the name Grimes. The painter Ezra Gray lived a couple blocks down, and the filmmaker Emily Kai Bock was on Parc closer to Bernard. Poet and publisher Ashley Obscura, whose Metatron Books published my poetry collection, lived nearby, as well as actress and model Dana Drori. Sean Nicholas Savage lived in the neighbourhood and would often randomly come in through our fire escape, further making our lives feel like a sitcom.

The video for "Double Vision" by TOPS is a great example of what life was like at our apartment. Filmed by David with his omnipresent VHS camera, it's essentially a supercut of every house party we ever had, featuring us all goofing around, eating snacks, doing YouTube karaoke, and dancing around in our shabby little abode. Raphaelle Standell-Preston and the rest of the Braids crew lived close by. Across the hall from us were Olivia Whittick and Claire Milbrath, who went on to start the *Editorial Magazine,* and Madeline Glowicki who later played in TOPS. On the second floor was the late writer Trevor Barton. We were joined in our apartment by fellow Edmontonian and filmmaker Evan Prosofsky.

I'm sure that every anglophone who moves to Montreal feels like they've happened upon a heretofore undiscovered magical artistic paradise, only to swiftly move back to the R.O.C. (rest of Canada) after graduating from Concordia with a couple regrettable tattoos and some nice memories. But it's undeniable that people do come away truly changed by their time living in this metropolis. Montréal is a romantic city that places real importance on the arts at the municipal level. Seeing an event like Nuit Blanche where you could go out all night looking at different art exhibits promoted as a mainstream activity amazed me. Quebecers really know how to live and their European-style appreciation for good food and fine art can be intoxicating to be around.

Back then, the cost of living was low and the quality of life was high in Montréal. Apartments were inexpensive and plentiful. Sure, you might have a leaky roof or a literal hole in the wall that your landlord was reluctant to fix, but it was a small price to pay for ridiculously cheap rent. Everyone I knew was applying for Jeunes Volontaires grants from the Quebec government to learn skills from more established artists and earn money for it. You could easily get by with just a few DJ sets a month as your only income, which is exactly what I did.

There was also an inspiring thread of civil disobedience in Montréal that culminated in the 2012 Quebec student protests, the Maple Spring. Thousands of people of all ages filled the streets, banging pots and pans to protest university tuition increases. Quebecers are always down for a protest. We all wore a red square in solidarity with the movement that year. On top of the spirit of the province itself, something about the ridiculously high concentration of artistic talent on our block felt intangibly unique. The diversity of the creative energy made our neighbourhood feel like a cross between the Factory and the Brill Building.

Life took on a cinematic feel. It felt like *Downtown 81*. The days were full of possibility and adventure. I became the de facto DJ for everyone's shows and afterparties. We formed a tight bond in a short amount of time, hanging out excessively and collaborating frequently. I was even inspired to try my hand at putting on an art exhibition. It was called Alternate Rollalities. I wrote different life stories for alternate versions of myself: what would I be like if I'd grown up in New York like my dad? What would I be like if I was back in Nigeria like my ancestors? Artist Matt Goerzen created 3D models of these different Rollies and we projected them at Eastern Bloc while I read their stories.

My friends and I made books, music videos, and albums; pub-lished magazines; threw conceptual parties. There was a feedback loop where one of us would release an album and the rest of the crew would be inspired to respond with their own work. It was an environment that provided constructive competition and encour-aged us all to step it up and make stronger art. But it somehow never felt overly critical or negative. I saw reflections of the '70s and '80s New York scenes I read about in books in our Mile End scene and felt a strong desire to document it in some way, whether it was through music or something else.

My life was pretty relaxed when I was in MTL. I'd start a day hanging out with one person at the park and end up having collected twenty new friends by the end of the night. Walking from Parc to St. Laurent on St. Viateur, a seven-minute distance on foot, could take over an hour, depending on how many times you'd run into someone and stop for a conversation. There's even a name for this phenomenon: getting Mile-Ended. I might pick up a chicken salad sandwich at Boulangerie Clarke, go to Parc St. Viateur, and write some poetry. Maybe I'd go to Cinequanon in the early evening, a free outdoor film series that showed chal-lenging films I likely never would've seen otherwise, such as *La Haine* and *Man Bites Dog*.

I worked on music in my bedroom, practised DJing, or hung out at La Brique, the nearby loft that many of the bands used as a jam space. Run by francophone artists in the scene such as Essaie pas (Marie Davidson and Pierre Guerineau), Xarah Dion and Asaël Robitaille (a.k.a. Bataille Solaire), it also fea-tured live shows and was frequented by a diverse array of musicians including Ellise Barbara, Bernardino Femminielli, Dirty Beaches, RAMZi, Mozart's Sister, d'Eon, Institutional

Prostitution, Pascale Project, and Antoine93, helping to bridge the Anglo-Franco divide.

David and I would often grab a giant slice from Pizzeria Van Horne for lunch. We'd drink forty ounces of malt liquor and whatever else was on offer at Dépanneur Pannu by night, having extensive conversations about everything and nothing. We cut a hole in a fence in Parc Ex and drank beers on top of a towering pile of rubble alongside the train tracks in a rarely used industrial area that would be completely overhauled and turned into Université de Montréal's MIL campus a decade later. Even though I was once again one of the only Black people in the scene and the only rapper, I still felt like I belonged more than I did back in Edmonton. I saw a context for myself in the past, feeling like I was Grandmaster Flash in that Laura Levine photo where he's arm in arm with Tina Weymouth from Talking Heads.

Having not released an album for a couple years and subsisting solely on publishing royalties from my old records, freelance writing, and whatever DJ gigs I could get, I started doing experiments for money at McGill University. I'd go up to the campus, they'd analyze my speech patterns while I said certain predetermined phrases, and I'd walk out an hour later with ten dollars. One time I took part in a transcranial magnetic stimulation study for thirty dollars. Another time a doctor monitored the motor control response of my right hand. I'd try to stack a few of these sessions back to back to make the journey across town more worthwhile.

We'd dig discarded vegetables and stale bread out of dumpsters. I remember one particularly jubilant day when Seb found a large quantity of perfectly fine mozzarella cheese that had been recently disposed of. He called us up and we shared the cheese equally. This somewhat chaotic lifestyle was a small price to pay for freedom. A little money went a long way because the cost of living was so ridiculously low. It allowed me more time and space to be creative than I would likely ever experience elsewhere. Not yet able to find a decent Black barber, I cut my hair into an afro mohawk. I started wearing vintage blazers and dress shirts with increasingly garish patterns. I felt free to openly express myself without fear of judgment, emboldened to envision myself as a Real Artist without fear of reprisal. It was something I had never experienced before.

Similar to the scrappy young bands in Edmonton, the bands in Montréal's lo-fi electronic pop scene often had a wild, ramshackle quality to their music. It was a new kind of electronic music that was not particularly influenced by house or techno, gaining popularity due to the proliferation of pirated music software and cheap, powerful laptops. Chillwave was happening around the same time with artists like Neon Indian, Toro y Moi, and Washed Out making bedroom pop songs using samples. Animal Collective seemed to be the most influential band in our world. Musicians copied their mysterious formula of classic pop songwriting and hypnotic sampling. Roland SP-404 samplers were so omnipresent that I used to jokingly call them Mile End doorstops. Ariel Pink's inscrutable homemade psychedelic rock songs were also an inspiration to many of the bands in the scene.

The lo-fi era felt like a response to the polished, artificial nature of mainstream pop music at the beginning of the 2010s. Releasing a crappy-sounding cassette tape where you could barely hear the lyrics over the hiss with a hastily scribbled drawing on the front cover seemed like a direct affront to the mainstream. Much of it was made this way out of necessity with the rudimentary tools that were available to these underground artists. It felt real, more authentic, the opposite of Auto-Tune. *Pitchfork* was all over it. This method of making music could also be seen as a way of obscuring a lack of musical proficiency. You could sometimes dodge scrutiny from music critics and fans if you were perceived as purposefully trying to make bad-sounding music.

The city was filled with characters. There were folks like Beaver Sheppard, a chef and painter transplanted from the Maritimes who played the ukulele and sang achingly beautiful songs with a high, reedy voice. He once chased me around Casa with a coke spoon full of ketamine in his hand. Matthew E. Duffy was a strange boy from small town Ontario. He had an intense gaze and only wore robes and gowns. He had cult leader energy. Artists of all stripes would come to his messy home on Van Horne where he would occasionally throw parties. I would DJ there with my laptop sometimes. It was a bit of a flophouse with mattresses on the floor in the living room. The walls were stucco, one was painted black and another was blood red. It looked like a horror movie set. There was a chef's knife stuck in the wall near the bathroom.

Duffy wrote prose and poetry in a lowercase gibberish language of his own making, some of which was published in a book by Metatron. He made music under the name Belave, used to dance on stage during Grimes shows, and was briefly a member of Majical Cloudz. He's photographed shirtless on the cover of the Pop Winds album *The Turquoise*. He once put on an abstract play with Kiki Barua called *ézx-ika'lz: de courtes vignettes; en chœur et mood* at La Brique in which he started fires and rolled around on broken glass. It was unclear how he managed to make rent every month, but I suspected he had some help from his parents. Duffy was well acquainted with musicians like Cop Car Bonfire who would set up on a random street corner and make experimental noise with samplers.

The indie scene was very Anglo; young people from all over Canada came to escape whatever artistic oppression they'd experienced in their hometown. Many of these kids came from affluent backgrounds but pretended to be poor, dressing in shabby thrift-store clothes and slumming for a few years before moving to whatever other city they wanted to and to whatever well-paying job awaited them there. Montréal was more culturally diverse than Edmonton with a large Haitian and Afro-Caribbean diaspora but the music scene was still firmly segregated.

Nearly all the artists signed to Arbutus were white. I got to DJ between bands at shows and at the afterparties but Seb never asked me if I would be interested in putting out records on the label. When I went out to shows, I was frequently mistaken for a number of other Black musicians that I don't resemble at all, such as Lunice and Markus Floats. There was one Halloween where I was harangued by a random partygoer for refusing to admit that I was Kaytranada. It felt like a way of destabilizing me, taking my personhood away. Ironically, the plaid-wearing, bearded white guys who would do this to me usually looked a lot more alike than any of us did.

The local rap scene was primarily white and francophone and not really into collaborating with outsiders. There seemed to be no infrastructure whatsoever for an English-speaking Black rapper like me to gain any measure of success in the province. In Quebec, they'd developed their own awards, their own grant systems, and their own culture with their own TV shows, films, comedians, and musicians who could be hugely successful without any out-side exposure. But if you were an anglophone artist in Quebec, there often seemed to be a glass ceiling that you could never truly break through.

Xenophobia and Islamophobia seemed to be steadily amping up in Quebec when I lived there. I quickly realized that they had rednecks there who were just as intolerant as the folks in Alberta I'd moved across the country to get away from. Théâtre du Rideau Vert featured a white actor in blackface playing P.K. Subban in 2014. In 2017, a mass shooting by a white domestic terrorist at the Islamic Cultural Centre of Quebec City left six people dead and nineteen injured. The Quebec government introduced Bill 62 the same year, a law that banned wearing face coverings while receiving public services, which seemed designed to spe-cifically target Muslim women who wear burkas or niqabs. This bill was related to the failed Charter of Values that was intro-duced by Parti Quebecois in 2013 that hoped to encourage "religious neutrality" by limiting the wearing of religious sym-bols by public sector workers.

Police in Montreal were unnecessarily confrontational, especially towards young people in the wake of the student protests. I'll never forget seeing a particularly imposing officer in NDG with a bald head and a massive fleur-de-lis tattooed across his neck. One quiet night, we were leaving La Brique after a birthday party. On the way around the corner, I briefly sat down on the curb to chat with my friend Anna. Suddenly, we looked up and were sur-rounded by police. There were very few residential units around so it wasn't as if someone called them. It seemed that maybe they had been randomly patrolling the area.

A cop aggressively asked me what I was doing there and I said we had just left a birthday party. She accused me of drinking outside (which I wasn't) and asked for my ID. The cops totally ignored Anna. I didn't have my wallet because I lived only a block away on Van Horne. I was particularly scared because this was around the time of Stephanie Trudeau a.k.a. Agent 728, the notoriously violent Montréal police officer who was suspended and convicted of assault after years of excessively brutal conduct. Jane came back after noticing I hadn't caught up with the rest of the group and boldly asked if they were charging me with anything. They said no and she said, "Okay, so we're going," and then we left. It was a jarring moment. I often wonder what might've happened to me if I was alone.

Despite all the ups and downs, I often sensed that something big was just on the verge of happening in our scene. A feeling of possibility. I felt like I was in the right place at the right time for the first time in my life. Everyone I met was an artist of some discipline. My life completely revolved around art. Live music, art shows, making music, dancing, reading. We all shared art films and obscure albums with each other. We lived in an alternate reality where the *Billboard* Hot 100 had been flipped upside down and Prefab Sprout and Orange Juice were the most influential bands from the '80s. I started to notice parallels between musicians I knew and the obscure artists of the past, sensing that certain people had intangible elements that would help them make it big and others were destined to be rediscovered thirty years from now as a cult classic or be completely forgotten.

One day during the summer of 2011, Claire Boucher asked me to come over to her apartment on Parc to check out an album she had been working on. I was a huge fan of her debut, *Geidi Primes*.

Claire's music, which she released under the name Grimes, had a warped alien quality to it that reminded me of the rawness of my first album. After meeting at a house party at my old place on Duluth a couple years before, we'd often hang out and send each other mixtapes online and talk about music. I sent her some trap and U.K. grime; she put me onto lots of classical music. I remixed her songs "Dark Heart" and "Crystal Ball," and she returned the favour with a wild reimagining of my song "Conditioning."

Claire had holed herself inside her apartment for several weeks, making a new album with GarageBand on her MacBook. It was early in the day but we went and picked up a bottle of cheap white wine from the nearby dépanneur and returned to her place. The blinds were closed and she left the lights off, but I could still see the black outlines of abstract gothic drawings of mythical creatures she had painted onto the walls. It seemed like maybe she hadn't slept in a while. She mentioned that she'd been doing lots of speed, but that wasn't anything out of the ordinary for people in the scene back then. I sat beside her on her bed, poured a glass of wine, and listened to the album from front to back.

The production was much more focused than anything she'd made before. The music gave me that exciting sensation of hearing something that was truly original. I asked if I could rap over the instrumental for a song she had called "Eight," and we got Seb to send it over. I later put my version up on SoundCloud as a bootleg called "88."

Her voice on this album was clear and present in a way it had never been before and the songs were haunting, otherworldly, and addictive. It was truly stunning. She sounded like a futuristic version of Kate Bush. It gave me dual feelings of instant familiarity and the shock of the new. I told her that she should be stoked about the album. I said, "I think people are really gonna like this." Talk about an understatement.

Her profile as a musician had been steadily increasing. She was touring more and more, and it seemed like she was being asked to play a huge festival in Mexico or some other country every other weekend. It made sense that she'd have a big record at some point soon. But when *Visions* dropped on January 31, 2012, it was a seismic event. Aided by the instant-classic video for "Oblivion" shot by Evan Prosofsky and directed by Emily Kai Bock, the album threw Grimes into the stratosphere. Claire had something that you can't teach: star power. Call it charisma or whatever, it was always there with her from the beginning.

She had this uncanny magnetism to her. Claire sometimes acted naïve, anxious, or oblivious. But I always had an inkling that she was more aware of how powerful she was than she let on. People easily became obsessed with her. They stared intently as she walked down the street. If she messed up during one of her wildly inconsistent live shows, no one cared; she would somehow always get away with it. There seemed to be a magical aura around her. After *Visions*, girls started dressing like her, dying their hair into vibrant colours and cutting it into baby bangs. It became increasingly difficult for her to lead a quiet life in the Mile End, and she essentially moved back to Vancouver when she wasn't on tour.

In March, I DJed an afterparty with her at a bodega in Bushwick and I could feel the hordes of people surging forward inch by inch, desperate to get closer to her like clout-thirsty zombies.

It was like Beatlemania. The last time we were in Brooklyn together, she was playing with Silly Kissers at Glasslands on a Sunday with six people in the audience. Two years later, she was the hottest act in music. If you would've told me at that bodega show that she might one day end up dating the richest man in the world, I wouldn't have been hugely surprised. The next week I DJed at another afterparty celebrating her album release in Montréal, and Win and Régine from Arcade Fire spent all night talking to her. It felt like a torch passing.

Claire was photographed by Hedi Slimane while wearing Givenchy for the strikingly glamorous cover of the April 2012 issue of *Dazed and Confused*. The online gallery for the interview has photos of show posters she designed and candid images, including one with the back of my mohawked head watching her perform. She performed "Genesis" live on *Late Night with Jimmy Fallon*. At the beginning of the summer, we both played Primavera Sound in Barcelona, where I watched her entertain a dizzyingly huge, rapturous audience.

In July, it was announced that *Visions* and my album *Hope In Dirt City* were both shortlisted for the Polaris Music Prize, pitting us up against albums like *Take Care* by Drake. In the press room at the ceremony in September, it felt as if every media outlet in the world had come to Toronto just to talk to Claire. She seemed exhausted by a hectic year, and her relationship with Seb and Arbutus had become strained. I thought she was a shoo-in that year but Feist ended up winning the award.

Back home in Montréal, reverberations from Claire's ascent were echoing. Sure, there had been a previous surge in attention brought to the city by the world-conquering success of Arcade

Fire in the mid-'00s. But that hype had largely dissipated and the local music scene had entered an ebbing period for a few years. After *Visions*, our little corner of MTL swiftly became the centre of the music world. *The Telegraph* in London declared "Montreal is the new Brooklyn" in an article about Grimes and Mozart's Sister playing at SXSW 2012. Foreign journalists came to town to document what was happening in our scene. *Spin* magazine published a feature titled "Burning Down the Loft: Inside Montreal's DIY Scene" that I was interviewed for in June. Australian filmmaker Tim Kelly made a documentary about the Montréal music scene that I was in called *A City Is an Island*.

Claire's meteoric rise put pressure on all the other bands in the scene to match her success. It cast a shadow over the whole scene. Some bands felt as if she'd used the community as a stepping stone. There was jealousy and envy. It hadn't previously crossed anyone's mind that they had a chance for international fame. But once that was seen as a potential outcome, it seemed to poison the purity of the scene, capitalism ruining the spirit of open collaboration that had made it all possible in the first place. It inspired unhealthy competition between us. It felt like a gold rush with people chasing fame. It seeped into the process.

Kids started moving to town from places like Minnesota in an effort to become the next Grimes. American and U.K. labels came searching for the next big thing, signing Grimes-adjacent bands like Majical Cloudz, Doldrums, and She-Devils. Instead of just creating to impress each other and our community, making art for art's sake, we were producing music for a worldwide audience that had taken a keen interest in everything that was coming out of the city. More and more musicians made the jump from Edmonton to Montréal around this time: Purity Ring,

Mitch Davis, Peter Sagar of Homeshake, Alex Calder, Garrett Johnson, Renny Wilson, and Mac DeMarco.

Spending his formative years in Edmonton, Mac moved to Montréal with his girlfriend, Kiera, in 2011 after a stint in Vancouver. As a member of Makeout Videotape, he made ragged yet tuneful garage rock and was highly respected by other bands in Edmonton. To many of us in the Edmonton scene, it wasn't a matter of if he was gonna blow up, it was when. A spot opened up on the first floor of our apartment building on Van Horne in Outremont and we managed to secure it for Mac when he moved to town. Mac looked like a 21st century update of Alfred E. Neuman from *Mad Magazine* and seemed to take nothing seriously. He had a Dennis the Menace vibe and an impish sense of humour that would lead him to do anything for a laugh.

I'd walk downstairs to Mac's apartment from time to time to see what he was cooking up. He had started accumulating analog recording gear that covered every available surface in the apartment. Instead of using the digital recording processes that had become popular and more readily accessible, Mac committed everything to reel-to-reel tape. Using this gear, he wrote a song in my honour, dubbed it to cassette, and gave it to me as a birthday gift. He looked a bit like a mad scientist fiddling with all the equipment. He chain-smoked like a human chimney and would typically be in only his underwear. He worked the late shift at Segal's, unloading pungent dried fish and stocking the shelves of the cramped grocery store until the early morning. Like me, he would also occasionally do experiments at McGill for money.

One day he mentioned that he wanted to start releasing this new music he was making under his real name, instead of Makeout

Videotape. I thought this was a great idea. Be yourself. He showed me some of the songs and they all featured him singing in a goofy crooning voice, sometimes pitched down with vari-speed. It sounded like an Elvis impression. One song was titled after his nickname for Montréal "European Vegas." There was another track about a man obsessed with blue jeans. Was he seri-ously planning to release this stuff? Evidently so. He called the album *Rock and Roll Night Club* and it was released by New York label Captured Tracks. My roommate Evan took a photo of him putting on lipstick for the album cover. It felt like his sense of humour was truly coming through in his music for the first time.

Mac recorded another album in his apartment right away. He was rapidly improving at recording himself, his music sounding more professional every day. His album *2* came out in October 2012 and was an instant sensation. The album was picked for *Pitchfork*'s Best New Music and was later rated as one of the best albums of the 2010s. Mac was always really chill and very fun to be around and his music started to reflect that more. The songs were easy to like, just like Mac. People always wanted to be around him. He has gone on to sell over one hundred thousand records, start his own record label, and perform on *Conan* and *The Tonight Show Starring Jimmy Fallon*.

His natural affability translated well to building a fanbase. After moving to New York, he gave out his home address at the end of his 2015 mini-album *Another One*, inviting his fans over for coffee. Dozens of fans came by. At first, his fans just wanted to hang with Mac and then they wanted to become him. He was what every guitar-playing skate bro wished he could be. Famous for his "Ode to Viceroy," he's probably responsible for a rise in smoking among young white males in North America over the last decade. Kids everywhere started dressing like him and Kiera. You'd see little doppelgänger versions of them around the Mile End. He basically wore the same combo of shredded dad cap and vintage Carhartt jacket every day, which no one ever considered fashionable before. He had become undeniably influential. I went to a show with him in L.A. a couple years ago and he got interrupted countless times to take photos with fans.

Mac and Claire arguably became the voices of their generation. The *Globe and Mail* called Claire "the coolest girl in Canada." *Pitchfork* called "Oblivion" the second-best song of the decade. It's hard not to compare your own success to that of your friends of a certain stature, even if it's a total apples and oranges situation. No one has ever wanted to look or dress like me. Hell, my Wikipedia page barely gets updated. Knowing people who are actually famous can be surreal.

For some folks in the scene, it was hard to deal with the cognitive dissonance of seeing someone you used to eat lentils with getting photographed at the Met Gala. The way their success dovetailed with capitalism was strange too. Mac's song "Moving Like Mike" was in a Target commercial. I once saw a mannequin at Urban Outfitters dressed to look just like him. I remember being on tour in the U.K., waiting for the bus, when I saw a massive Apple billboard towering over me on the other side of the street. It was of Claire making music on her MacBook, a portrait of a bedroom musician who took over the world.

The explosion in popularity of our music scene also coincided with the gentrification of the Mile End. Video game developer Ubisoft Montreal moved to the Mile End in 1997, bringing a burgeoning industry powerhouse to an area in economic decline.

The scrappy neighbourhood we moved to for cheap rent had suddenly been branded by the press as an artistic haven and the coolest place in the world. Maybe it *was* the new Brooklyn after all. Rent became more expensive. You started seeing groups of tourists being led on walking tours along St. Viateur. Beloved local businesses were pushed out by greedy landlords hoping that wealthy chains might take their place for drastically increased rent. People started getting priced out of the neighbourhood and the music community became less centralized.

Were Arbutus Records and the Mile End music scene a gentrifying force? Young artists moved into a neighbourhood that was seemingly full of abandoned warehouses and unwittingly helped to market it to corporations as a future site for development. But when did it begin? Was it Ubisoft's fault? Were printmaker Kiva Stimac and Godspeed You! Black Emperor members Efrim Menuck and Mauro Pezzente gentrifiers when they started Hotel2Tango and Casa del Popolo and took over La Sala Rossa? Was POP Montréal when they made Mile End the home base for their festival? Is it possible to build an artistic scene without displacing other people in the process?

Neither Mac or Claire could've blown up without the infrastructure that the city and the scene built for them. Their success also required a particularly unique confluence of events that probably can't be replicated: a thriving local artistic community + low cost of living + affordable music gear + free time and space to create + the intangible elements of innovation and charisma = decade-defining music act.

Music scenes can mean many different things to different people. They can be a respite from a world that doesn't appreciate art, a reflection of or reaction to the larger community outside of them. They can be a talent incubator that provides all the tools needed to create impactful work. Or they can represent a patronage system where a scene supports the endeavours of an artist or label they want to hear more music from. I'm very thankful for the support of Edmonton journalists like Fish Griwkowski and Sandra Sperounes and promoters like Eli Klein and Brent Oliver early on in my career whose important roles in a music scene are often forgotten.

It's not hard to notice that those who benefit the most from music scenes are usually white people, particularly white men. In the past, music scenes seemed like they were just a way for guys to make some pocket change and meet women. It's a system that's ripe for predation and sexism, and that aspect has only started to get rooted out in recent years as music communities have become healthier, more equitable, more thoughtful, and more racially diverse. The new artists, labels, and publications coming out these days make me envision a better future, one where music scenes that function solely as exclusionary hierarchical power structures might soon be a thing of the past.

9

UNIVERSAL HEARTBEAT

The first time I ever DJed was on the radio to hundreds of listeners, when I was just fifteen years old. It was early 2001 and my father had invited me to join him during an edition of his show on CJSR 88.5 FM, *The Black Experience in Sound*. It aired every Saturday night and had become appointment listening for local hip-hop heads. His strange melange of contemporary rap and R&B crossed with obscure '80s funk and soul blared from car stereos all across Edmonton. Coming along to hang out while he did his radio show wasn't peculiar; I'd done it several times before. But this time was different. On the drive over, he casually asked me if I wanted to help him pick what was played that night. I remember pulling up with him to the mostly dormant University of Alberta campus that icy evening. Teddy had a crate of records and a bag of promo CDs that I helped him carry in.

My dad didn't tell me anything about his process for selecting tracks or give me any advice about what to play. I was excited and anxious, but luckily by the age of fifteen, I had already started to hone and develop my own personal musical taste. The CJSR station was comparable to most college radio stations in North America: walls covered in CDs and vinyl records arranged in alphabetical order, a red illuminated On Air sign outside the studio door, various band posters and stickers on every surface, flyers for station fundraisers and events, tchotchkes on the desks leading to the control room, which had a large vault-like door to keep background noise off the air. We took our seats and got to work.

My dad's musical perspective was very influential on me. Having a DJ for a father meant I grew up around a diverse library of records. For Teddy, there were no barriers between genres. If it was funky, he would play it. Listening back to recordings of his old DJ sets can be dizzying. He would play quiet storm R&B, freaky new wave rock, wiggly boogie funk, and the hottest East Coast rap of the moment and somehow pull it all together into something coherent.

I used to love going back to New York with him. It felt like we were at the centre of the universe for the music that we both loved. Everywhere we'd go, we'd collect mixtapes along the way. He'd visit some friends in Harlem and I would pick up a Diplomats CD while we were there. Teddy would take me to Canal Street in Manhattan, where all the vendors pulled their wares out of tattered suitcases and would place them on blankets or large plastic tarps. We'd buy mixtapes from street vendors, gaining access to unreleased tracks before anyone else. Maybe I'd pick up an Akademiks sweater that had fallen off the back of a truck as well. One of the only songs I can remember playing when I hopped on the radio with Teddy is a track from a promo copy of DJ Clue's *The Professional 2*. Street mixtape culture was just starting to get commercialized by major labels and Clue was one of the New York jockeys leading the way. Sometimes the songs on the mixtapes never officially came out at all! It felt like being part of a musical world that no one back home was aware of. The DJ Clue promo CD I was playing on CJSR, however, wasn't a Canal Street bootleg; it came straight from Def Jam. It was silver and had no booklet, just the artists and track titles printed in black text on the top of the disc. I played "Cream 2001" featuring Raekwon and Ghostface Killah, a throwaway track that's saved only by Ghost's verse where he receives advice from the late Marvin Gaye while praying over his grave.

I'll never forget that buzzy feeling of knowing that the songs I picked were being instantaneously beamed over the airwaves to be heard by a mysterious constellation of listeners across the city. That feeling of connection, that shared spirit of excitement, the transference of energy: it's something I've experienced many times since but it never gets old.

After the show was over and we were leaving campus, my father ran into one of his fellow disc jockeys. Meeting at the bottom of the stairwell, the disc jockey bent down and asked me, "Hey, heard you on the radio just now. Do you think you're gonna be a DJ when you grow up?" Before I could emphatically answer "Yes!" with all the enthusiasm I could muster, Teddy answered for me, "Naw, man, he doesn't wanna do that. He's gonna get a *real* job instead." That's the thing: my dad never encouraged me to become a DJ. In that particular moment, seeing my expression as I was asked the question, he probably regretted putting me on his show in the first place. Because to him, in many ways, being a DJ was a drag.

When he was in college with my mom at Shaw University in Raleigh, North Carolina, from 1969 to 1973, Teddy had a radio show on WSHA 88.9 FM under the name Broadway T. He'd throw parties out of the Kappa Alpha Psi frat house. In the '80s and '90s, DJing wasn't really a proper occupation yet. My parents moved to Washington, D.C., in 1974 for a few years and then permanently settled in Edmonton in 1980 after having my sister Gena. That's when Teddy started *The Black Experience in Sound* at CJSR, but college radio shows didn't pay. He'd throw the occasional community hall party, but club gigs were not as plentiful. Clubs barely existed in Edmonton back then. People weren't as hip to the music he was playing as they were in the States either.

I often think of what it would have been like if my dad were coming up as a DJ today. What he would've thought about technology like Serato that made travelling with a large library of music more manageable, how he'd marvel at CDJs and their USB capability, what he could do in a world where DJs had booking agents, toured the world, and were paid and respected for their craft.

He didn't live long enough to witness the rise of the superstar DJ, but who's to say he would've wanted to become one in the first place? He was definitely well aware that he probably had a better voice and sharper musical taste than anyone else on the air in Canada. (He was posthumously inducted into the Stylus Awards DJ Hall of Fame in 2010.) He'd gotten scouted by our local mainstream pop radio station Power 92 but turned them down when he found out that he wouldn't have any say over what he'd get to play. Time and time again, my father refused to compromise. Unfortunately, this stubborn attitude left him without access to a larger platform. As I was growing up, it often seemed to me like my dad felt underappreciated. And he didn't want me to suffer the same fate.

But it was too late. I had a fever for the flavour. About a year after my on-air debut, I somehow became affiliated with members of my high school student council despite being unelected and not particularly popular. As a result, I got to play some tunes in the school cafeteria area during lunchtime. Like with most things, I attacked this challenge with an unnecessarily high level of intensity.

I burnt CDR after CDR, each disc filled with my favourite rap songs. These tracks weren't the typical gangster rap singles you might hear at a Much Video Dance Party but they weren't experimental underground cuts from the Anticon catalogue either. If I couldn't find a clean version of a song on Kazaa, I'd try to make my own by cutting out the offending swear words using the rudimentary sound-editing software on my computer. This process would leave huge, inelegant gaps in the songs but at least I'd be able to play music that I actually liked for the entire school without getting in trouble. The equipment provided to me by the school was a front-loading CD unit that was the size of an inkjet printer (it was probably more commonly used to play "O Canada" during school assemblies).

Nonetheless, I was able to make do with what I had. Becoming the lunch-hour DJ was empowering. It was a way for me to be socially involved without having to actually put myself out there and talk to other kids. Sure, my songs were occasionally cut off by announcements coming in over the school public address system. My lacklustre editing ability meant that my homemade clean version of "Guess Who's Back" by Scarface, Jay-Z, and Beanie Sigel sounded like an experimental cut-and-paste sound art project. DJing for free at lunchtime also left me with barely any time to eat. Who cares?! I was living the dream!

After years of skimming through my dad's discarded promos and scouring new releases for that one decent song from a twenty-four-track album, I finally had a real-world application for the musical knowledge I had acquired. The whole enterprise made me feel like I was getting one over on the Man. I couldn't believe that they were letting me do this. Had they even *heard* what Cody Chesnutt is singing about on "The Seed (2.0)"? I was playing songs about *sex* AT SCHOOL! I was already wondering how I could possibly keep getting chances to do this.

The impulse to share music with people became so all-consuming that I was willing to break the rules in order to do it more. When my mom travelled to China with a group of her friends, I threw a raging house party that I wrote about in my song "Oliver Square." My family rented an unassuming, small house in Meadowlark at the time, a greyscale suburban area bookended by two different mini-malls. While her dirtbag boyfriend "looked after me" (a.k.a. did drugs in the bedroom with his one-eyed gangster friend), I set up my computer speakers in the basement and cracked a beer, envisioning that maybe twenty of my fellow students might come through. I was mostly excited to play a few friends some tracks from Jay-Z's recently leaked and still-unreleased double album *The Blueprint 2: The Gift & The Curse*.

As the tropical flutes and vocal samples from Kanye's beat for "Poppin' Tags" rang throughout the house, I watched as teens streamed in. Word had travelled. It wasn't just folks I knew from St. Francis Xavier who were showing up but also kids from Ross Sheppard and Jasper Place as well. Things quickly grew out of control. Jocks started smashing nerds in the head with rocks from my mom's flower garden. Strangers put holes in the walls with their fists. Drunk kids relieved themselves in our next door neighbour's decorative well.

Suddenly, my mom's boyfriend emerged shirtless and wild-eyed from the bedroom. He was brandishing a baseball bat, screaming at everyone to leave. The cops arrived after everyone had already left, sticking me with a noise violation ticket that I later beat in court because the ticketing officer never showed up. I got grounded within an inch of my life when my mom returned to Canada. This briefly put an end to my party-hosting career. But I kept trying to conspire ways to legally play music as loudly as possible.

◆

It was 2005, and my friends and I often spent our weekends at Halo where Travy D and Blue Jay would throw their Mod Club night every Friday. It seemed as if they played almost exactly the same set every week, a mix of northern soul, Britpop, new wave, and indie rock that had the crowd rocking. They'd close their sets with "I Am the Resurrection" by the Stone Roses. Their performances were like a weekly education in a world of music that I'd always enjoyed but didn't really know very much about. I'd bug them in the booth while they played, watching them operate, soaking in the atmosphere of their hallowed position at the back of the club.

The more DJs I met, the more I felt like they were members of an exclusive club that I wanted to get into. There was a certain magic to what they did, how they used sleight of hand with the turntables like they were a set of cards. As Simon Reynolds said in his seminal rave tome *Energy Flash*, the DJ can sometimes seem like "a shaman or dark magus." DJs are always talking about vibes and are borderline superstitious about the dire consequences of playing the wrong song at the wrong time.

I loved how being a DJ involved accessing two opposite sides of one's personality. The introverted archivist digging for records, obsessively filtering through dusty discs on a solitary search through the muck, on the hunt for songs that shined more brightly for them than anyone else. The extroverted entertainer behind the decks, sharing their spoils with an unsuspecting audience, providing the crowd with a hard-earned respite from the workaday world.

Nik Kozub had a night at the Victory Lounge on Thursdays and it became a gathering place for the local indie rock and electronic music community. I'd show up and watch him every week. Victory Lounge was the basement club attached to the Starlite Room, a notable downtown music venue that once hosted Nirvana back when it was called the Rev. I cold-called Wayne Jones, the booker of the Victory Lounge, to see if he might meet with me. I somehow managed to convince Wayne that I was about to become a big star and I knew enough people to float a weekly DJ night. I must have impressed him (or seemed impressionable) because he also offered to hire me as his promotions manager. This meant that I got to print and drop off flyers and put up posters for every event at the club. But most importantly, I had secured my first residency.

Starting in August 2005, I played every Tuesday at Victory Lounge and made the princely sum of fifty dollars a night. I called my party the Youth Beat and designed posters with not one but two drawings of my face on them. The quality of the DJing itself was not my focus at the time. I'd just play some cool tracks one after another and hope that some people would show up. Attendance was inconsistent but there was often a decent crowd. The place would be completely packed if there was a live show happening upstairs. Things could get chaotic. I DJed there on my twentieth birthday and my friends tried to get me to consume twenty shots. I was running back and forth between the stage and the bathroom trying to puke. One time, coming back from the toilet, I tripped over my headphone cable and landed head-first on my metal record case. I woke up with a large purple bruise on my forehead and no idea how I'd gotten back home.

There was one particular conversation that I had with Wayne that really made an impression on me. Meeting with him at the end of the night to collect my pay, Wayne pointed something out to me that was surprising at the time but painfully obvious in retrospect. "You realize you can't mix, right?" he said. I protested, but I knew he was right. I had no idea how to transition between songs. I would try to hide this by slowly changing the volume between tracks or stopping one track and dropping the next song immediately. The thought that I might need to do more than that hadn't yet occurred to me.

I grew up around my dad who was a selector first and foremost. Being able to match beats didn't become an expected skill for a DJ until the late '80s. David Mancuso knew how to mix but chose to play songs in their entirety in order to retain their purity. John Peel couldn't mix two records together. I had probably never even witnessed a world-class house DJ spin at that point, having previously only been aware of the hip-hop world of scratching and turntablism. Wayne was actually a bit of a raver in his heyday, intimately familiar with the art of real beatmatching. Though I was starting to develop a local following through my music, I might never DJ anywhere other than his dingy basement club if I didn't figure out how to mix properly.

My roommate Eric was a punk with a septum piercing whom I'd met while working at the vintage clothing store Divine Decadence. He seemed to revel in saying surprising things to people just to see what their reaction would be. He had a wonderfully twisted sense of humour. But on top of all that, he was the proud owner of a full DJ setup including two Technics 1200 turntables. His genres of choice were jungle, drum and bass, and breaks, all of which I'd had little to no exposure to. He was kind enough to let me play around with his gear, my first time having extended access to these tools of the trade.

By that time, I was collecting vinyl, mostly picked up at Play de Record on trips to Toronto. I'd attempt specific mixes repeatedly until things started to line up. I remember wheeling back the 12-inch single of Tiga's version of "Louder Than a Bomb" over and over and over until it would stay synced up with "Hustler" by Simian Mobile Disco. We would throw house parties from time to time so we could hone our skills, alternating between Eric's obscure selections from the hardcore continuum and my pop rap cuts and club records. One of us would run to the bathroom or hold court with the guests while the other person hopped on the decks.

When I first learned how to mix with actual records, I started to see music from a completely new perspective that changed my life. I came to the realization that all music was part of the same continuum, the same universal heartbeat. It was a spiritual discovery for me. The only thing that separated Fleetwood Mac's "You Make Loving Fun" from "Patrick 122" by Mr. Oizo was thirty years. With a little practice, you could make these songs melt into each other (and this was the late '00s so I probably tried to do this particular mix at some point). As I practised more, I noticed that certain songs just felt right together. I started to chase that feeling of synchronicity.

The *Disco Not Disco* and *Mutant Disco* compilations helped to inspire my taste early on. They highlighted a specific style of off-kilter disco and funk tunes that ruled the underground clubs of New York in the early '80s, songs that straddled the line between organic and computerized production and prefigured the sound of DFA Records and LCD Soundsystem. I poured myself into research, reading Tim Lawrence's *Love Saves the Day* and *Last Night a DJ Saved My Life* by Bill Brewster and Frank Broughton in rapid succession. I became more and more attracted to the countercultural aspects of dance music, amazed that songs without any words could function as radical protest anthems. There was a sense of personal freedom in club music that I hadn't really seen elsewhere.

I also started paying more attention to the natural rhythms of life, such as the way the chirps of birds would mix with the trains rushing along the tracks or how honking cars might merge with the signal beeps as I crossed the street. The cyclical nature of existence was mirrored by the overlapping loops of the music. But just as there is harmony in nature, there can also be dissonance. The same duality holds true while mixing records.

The other side of the euphoria of the perfect mix is the ever-present terror of trainwrecking. That's the term for when you play two records and they clash with each other, increasingly going out of time to create a cacophony of noise. Some DJs call it clanging and that's what it sounds like. When two songs are playing out of sync, you'll hear a rhythm that sounds like two galloping horses jockeying for position. And no DJ wants to play something that clears the floor, a taste miscalculation that causes an immediate audience exodus. Whether live or on the radio, letting a song play out in full duration and leaving silence in its wake is a common fear (no matter how long a song is, the possibility of your mind wandering until the CDJs start flashing at you like a submarine's missile jettison alarm is always there). A skipping record (or a faulty USB causing your CDJ to go into Emergency Loop mode) is always a vibe killer. The list of DJ nightmares is long but they're a small price to pay for the catharsis and spiritual uplift of the right mix at the right time in front of the right people.

As soon as I started to figure out mixing, DJing became my obsession. I started playing every weekend at the Black Dog in the basement, where I'd cram as many people as possible into the small room and play Alan Braxe and Fred Falke tracks for frothing, maniacal audiences. I'd play on all three floors of the pub, teaching myself to mix with the archaic front-loading two-disc CD player on the main level. I eventually picked up my own gear, a used pair of Denon turntables and a sketchy, neon-tape-covered Vestax two-channel DJ mixer that I bought from Chris Waterton before he moved to L.A. I practised constantly.

My music manager got me tickets for the biggest tour of 2007: the Daft Punk pyramid tour with the Rapture opening up at

Arrow Hall in Toronto. It was impossibly inspiring. I still remember when kids used to call me gay for listening to *Discovery* back in high school. Just a few short years later, it felt like electronic music was taking over the world. I played everywhere that I possibly could around Edmonton over the next couple years: Fluid, Red Star, New City, the ARTery, kHz, Prohibition, Rose Bowl Pizza, the Hydeaway. I'd play nightclubs and pubs, at DIY spots between bands at indie rock shows, at house parties. Nik and I even threw a jam at an old-fashioned family steakhouse downtown. We had a group together called New Strathcona. Every week I'd comb the blogs, burning fresh CDRs and printing the track lists off iTunes. I'd hang out on the Hollertronix message board, picking up bootleg remixes and mashups from the members there.

This was all near the beginning of the nu-rave era, a roughly three-year time frame in the late '00s when it seemed like everyone in the Western world wore neon American Apparel outfits, drank PBR, and listened to trashy electronic music. VICE magazine's dos and don'ts section was our style bible. The music turned out to have very little staying power. So much from the era was made to be disposable. But there's still something to be said for the loose, chaotic nature of the parties themselves, where crosspollination of genre was encouraged and celebrated. I got to rap on stage with Klaxons at SXSW in 2007. Nobody could tell me shit for months.

But for all the superficial aesthetic trappings associated with this scene, nu-rave was surprisingly unpretentious. Along with the parallel scene of nu-disco, the melding of sounds and cultures at the parties felt like a reflection of society coming together in a broader way. What I loved most about this era was how the parties pushed to break down the rigidness of genre. Mashups were revolutionary. To this day, those moments when I saw DJS loosen themselves from the constraints of genre have been some of the most memorable times I've had raving.

The Hollertronix and DFA parties I got to attend back then were hugely inspiring. In many ways, this period was reminiscent of the '70s and '80s, when going clubbing wasn't as inflexible as it is today. If you went to the Loft in 1974, you wouldn't just hear disco, you'd get a survey of all the danceable music of the time. If you went to a party in Detroit in 1987, they wouldn't be strictly playing techno. You'd also be dancing to funk, Kraftwerk, Yellow Magic Orchestra, and other tracks that informed the techno sound. The DJS at Halo even had that spirit back in the day, aiming for pure pleasure by playing a wide variety of genres.

Touring Europe as a rapper gave me access to more and more interesting music for DJing, expanding my knowledge base in a way that merely digging around online could never do. Performing at Fabric in London and raving in Berlin showed me that there was so much more to dance culture than what was happening in my backyard. My old Edmonton pal Juliann Wilding moved to Toronto with her husband, Henri Fabergé, so whenever it was Canadian Music Week or I was in town for some other event, we'd throw a party at their house. Essentially in the style of an old school rent party, we'd decorate the place, charge people at the door, and throw the best party in town. Coming out of the nu-rave era into something more nebulous and mature, I found myself playing more classic disco, '80s new wave hits, and contemporary indie rock.

We had one party that was themed after the film *Liquid Sky* where everyone ate weed brownies. It was fun to play some classic pop songs at top volume in a house like that. Fuck being cool: I'd play Rod Stewart if it felt like the right thing in the moment. That corner of Bathurst and Dupont was legendary for a while. Sometimes I'd be thinking more about the afterparty than about the live show that I was actually in town for.

On the other side of things, there's nothing worse than a corporate party. I hated when commerce got in the way of a good time. Nothing could kill the vibe faster. I remember playing at the Drake Hotel in Toronto when a guy in full Bay Street regalia (think Patrick Bateman) came up to the booth. He said he'd give me one hundred dollars if I played "SexyBack" by Justin Timberlake. I accepted (he somehow didn't realize that it was 2006 and I would've gladly played it for free), but I still felt weird about the transaction. What happened to trusting the DJ? I believed in the spirituality of this art form and hated to watch as it rapidly became more and more commodified.

The more popular I got, the bigger the clubs I got to play. I opened for Diplo in Edmonton and jumped on stage with him to rap over "Paper Planes" (this might be the most '00s sentence ever committed to print). Unfortunately, in most cases, the bigger events also ended up being less fun. I started DJing more for money than out of sheer enjoyment as it was income that my label usually wouldn't take. Sometimes I'd get way too drunk out of a combination of stress and boredom, even occasionally falling asleep behind the decks. Around 2010, it got to the point where I was DJing more than I was rapping live.

◆

I met a guy named Phil Karneef who was the touring drummer for a band called Mixylodian when they came to Edmonton to play at the Hydeaway. He was tall and shaggy and punctuated his sentences by jabbing the air with his index finger. He looked like a cross between a werewolf and Kramer from *Seinfeld*. Everyone called him Karn. He was a real character. His family was Lebanese and based in Ottawa, but he lived in Montréal and it felt as if he had always been there, like a statue or an old piece of furniture.

He had a multitude of different hustles. He used to fix computers and other electronics. One time he brought hundreds of samosas to a rave and sold them at an inflated price. He started a jazz fusion group called Karneef in which he was a demanding James Brown–style bandleader/tyrant. We later wrote a song together called "So Trippy."

I already knew that people partied differently in Montréal. I remember going to a Megasoid afterparty in 2007 at a loft in Old Port during POP Montréal and being blown away. Megasoid was a group that featured Sixtoo, a well-known underground rap producer from Nova Scotia, and Hadji Bakara from Wolf Parade. They churned out dark, mutant, synth rap beats almost a decade before Kanye came out with *Yeezus*. They quickly became local party legends for the outdoor Bridge Burner parties they'd throw with Ghislain Poirier every Saint-Jean-Baptiste Day underneath the Van Horne overpass. The event during POP Montréal also featured Subtitle, Daedelus, and the Glitch Mob. The tables were covered with vintage synths and drum machines. I jumped on the mic alongside fellow rapper and kindred spirit Giovanni Marks and rapped along to the group's gnarly improvised synth jams.

The whole night felt like being in a movie. I even wrote an article about it for *Vue Weekly*. It wasn't just the music; the vibe was different as well. For the first time in my life, it felt like I was at the greatest party in the world at that very moment.

When I moved to Montréal, Karn introduced me to the DIY electronic scene in the city, starting off with a house party he was playing with Thomas Promise. There was a freewheeling, scrappy quality to the DJing in Montréal that I hadn't encountered in Edmonton. While DJing with vinyl and turntables was a purist prerequisite back home in the '00s, I remember being gobsmacked when I walked into a typical Mile End apartment to see Thomas hunched over a kitchen table, headbanging along to the laptop that he was playing music out of. He had the party rocking, with not a single person lamenting the fact that this man was playing a crusty-sounding mp3 from his portable computer's headphone jack into a nearby stereo's auxiliary output. Was nothing sacred? Apparently not. I started playing back to back with them, searching the computer's VirtualDJ program for tracks that I recognized.

Back in 2005, I had tried to start an electronic pop band in Edmonton. The jaded old rock bassist I talked to about joining my group said to me, "What are you gonna do on stage? Play the laptop?" He started laughing hard, pretending to play a keytar, air-typing horizontally as if it had a computer keyboard on it. In just a few short years, nearly every live music show I'd see would involve a laptop in some way. By the turn of the decade, a confluence of events further democratized the world of music.

Microchip technology had improved to the point that most computers could run sophisticated programs without any lag in response time. Internet speed had skyrocketed and music software was easily and liberally pirated. Illegal filesharing had become more prevalent and less scrutinized than ever, allowing members of message board communities and private torrent sites to build vast collections of obscure music. Combine all this with a bunch of millennials with a load of free time and you've got yourself a music scene.

I loaded up the Dell Inspiron I got at Lollapalooza with a cracked copy of VirtualDJ, got an Akai MPD24 USB controller, and started barnstorming lofts around the city with Karn. We'd do ecstasy and party into the early morning. I'd never done drugs like that before. In fact, I was virulently against drug use when I was growing up in Edmonton. It had certainly been available. I knew kids who did meth. I didn't even smoke weed. I had never (and still haven't) smoked a cigarette. But something about being in Montréal made indulging in substances feel like second nature.

When I took MDMA (or "da" as we called it) under controlled circumstances, it would give music this electrified fourth dimension that wasn't previously accessible to me. Old favourites took on new significance. It made you feel warm and close to God, like there was an invisible forcefield around you. It produced total euphoria that was tailor-made for the pulse of the club and filled you with a massive sense of empathy for everyone around you. Unfortunately, the comedown was worse than anything I'd previously experienced, leaving me depressed for days after.

My friends and I congregated around the constellation of loft venues that were springing up across the Montréal nightlife landscape. Silver Door was a second-floor walk-up, a complete hole in the wall on a seemingly barren corner of Parc and Beaubien that went through many different incarnations, having been shut down by the police and resurrected innumerable times over the years. Live bands would play, the illegal bar would sell PBR, and if we were DJing afterwards, dance punk records that featured real instruments were the order of the day. I started refining my collection with more Italo disco and boogie funk and got deeper into classic Chicago house, Detroit techno, and acid. I made edits of '80s new wave hits using their extended and 12-inch versions. I became obsessed with dub mixes. We'd make remixes for local artists in the afternoon, excited to play them for ravers the same night.

There was very little subtlety in the way we were playing. I once got one of the oddest requests I've ever had while playing at Silver Door: "Play something at a different speed!" We must've been locked into 124 beats per minute for what probably felt like an eternity with no indication that we would ever bring some variety. Local tracks like "Sweet Sixteen" by Think About Life would tear the house down. We raided Larry Levan and David Mancuso playlists as a response to the increasingly disposable, computerized nature of nu-rave. There was a hunger for something more organic. There was a lot of electronic music, but spiritually it felt like the rebirth of disco.

The open nature of the scene inspired me to create my own event series that I called Mood Management: I'd find a different venue every month and pair a local band with a specific genre of music that I would play for the whole night. This challenged me to up my expertise in genres that I wasn't already familiar with. I'd decorate the rooms differently every month. I had a night where I played only African highlife and afrobeat. I stole a few small palm trees from Rona at night and dragged them to Eastern Bloc for the occasion. I threw this one party at a loft on Van Horne that I called the Rite of Spring where Flow Child played and we hoisted a giant paper sun up to the ceiling. We threw a different event at Eastern Bloc where we projected video of CGI dancers from YouTube on the walls and I played acid house all night long.

That year during Christmas, I tried to throw a similar event back home with my fellow Edmonton expats who had also moved to Montréal. It was a variety show at the Pawn Shop with bands playing and me DJing and hosting. Unfortunately, the vibe wasn't quite transferable. People weren't really appreciating what I was playing and I was frustrated.

Talking to my sister Gena about it afterwards, I came to an important revelation. At that time, I just wanted to show people all the cool songs that I knew. My sets were searching for valida-tion, as if I were screaming, "Come see how cool I am and listen to all the crazy music I know about!" Gena pointed out that I wasn't really connecting with the audience. I would blame them when they weren't into it. "They are behind the times; they don't know enough about music." Maybe there was some truth to that, but an inflexible DJ is destined to end up back home alone, playing their weird-ass tracks for an audience of one. I was misreading my role as a DJ.

See, sometimes DJs can be selfish. They can be single-minded and obsessive to a fault. Some are stingy with their time on stage if there's more than one of them on the bill. There's the legend of DJ Kool Herc soaking off the labels of his records so rival DJs in New York wouldn't find out what breaks he was using, a tech-nique taken from his native Jamaica. So much of being a DJ is about finding an edge or developing a niche that works for you but another big part of it is being open and having the willingness to share. Maintaining this balance is crucial.

By 2011, I had mostly abandoned my rap career to focus primarily on throwing parties. *Afterparty Babies* had come out three years earlier and I'd lost whatever industry buzz I had been building up. I didn't really care. I was intoxicated by the Montréal afterparty scene. Despite not making much music of my own, I was still very inspired by my time in the city. I experimented with making instrumental electronic music, had noise jams with techno freaks, and learned about subcultures of music that I previously didn't even know existed.

My views on individuality, creativity, and artistry were forever changed by my time there. I traversed the entire galaxy of loft venues across the city. I drank beers in the hideaway hole above the stage at Silver Door, nearly fell off the roof at Friendship Cove, and hopelessly tried to fill the cavernous institutional space at Eastern Bloc. I came home smelling like cigarettes after a night at Tarot, hung out by the train tracks behind La Plante, and walked up Tobin's spiral stairwell at Bella Muse, feeling as if I'd reached the party at the top of the world. One time Sebastian Cowan and I threw a rave in the middle of a forest in Laval, a suburban area outside of the city centre. Vans picked people up to drive them to the location; we had cut down tall grass, dragged a generator into the clearing, set up a PA system, and threw a party that went into the early morning.

Most of the places I played in Montréal were large industrial buildings that had been left in abject disrepair for years, recently rediscovered and turned into multiuse spaces by intrepid artists. People lived there, worked there, created there, partied there. Dancing in these abandoned warehouses felt like a direct affront to corporate greed, as if we were celebrating the fall of capitalism. And the electronic music of the time fit perfectly with the environment. It was called "deconstructed club." The tracks being played were becoming sleeker and more futuristic, incorporating elements of rap, R&B, international rhythms, and literal urban noise, released by labels like Night Slugs.

We were living a secret life. The other nine to five. These buildings that looked barren during the day came alive at night. It was like a secret city. I shared an apartment with the artist Rachel Shaw, and my friends and I would occasionally hang there during the early part of the night, have a few drinks, take a disco nap together as a group, and then we'd head out to the loft at around two in the morning. There was a social hierarchy and economy of the night that was like a funhouse mirror reflection of the waking world. The only difference was that it didn't matter what day of the week it was. Sometimes you'd look up and it was somehow Tuesday afternoon. And there were no consequences because living in Montréal provided you with an incredible quality of life for not much money. My rent was around four hundred dollars a month and I could sometimes make that in a single night playing an afterparty.

The nights were often hedonistic, drug- and booze-fuelled. We were doing da every weekend. I remember going to a New Year's Eve party where a mason jar full of pills got passed around before midnight. Places like Torn Curtain hosted sex parties. They'd have trapeze artists rehearsing in the main room during the day.

That spot was really the apex of the loft era in Montréal. During the times I got to play there, it felt like it was the Hacienda or the Paradise Garage. Epic and cinematic, there was a skylight in the roof so you could see the night gradually turn into day. The place was run by a mysterious figure named Phil Borden. The audience was a mix of normies and freaks, starting off as a primarily queer scene that gradually became straighter as it got more popular. The door people were usually Cami and Sarah, two glamorous, notoriously tough ladies who helped to control the flow of the room.

At the Torn Curtain, the music and clientele might be completely different night to night, but no matter what was happening, there was a special energy in the air. DJs like Jacques Greene, d'Eon, Adam Wilcox and Thomas Promise would hold the party down. Imagine a massive warehouse filled with weird artistic kids with a line around the block and cabs outside like it was a legal nightclub. But this wasn't a meat market like the clubs on Crescent. What we had felt more like a contemporary answer to the salons of nineteenth-century Paris: painters, musicians, writers, actors, thinkers, and filmmakers all congregating in the same place, scheming together about future collaborations.

In his 1993 essay "The Booth, the Floor and the Wall: Dance Music and the Fear of Falling," Will Straw uses the term "chaotic populism" to describe the '70s Montréal disco scene. This statement also fits the '00s loft scene perfectly. It was an ideal blend of art and commerce. We were pulling in hundreds more in income than you'd ever see from playing at a regular venue. And the parties were way looser and much more fun than playing at a legit bar. My sets were becoming more dramatic and feeding off the energy in the audience. I copied tricks I'd read about in books about disco, like playing songs with long intros with the lights completely turned off.

Unfortunately, Torn Curtain couldn't last forever. The place wasn't up to code. They were selling alcohol without a licence. There were often upwards of three hundred people in there at a time and only one visible exit. Sometimes it felt like a catastrophic accident was right around the corner. The news of drummer Jerry Fuchs falling to his death in an elevator shaft during an event at an industrial building in Brooklyn in 2009 hung over us all and served as a cautionary tale that felt grimly possible in our scene.

The artful, free spirit of the place eventually gave way to a sleazier element. Drug dealers and other members of the underworld started frequenting the events, looking for a cut of the action. Sean Nicholas Savage once described it to me as the "bottom of the funnel for all the other clubs around Montréal. All the druggy people in the city seemed to drain there." Drunk people started showing up from the mainstream clubs downtown after they would close, bringing further unwanted attention to the loft.

On December 2, 2011, I was throwing one of my Mood Management events at Torn Curtain. It was myself, a couple newcomers from Vancouver, and the Cowan brothers from Arbutus Records performing. Things were going well as I watched the room gradually fill up with ravers. The vibe was mellow and promising. The party lights bounced around the room, briefly illuminating the PBR containers below the bar. It felt like we were in for a perfect night when suddenly the lights came on. At almost the exact moment that I began to peak from the da I'd taken earlier, the place got swarmed with dozens of cops.

Turns out they had been scoping out the venue for months, sending in undercover officers to build a case. The police were mainly hoping to catch the dealers who had been operating with total impunity out of different corners of the loft. The cops lined everyone up, processed us all, and took photos. I somehow successfully avoided prosecution by telling an officer my name was Ed Miles. Many ravers received fines in the mail. Though this was just one of many busts around that time, it felt like a watershed moment.

The Montréal afterparty scene became splintered for a few years after the raid. For a while, things were too hot to take part in, so in order to survive, I had to go legit. Other than publishing royalties from my old albums, DJing was my only source of income. Through word of mouth, I started getting some atypical gigs. I was part of the entertainment at a bar mitzvah for the wealthy son of an art world figure. They also hired Cirque du Soleil to perform. They had us all wear matching custom jackets that were covered in multicoloured piping that lit up in different configurations with the flick of a concealed switch. As I played a predetermined combination of songs, the world-renowned troupe performed synchronized aerial ballet around me, all of us flashing and blinking like Christmas lights.

I was invited to DJ for Sacha Trudeau's birthday party at his home, a heritage building in the Square Mile area called Cormier House. The building was stately, with large pillars and high ceilings that made it feel like a museum. I played on the main floor, taking a few moments to stare at a massive painting of Pierre Elliott Trudeau wearing a cape. The downstairs area had a wood-panelled hallway lined with a variety of swords from different nations, leading to an indoor pool with gymnastic rings hanging from the ceiling. This was all a far cry from the house parties I used to play at in Edmonton.

Around this time, I also started playing at a couple queer clubs. At the Royal Phoenix, I played futuristic dance music and deconstructed club during a dance night called Hydromatic that I put on with the experimental artist Babi Audi. We had hosts and drag performances during our sets. At Notre Dame des Quilles, a bar with two small bowling alleys in it, I played mostly '90s rap and R&B jams, building momentum by playing progressively bigger and bigger tracks until people were screaming and dancing on the tables. Just before the bar would close at three in the morning, I'd often play the following songs in rapid succession:

> Usher ft. Young Jeezy, *"Love in This Club"*
> Justin Timberlake, *"Cry Me a River"*
> Aaliyah, *"Are You That Somebody?"*
> Destiny's Child, *"Say My Name"*
> Ginuwine, *"Pony"*

I had another residency on Tuesdays at Nouveau Palais. We tried to recapture the magic of the loft at legit spaces like Resto-Bar Kathy & Kimy, a Honduran restaurant with a small party room in the back. It wasn't much more than a drug front. We also threw some parties in this basement on Parc called La Gruta that was run by these older ex-convicts named Bones and Marco. But it was never quite the same.

Through a friend of a friend, I ended up DJing the wrap party for Xavier Dolan's film *Mommy* at Buvette Chez Simone. Playing a mix of '80s new wave classics and '90s rap jams that I'd mastered over the years, I rocked the house. The party went well and

I soon received an email from the bar owners, asking if I'd like to come back and play regularly. That's when I started picking up residencies at charcuterie bars. Strangely enough, this was the period when I probably learned the most about music and the importance of music in public spaces in my entire life. I came to realize that the true purpose of a disc jockey was one of service, my sister Gena's advice about connecting with the audience echoing through my mind.

Buvette, located on Parc Avenue in the Mile End, serves expertly arranged meat and cheese plates and other refined snacks. In the summer, artsy middle-class French Canadians sit on the terrasse and drink Aperol spritzes. It's a classy spot and all I had to do was maintain the vibe on the occasional Friday. I played at several similar gastropubs around the city, eventually spending more time playing in these environments than I did at clubs or afterparties.

I would set up my laptop and controller behind the bar so it looked like I was another bartender. I'd typically get more drink orders than song requests on any given night. DJing in these environments required a deep, broad spectrum of musical taste, stylistic flexibility, and a lack of ego. How little can you insert yourself into the equation while still creating a vibe? Playing these gigs, I learned how to be subtler in my approach. There are things you can do to make the night easier for yourself. When the drunk requests start rolling in, be sure to listen with grace and not anger. If you don't have the song and it's actually a good request, make sure you have it next time. Try to have only one drink per hour and avoid taking shots until the end of the evening. Be mindful of maintaining the vibe throughout the set, but be prepared to amp things up when the time comes.

You can't just walk into a bar with a planned setlist and assume people will fall in line. You've got to read the room. Feel people out. Play something that displays some curiosity but isn't wilfully obtuse. There's an element of surprise and delight involved in performing for an audience in this way.

Unfortunately, these charcuterie gigs made it clearer than ever that DJing could also feel like just another underpaid service industry position. And despite the occasional patron curiously asking what I was playing or the odd night when I received excessive plaudits from the staff, the truth is that no one actually cared.

In fact, in many cases, no one could even hear the music at all. At the bar, there was a constant battle between what was coming out of my mixer, customers talking among themselves, and ambient street noise. Sometimes it felt like these establishments liked the idea of being a charcuterie bar that had a DJ more than they actually wanted to have one. A neighbour who bought the condo above Buvette, ostensibly so she could move into a vibrant artistic community, quickly decided that she preferred that the entire neighbourhood be silent. She called the cops several times a week, complaining about the bass. So, when I played my sets, I was forced to perform at a significantly reduced volume that was completely devoid of low end. I dealt with similar circumstances at my other gigs as well.

None of this stopped me from preparing for every possible situation. I wanted to be capable of going in any direction if necessary. I hoped to create a contemporary approximation of what post-disco New York was like in the mid '80s: a mix of new wave oddities, synth funk workouts, jazz fusion bops, and electro rap jams that wouldn't quite make you pause your conversation but might pique your interest if you momentarily focused on the music. I guess it was somewhat ironic that this highly curated soundtrack that I'd spent years compiling was barely audible.

Playing this whisper music as the people around me loudly chomped on *rillettes de canard* and quaffed goblets of pear liqueur on ice was a little depressing. I'd usually get paid around $140 for a four-hour set. Playing for such well-heeled crowds put my economic difficulties into sharp relief. The faint whiff of melodic sound vapour I was playing would waft around the room like recently sprayed cologne, creating the sonic equivalent of tacky patterned wallpaper, the ideal camouflage for meaningless chitchat. My legs would ache from standing up for hours at a time.

I was playing gigs like this twelve to fifteen times a month. The lifestyle started getting to me. I subsisted on hefty plates of rich fried food and would typically work until three in the morning, preventing me from getting quality sleep. More often than not, I'd head out to an afterparty when I was done, meaning even later nights. I drank lots of strong, sugary cocktails and rarely turned down a shot. One time, after DJing at a bar in Old Port, I hopped on the bus to go home and woke up at the bus depot.

The days when I wasn't DJing were spent either hungover and unproductive or doing research for the next gig. I was making okay money but I wasn't saving any of it, occasionally going over my tab and paying for additional food and drinks while I was working. The weirdest thing about filling up my schedule with so many of these sets was the fact that it wasn't generally considered to be a respectable form of DJing. I was paid comparatively very little to play barely audible music off my laptop to non-dancing patrons. It wasn't even really practice. Practice for what?

Being a charcuterie DJ made me question the purpose of music in the first place. When you're out somewhere and the music is good and presented with grace, you don't really notice it. The next day you'll probably tell people that you had a lovely time the night before and not recall exactly why. People only seem to appreciate music when it's not there anymore. Think of a time you've been out to eat and there was no soundtrack at all. Background music is important. I can't help but think of the *New York Times* article by Ben Ratliff about composer Ryuichi Sakamoto feeling the need to make a playlist for his favourite restaurant Kajitsu:

> *[Sakomoto] went home and composed an email to Mr. Odo. "I love your food, I respect you and I love this restaurant, but I hate the music," he remembered writing. "Who chose this? Whose decision of mixing this terrible roundup? Let me do it. Because your food is as good as the beauty of Katsura Rikyu . . . But the music in your restaurant is like Trump Tower."*

The other side of this coin is when background music becomes a form of cultural appropriation. When playing golden age '90s hip-hop at trendy restaurants became popular, I found it disturbing. It felt like a cheap way of adding some streetwise hipness to otherwise bland establishments. The cultural dissonance of listening to Black music at a Canadian taco restaurant with no Mexican employees that was primarily owned, operated, and patronized by white people was jarring to me. Not that long ago, rap was barely even on the radio in our country. But like jazz eventually sliding into waiting rooms and elevators, time and capitalism have a way of defanging Black art forms.

It was all the fun and danger without any of the pathos, the pain, or the struggle. Stripped of their urgency and context with the volume turned way down, the rappers sounded trapped inside of their own songs, forced to conduct a canned performance of their fraught life experiences in perpetuity for the enjoyment of those who had gone on to gentrify their neighbourhoods. When I played classic rap songs during my restaurant DJ sets, I had to contend with the fact that white people think they're allowed to say (scream) "nigga" as long as they're singing along to a recording of someone Black doing it. I tried to politely check people for it, but it felt futile. Playing these songs of Black celebration for a wealthy, mostly white audience was spiritually damaging.

At the time, I was feeling quite down about playing gigs like this in the first place. I was in a holding pattern when it came to my artistic career. But this period of time had the unexpected benefit of building up my musical knowledge and repertoire to a ridiculously detailed level. I was getting into more and more obscure subgenres: Japanese city pop, Brazilian boogie, African funk, instrumental library music. This variety is something I still draw from during my sets today.

◆

In 2018, I was asked to play a Torn Curtain tribute set for the Arbutus Records tenth anniversary party during the Red Bull Music Festival in Montreal. I dug through my closet and pulled out my heather grey Think About Life T-shirt that said the word *Family* under a drawing of a dog's head. The venue was a massive furniture warehouse in St. Henri that had been rented by Red Bull for the evening. My set time was at five in the morning and there were several bands and DJs on before me. I remember lying down on a couch in the green room, trying to get some rest like back when we used to take disco naps before the rave. The night was filled with so many old friends and familiar club characters and the production for the event by Shaydakiss and A-Rock was perfect—smoky with dramatic lighting like the epic discos I'd read about when I first started DJing. For my set, I asked for a golden light behind me that would signify the sunrise.

When the time came, I walked up to the decks and started my set with "There's Something Better" by Free Life, a euphoric, religious-tinged soul track. I had practised for months leading up to this set, crafting the narrative of the music, thinking of songs that would appeal to tired dancers. I wanted it to feel like an alternate reality Sunday morning church service so I drew from gospel disco and played songs with a spiritual feeling. I visualized my performance going well before it happened, imagining myself as part of a lineage of underground party rockers, hoping to manifest the spirit of goodwill that made the Loft and the Paradise Garage such timeless clubs.

At one moment, I was playing "Such a Feeling, Pts. 2 and 3" by Aurra, a Shep Pettibone dub version of the original boogie funk track. The intro of the song features only dubbed-out vocals from the original track, but I pumped up the delay effects even more using the mixer. The first minute and a half of the song has no drums so people started clapping along. Then they started jumping and stomping. By that point, the DJ booth had turned into a separate club of its own with people moshing and thrashing with their arms around my shoulders as I played.

I sensed an intense longing for release and relief in the audience that I hoped to seize upon. I kept the BPM slow throughout the set but gradually sped things up, playing some disco near the end. I featured a couple songs that I played during the Torn

Curtain era, but many of them had been imported directly from the '70s and '80s parties that built the foundation for the events we were doing. These old songs still work and can elicit the same reaction, no matter how much society and culture changes.

They've been passed down and shared through playlists, mixes, compilations, and books as if they were ancient folktales, a part of our oral tradition. I'm still playing some of my dad's old records and I'll definitely tell stories about what my dad used to play to my kids. I closed my set with "The Pressure Pt. 1 (Classic 12" Mix)," a Frankie Knuckles remix of a gospel house anthem by Sounds of Blackness that I first learned about when the Blessed Madonna played it during her Red Bull Music Academy lecture in Montréal a couple years before. We all sat there in silence. I cried when I first heard it. The great continuum, that universal heartbeat goes on and on.

One of the things I love most about DJing, the thing that generates so much of the mysticism I associate with it, is the fact that I could play that exact same set from that night in the same exact order again somewhere else today and it wouldn't come close to having the same emotional impact. I listen back to the recording of that party and I can still hear the spirit of that particular evening. But listening to the individual songs won't do the same thing.

You can try to replicate what you hear in a recording of Larry Levan spinning at the Paradise Garage that you found on YouTube. You can take "Bourgie Bourgie" by Ashford and Simpson and put it on your USB and make it the first song of your set, but there will always be something missing, some intangible element that you can't quite grab a hold of. The song feels different when you're playing it. That transcendent feeling, that sense of being part of something larger than yourself, that out-of-body experience—this is what we're searching for when we go to the rave. The moments when I've felt that shared catharsis, I'm still trying to wrap my arms around those memories. When I DJ, I want to give that feeling that I've felt to other people.

After the Arbutus party ended, we all went back to their office. We piped some songs onto the roof with a speaker that Seb had put up there. Standing on the rooftop, looking out at the greening copper domes of the churches, feeling the morning chill as the hazy dawn climbed up the edge of the mountain, it felt like I too had reached a climactic point. No matter how far you get in this world, a journey in music is one that has no end, as the search is never over. As I rushed to catch an early morning bus back to Toronto, I noticed that I didn't have any of the nagging critical feelings about my performance that I typically would have. I just basked in the warm glow of the amorphous connection I had formed with everyone there and thought about when I might get a chance to try to capture that feeling once more.

10

HOPE IN DIRT CITY

Around the same time that I was serving my term as poet laureate of Edmonton, I was working on some demos for an album I was calling *Roquentin*. Named after the protagonist of Jean-Paul Sartre's *Nausea*, I intended to make a concept album inspired by the book after picking it up at an airport. Maybe it was growing up with the cold, isolated Edmonton winters but I felt compelled to follow up my carefree club record with a dark, existential journey. I was also planning a totally new process for how I would create the music. Inspired by the production of Organized Noize and UGK, I wanted to make demos at home, re-record them with a live band, and then use the live instrument recordings as a sample source for my beats.

This would be another major departure from my previous album, which was made primarily on my laptop. I was also heavily influenced by the Compass Point All Stars, a studio band built around

Jamaican reggae legends Sly and Robbie and created by Island Records' Chris Blackwell in the Bahamas. It seemed like every time I found an album I liked, I'd look in the liner notes and see it had been recorded at Compass Point Studios with some or all of the All-Stars involved. Records by Grace Jones, Ian Dury, Tom Tom Club, Lizzy Mercier Descloux, and Talking Heads all benefited from the Compass Point magic. I loved how these records combined a rock sensibility with reggae rhythms and new wave electronics.

To execute my idea, I needed to put a band together. Upper Class connected me with some session musicians in Toronto: my old friend Jered Stuffco from Dietzche V. and the Abominable Snowman on synth, Paul Prince on guitar, Ian Koiter on bass, and Eric Lightfoot, the metalhead son of Gordon, on drums. I would travel back and forth between Edmonton, Montreal, and Toronto and jam with them at Rehearsal Factory at Bathurst and Richmond in Toronto. I'd work on demos at home, email them to the band, and we would rearrange them so they made sense for real instruments.

My managers encouraged me to stay with friends in Toronto instead of getting hotels to save money. I couch-surfed and slept on floors for quite some time, staying at so many different places during the making of the album that I devoted a whole section in the liner notes to my "housing association" with twenty-two names on it. As nice as it was to work on music in Toronto and hang with friends, it was stressful living an itinerant lifestyle for months while also having rent, bills, and poet laureate duties to tend to.

After becoming poet laureate, I essentially stopped performing live until a show at the Garrison in Toronto with the band for

Canadian Music Week 2010. The new songs we had been working on were well received. I always had a punkish edge to my
performance and attitude, but it was teased out even further
with these new compositions. I had my afro mohawk and I was
wearing a chambray cowboy shirt and a brown belt with a large
decorative gold buckle. Our songs ran the gamut of punk, disco,
blues, art rock, funk, metal, prog—sometimes all within the
same song.

Following CMW, the band and I met the guy who would be producing the album with me, Michael Musmanno. Michael was
a stereotypical caricature of a producer. He wore shades indoors,
had a raspy New York accent, ripped through cigarettes, and had
a bit of Phil Spector energy to him. Upper Class had asked him
to come from New York to produce the record with me because
of his work with Lilys, some rock band that my music manager
liked. It wasn't really my vibe but I appreciated having someone
involved who knew how to work in the studio with live musicians. Having external input for the first time pushed me to record
better performances. Michael would have me record my verses
countless times so he could comp together the best parts, an
approach I'd never taken before.

During these studio sessions, Upper Class finally got me a stable
sleeping situation and paid for me to sublet a room in a condo
for two weeks. We recorded at Chemical Sound in Toronto's
Leslieville neighbourhood. It was the most professional recording
studio I'd ever worked in. It was filled with vintage equipment
and had a huge live room that made me feel like we were the
Beatles at Abbey Road. We recorded onto analog tape. I'd see
weird instruments in the room like tubular bells and be like,
"Fuck it, let's put it in there." The studio was run by Dean Marino

and Jason Sadlowski and they were super helpful, kind folks. I'd never worked with producers, engineers, and technicians like this on an album before. There was an air of authenticity that hung over the proceedings, like I was finally making a real album with some real musicians in a real studio, instead of the bleeps and bloops I made on my computer in my mom's attic.

We had DJ Nato record my uncle Brett remotely from Edmonton, doing saxophone overdubs on a few of the tracks. Paying for all this had to be expensive for Upper Class, but none of that information was shared with me. When the recording sessions were over, I travelled to New York in May to hang with Michael while he mixed the record at Between the Bridges Studio in DUMBO; I stayed with my friend Maria in Brooklyn. The songs were sounding great, and after the mixing sessions, I was confident that the album was close to being finished.

Over the summer of 2010, I took part in some unusual collaborations and performances. At the end of May, I returned to Toronto to take part in a roundtable discussion with the *National Post* about Canadian hip-hop and how it was starting to supplant indie rock as the biggest music coming from the country. Canadian rap had skyrocketed to global recognition with the meteoric rise of Drake. It was me, Shad, Maestro Fresh Wes, Buck 65, Saukrates, D-Sisive, and others, and we all kicked verses—Drake was the elephant in the room. I fumbled through some lines from an unfinished song called "Hope in Dirt City." I was the only rapper invited from west of Ontario, which was a point of pride for me, but I was barely involved in the conversation and felt like I didn't have much to contribute. I still had an inferiority complex about my place in the wider world of Canadian rap. I was just happy to be there.

In June, I went to Waterton Lakes National Park in Alberta to take part in the National Parks Project, an initiative that brought Canadian musicians to different national parks to create original music for the hundredth anniversary of the creation of Canada's national park system. I teamed up with Laura Barrett and Mark Hamilton, and the whole experience was filmed by director Peter Lynch and turned into a film. It was an unforgettable experience. We rode horses across the Alberta plains. I was amazed by how similar it was to riding a horse in *The Legend of Zelda: Ocarina of Time*.

We visited glaciers and combed through the mist to see the buffalo in the early morning. We recorded in a teepee as well as in a church. I had a solar-powered backpack that gave me access to electricity so I could use my laptop to contribute beats and samples to the songs we were making. I loved the contrast of making electronic music surrounded by the timeless majesty of nature. I felt like I was truly seeing Alberta for the very first time.

On Canada Day, I performed "The Morning After" with a fourteen-piece band in Ottawa on Parliament Hill. Queen Elizabeth II was in town watching the celebration. That was my final show of the summer, giving me some time to revisit the mixes from Michael and send notes back and forth on potential changes. Some of the songs had shifted drastically in a way that I wasn't happy with. I was starting to regret ceding control of the record. In the fall, I played university shows in Winnipeg, Thunder Bay, and Calgary; DJed the Secret City / Upper Class showcase at Pop Montreal; and performed at Supercrawl in Hamilton.

Around this time, I signed a management contract extension with Upper Class that would expire two years later. I didn't show it to a lawyer or think about it much. Despite not seeing much money during our first five years working together, my career seemed to be in great shape and we were in the middle of working on a new album. It felt like a foregone conclusion that I would continue working with Upper Class. I didn't feel like I even really had a choice.

During this brief period away from the road, I figured it might be a good time to try to get more organized financially. I asked Upper Class for expense reports for 2008 and 2009 and my SOCAN statements so I could get up to date on several years of taxes I was late on. My sister Gena was a financial analyst and had offered to help me pull everything together so I could file properly. Upper Class sent me an Excel sheet with receipts that I had given them of my tour expenses dating back to 2007 and advance statements that said how much they had given me over the years. But I never received anything that explained the accounting situation with regards to recouping my albums. There was no time to dwell on that between live shows, travelling, collaborations, and whatever personal life I could eke out. I was never stationary long enough to make sense of what was happening with the money.

I spent most of the winter out west, DJing a ludicrously fun New Year's Eve party with my MTL pals Grimes, Sean Nicholas Savage, and Mac DeMarco in Vancouver. I also recorded some songs with my prairie rap mentor mcenroe while I was out there and filmed a low-budget video for my song "Jukebox" with my pal Cole Kushner. I started 2011 off by performing with the Calgary Philharmonic Orchestra as part of a project called Acres of Dreams where I was commissioned along with three other songwriters to compose some music inspired by immigration to Western Canada.

I wrote one track from the perspective of the first European settlers to Edmonton ("Settlement") and another called "One Pound One" that was about Hudson's Bay Company fur trader John Rowand (yes, I bravely chose to centre the white colonial experience in my deconstruction of Alberta history). Still, it was exhilarating to have my computer compositions translated by dozens of classical instruments—my kicks transformed into timpani drums and my chopped-up orchestral samples expanded into real strings.

In February 2011, Michael Musmanno sent me the stems for the album. This was the part of the process where I was supposed to start sampling the recordings we had made at Chemical Sound and turning them into finished songs, but that was proving to be more challenging than I anticipated. Some songs were showing promise though: "Conditioning" was transforming from a bar band blues tune into a strange hip-hop hybrid that was exciting me. By March, I was back on the road with a new live set-up featuring DJ Co-op playing beats and samples and my wild friend from Montréal, Phil Karneef, on live drums and electronic drum pads. We played CMW in Toronto at the Opera House and followed that up with several shows at SXSW in Austin.

At the end of the month, I was invited to perform at the Hip Hop Summit at the Glenn Gould Studio in Toronto where the CBC was celebrating over twenty-five years of Canadian hip-hop. Drake wasn't involved but his massive stateside success over the previous year made it impossible for the Canadian media to keep ignoring the talent on our side of the border. I shared the stage with the giants of Canadian rap: Kardinal Offishall, k-os, Choclair, Michie Mee, Maestro Fresh Wes, Dream Warriors.

Other than the Rascalz, I was the only rapper from the west side of Canada invited. With Skratch Bastid on the decks, I played "Sharks" to sheer confusion from the typically screwfaced audience of Toronto hip-hop heads who had no idea who I was. Looking out of place in a thrift store bomber jacket and a New Era ball cap emblazoned with Los Angeles in cursive that I got for free at sxsw, I called Shad on stage and we performed our song "Baby I'm Yours." I clumsily bumped into him mid-song. Kardinal Offishall came on right after and absolutely levelled the place with possibly one of the greatest live performances I've ever seen. Oh well, back to the lab!

At the end of the night, we all kicked verses over one of Skratch's beats and then "Northern Touch" was performed and it devolved into absolute chaos—I was jumping around with all the other rappers on stage, wilding out. I couldn't help but feel like I was starting to find my place within the hierarchy of Canadian rap. I remembered when the Rascalz refused to accept their Juno for Best Rap Recording back in 1998 because the award wouldn't be televised. That suddenly felt like ancient history. In Canada, the powers that be were often a bit behind the times when it came to rap music. But at the Hip Hop Summit, it felt like we had all finally arrived.

In many ways, this particular night represents a demarcation line between the past and the future of Canadian rap in my mind. These were the artists I grew up watching on MuchMusic all in one place, finally getting substantial respect from our country's national broadcaster. But just on the horizon was a new era of Canadian rap that had no interest in waiting around to be acknowledged by the CBC after the fact.

My music manager and I continued working on alternate mixes for tracks on the album between my various festival gigs. In the summer, I played Folk on the Rocks in Yellowknife and Calgary Folk Music Festival, followed by POP Montreal and M for Montréal in the fall.

I worked on a video for "Conditioning" in Montréal with my roommate Evan Prosofsky behind the camera and Australian filmmaker Tim Kelly directing. It was shot on 35 millimetre, which was ridiculously expensive, but thankfully we got a MuchFACT viral video grant that helped us pay for it. The song is inspired by working out back at the Kinsmen Sports Centre in Edmonton, dealing with both the bleakness of the winter months and a semi-requited failed romance by trying to improve my physical condition. I cultivated images of overturned cars along Highway 2 as my old roommate Jessica drove me and Weez-L to Edmonton International Airport for shows. In the video, I'm running through the rain in a grey tracksuit, training for an unspecified title bout like the Black Rocky of the Mile End. We shot in my old roommate Ted's loft and at the abandoned building on the corner of Van Horne and Parc. I convinced Tim and Evan to let me do a slow-motion layup on the basketball court at Sœur-Madeleine-Gagnon Park. I would have a great new video to reintroduce myself.

Suddenly, it was 2012 and it had somehow been almost four years since *Afterparty Babies*. It had been two years since the *Roquentin* studio sessions happened. Chemical Sound, the studio where most of it was recorded, actually closed down before the album even came out. That's how long the process took. I was firmly living in Montréal. I was receiving beats from other DJs and producers I met at parties. I began thinking of a way to make my album a hybrid of the existing live-instrument songs and some stuff that was more in line with the deconstructed club music I heard out at parties.

I continued chopping up tracks in my bedroom over the winter, trying to make the two sides of the album make sense with each other. The organic live band music felt lyrically connected to Edmonton while the beat-based stuff had more of a Montréal vibe. By this point, I had abandoned the Sartre concept and renamed the album *Hope in Dirt City*, a reference to the self-deprecating nickname that some of my friends had come up with for Edmonton. I wanted to pay tribute to my home city: a gritty, working-class place that was proud of its rough and tumble reputation.

◆

Around February 2012, I stopped hearing from my music manager. Email responses came only from my business manager and an intern. The music manager's absence was not explained. It was as if he had been written off a TV show. This guy had been my day-to-day manager, the person whom I had started this whole journey with, so it was jarring to have him disappear like this. My business manager gave me lots of advice around this time, encouraging me to update my wardrobe and image and giving me tips on how to deal with the press more professionally. I felt like I was still in good hands. I focused on completing the album.

The next month I returned to SXSW and followed it up with Canadian Music Week, Kazoo! Fest, and Lawnya Vawnya. Work on the album intensified and a final track list came together. My friend Jody Zinner altered an image of me taken by photographer Richmond Lam to create the album cover, a crinkled, distorted picture that seemed to reflect my fractured state of mind during the sessions. It had been four years since my last release, and Anti and Big Dada weren't interested in releasing my next album in the U.S. and U.K. respectively. I wasn't too surprised, considering I hadn't personally communicated with anyone at either label for years. We talked to 4AD and XL to no avail so Upper Class ended up signing a U.S. distribution deal with Redeye for the record.

The video for "Conditioning" premiered on *The Fader* and was a hit, leading to a TV performance on *The Strombo Show* and an offer to open up for Japandroids, the Vancouver two-piece punk band. As reluctant as I was to take on yet another opening slot for a rock band, Japandroids were red hot and I would definitely have an opportunity to perform for more people than I had on any of my previous tours. Travelling with my old Edmonton pal Calvin handling DJ duties, we started off in Cardiff, Wales, and zoomed around the U.K. Their shows were all sold out, the venues positively crammed with white men. As usual, there was a polite tolerance for my electro rap that would melt into shocked enthusiasm after about three or four songs.

Likely boosted by being on a tour with Japandroids, I ended up playing Primavera Sound along with them as a late addition to the lineup. I chatted with Danny Brown backstage at his show. I went to see Buffy Sainte-Marie with Japandroids tour manager Melissa and we both sobbed profusely. I was given a purple-and-teal Jeremy Scott x Adidas kimono with surfing gorillas on it for playing at the Adidas Originals stage and I rocked it that very night during my set.

While I was in Europe, *Hope in Dirt City* was released on May 29, 2012, just two days shy of the Polaris Music Prize eligibility cut-off that year. *Hope* didn't get the same public response as my previous albums. Lacking the U.S. and U.K. labels' backing hurt me and a haphazard, rushed release meant there wasn't enough lead time to properly seed the record with publications. I think some of my fans are still unaware that this album ever came out. Bouncing from dub reggae to '80s new wave to sketchy disco to underground club music felt like a sonic representation of my duelling identities and conflicted sense of self-perception.

The sound of *Hope in Dirt City* was completely out of step with mainstream hip-hop, which had been incrementally tilting towards trap music. In stark contrast to the hype adlibs of Atlanta's hitmakers, my monotonous spoken-word vocals formed a dour atmosphere across my album, sounding like I didn't much want to be there at all. The songs on *Hope in Dirt City* continued from the direction of the National Parks Project and Acres of Dreams; I was singing and crooning more than rapping. My lyrics were obtuse, poetic, and oblique but not particularly playful. Listening back to this album is difficult for me because it returns me to the state of mind I was in when I made it: the uncertainty, confusion, and emotional tumult all come rushing back.

The sequencing of the album created an interesting sense of ambiguity for the listener, but I feel like I didn't completely achieve the live/sample balance within individual songs the way I originally envisioned. The songs that I wrote from other perspectives satirizing the rap world, like "(You Can't Stop) The Machine" and "Hype Man," were the most effective, and the songs where I reminisced about Edmonton (the title track, "Crash Course for the Ravers," "Conditioning") have a warm quality to them. But all around, it's probably my least fully realized album.

The Japandroids tour shifted to North America where we played major cities at sold-out midsized venues full of white rock fans. Brian and David were really lovely guys who wanted to bring my music to a larger audience, but like the tours that came before it, I felt like this one wasn't beneficial to my career. After our last show together in Minneapolis, I immediately joined Liars for a summer jaunt across the southwestern States. I was a long-time fan of Liars going back to 2001's *They Threw Us All in a Trench and Stuck a Monument on Top* and their dance punk anthem "Mr Your on Fire Mr." I got along great with Angus and appreciated their strange, uncompromising music, happy to join the tour and provide a remix of their song "Brats."

Right at the end of that tour, I found out that *Hope in Dirt City* was shortlisted for the Polaris Music Prize. It was gratifying to have an album that had such a fraught gestation get on there, especially with how late it was released. I was pretty shocked but quite proud. With the help of my pal Marilis and artist Renata Morales, I got hooked up with a futuristic black-and-white outfit by designer Denis Gagnon to wear while performing at the gala.

Despite once again not winning the big paycheque, I had built up plenty of momentum going into my fall North American tour with Fat Tony. Anthony is my American counterpart. We have a similar approach to our artistry and have continued to collaborate with each other and go on other tours together. By this point, I had reconnected with DJ Co-op and our live set-up had become very progressive. We'd play songs in rapid-fire fashion, bringing in random tracks we liked and other people's beats. We'd do random covers and make decisions off the cuff. He would try to surprise me with beats that were relevant to whatever city we were in. It felt very alive. It was something born of the mashup generation, but it felt fresh and unlike any show I had seen before. It's a shame we never got it on tape.

This was definitely the point when I started levelling up as a performer. I remember watching Radiohead's performances of "Idioteque" and "The National Anthem" on *Saturday Night Live* in 2000 as a child while sitting next to my parents and seeing a world of possibility in front of me. Nirvana's video for "Lithium" was my idealized view of a live show: controlled chaos leading to mass catharsis. I studied great performances on YouTube: Marvin Gaye at the 1983 NBA All-Star Game, the video for "Transmission" by Joy Division, Neil Young on the *Trans* tour in Berlin. I loved the electricity of a great concert.

I started to enjoy surprising and delighting the audience. I used to try to get by on novelty, intensity, or sheer enthusiasm, but I broke through into a different, deeper level of connection. I got to a place where I'd be on stage performing and I'd have an out-of-body experience and I could see myself rapping to the audience. When I got to that point, I knew the show was lit. Crossing from the physical to the spiritual realm wasn't scary: it was encouraging. I always felt that there was a spiritual covenant between the performer and the audience and this seemed to confirm it.

There's also a physiological response that happens over the course of a show. The adrenaline kicks in when I start the first song; it feels like taking off in a fighter jet. The anxiety is briefly unbearable until I reach flight velocity and my emotions stabilize. The more I played, the more comfortable I felt on stage. Now, I feel more at ease speaking on a stage than in an everyday conversation. It's the curse of the performer. After the show is over, I often feel emotionally sensitive, vulnerable, and throbbing like a raw nerve. My friend Patricia told me that the French have an expression for this—*à fleur de peau*, which translates to "on the surface of skin." I have trouble coming down from the experience and can seem distracted while I'm slowly sliding back into real life.

That fall, we went all out on the tour and gave everything to the audience. I played most of the shows while wearing a camouflage jacket and a custom black-and-grey fitted cap that had HOPE embroidered on the front. I felt like I was on a mission. I remember rocking the house at Glasslands in Brooklyn. Our routines and transitions were on point. Co-op would use samples that helped to explain the influences behind my songs to the audience in a compelling way. He'd drop in a dancehall acapella at the end of "Small Deaths" to emphasize that song's dub reggae elements. Or he might do a scratch routine using the "Rock the Bells" sample and I'd rap "Get On Down" over it, helping to emphasize my reverence for old school hip-hop.

We closed the show out with a raucous take on "Loft Party." Fat Tony joined me on stage. The shows on that tour had such vital energy. They were fast-paced and exciting, some of the most memorable shows I ever played. But I spent almost all my time on the road that year, which precluded me from maintaining healthy relationships and having a stable life.

Getting my SOCAN statements and advance documents from Upper Class for my tax filings gave me no further clarity about the status of my debt to the label. I wasn't seeing any money, many of our shows were still lightly attended, and I couldn't understand why. I was starting to suspect that my career was built on a house of cards.

On the *Hope* tour, in order to save money, we didn't have a tour manager so Co-op had to drive us almost the entire time. To try to alleviate the pressure on him, I attempted to get my driver's licence while in Edmonton between shows. After failing the driving test a couple times, I sat in the car and cried.

11

SELF-TITLED

Early in 2013, I emailed my business manager to ask about the location of an ACTRA cheque in my name for $1,446.57 that she had forwarded me only the cheque stub for. It seemed as if it had already been cashed. She asked me to scan the associated stub. I did so, sent it to her, and never heard about it again. This was a typical interaction with Upper Class Recordings, the increasingly disorganized label that was failing to capitalize on my Polaris Music Prize shortlist nomination the year before.

I had no U.K. or U.S. bookings planned. It seemed as if I was playing occasional Canadian shows to keep the machine running instead of furthering my career. In October, I sent Upper Class a long email with a detailed plan of action for the future of my career. I told them about demos I had made for an album I was calling *Dépanneur* with my friend Tyler Fitzmaurice. I also told the label that I wanted to change my artist name to Rollie as a way of getting away from the baggage of my previous records and starting anew. I used Chance the Rapper and Dean Blunt as examples of artists with great album rollouts and suggested a potential timeline for how we should introduce my new music in the new year.

My business manager said she'd absorb it and get back to me. This was her only response to the email. Going into 2014, the only show I had booked was a private performance at the Broadway Theatre in Saskatoon for three hundred high school students. As the months went by, I sent the label several demos. No response. Nine months after sending my detailed plan of action, I emailed my business manager again. I was working on new songs and wanted to see if I could get an advance to help pay for completing the album. She responded, "This is much more a conversation and obviously a reconnection so I can fully understand where you are and where you want to go."

I followed up in August and she said she'd call me but never did. I tried her again the next month and I was ignored. In October 2014, she forwarded me a SoundExchange cheque and said the label had been "chasing down revenues and waiting on these funds so a part can be earmarked for studio" and that we should talk after I received the cheque in the mail. We never ended up speaking. In November, I was in Toronto for a Raptors game and tried to schedule a meeting with my management in person to no avail. As the calendar shifted to 2015, I couldn't help but feel as if I'd lost a year of my career due to a lack of communication.

The radio silence from my business manager continued. I sent her a DJ mix I made, some new press photos, and a viral essay I'd written about the Grammys. No reply. Just as my music manager had disappeared without a trace, my business manager was becoming progressively less involved. The intern became my main contact at Upper Class in 2015. He and I started changing over my social media accounts to use the name Rollie and made some vague plans for an EP.

To the outside observer, it probably looked like I was having an identity crisis. I put on a couple haphazard DIY shows in Montréal to preview some of the new Rollie songs. They didn't go particularly well. I felt rudderless and had no idea what the future held for me. My career was falling apart, and my label and management were doing nothing to keep things together. Over WhatsApp, my business manager asked me to send her all the demos I'd made for my next project. She was in St. Maarten working on a "pretty big project" and was subsequently heading to Miami to see her parents. I sent the tracks and she didn't even download the zip file before the WeTransfer expired.

By the end of February 2015, I was fed up. Encouraged by my ex-girlfriend Coey, I sent Upper Class an email about the lack of support I was receiving and I asked if they still wanted to represent me. My business manager replied nearly a month later apologizing for the lack of responsiveness, citing personal and professional issues, which included a failing computer. I told her I'd be in Toronto in the spring and we should reconnect. We made plans to catch up but nothing really came of it. The last thing that Upper Class facilitated for me were the travel logistics for a movie role I took in a short film called *God's Acre*. From that point on, there was no communication. Upper Class had ghosted me and I was left alone to pick up the pieces of my career.

◆

I moved to Toronto in the summer of 2015 and shifted my focus back to journalism. I was interviewing artists as a free-lancer and spent the summer working on a book proposal, envisioning a future as a non-musician. But I had the nagging feeling that I needed to get to the bottom of what was happening with Upper Class. Coey introduced me to a polite, disarmingly friendly music lawyer she knew named Jared Leon. Over several months, Jared and I discussed my past and present dealings with my management.

I sent him all the contracts I'd signed over the years. For the first time in my career, I had the time and space to step back and look at my label situation on a macro level. I combed through thousands of emails, adding up all the merch money I'd sent Upper Class over the preceding decade, all the fees they'd received on my behalf, and every grant I knew that they got. Seeing all the numbers in one place was sobering, humiliating even. Not including the advances from Anti that added up to at least $80,000 U.S., Upper Class received around $255,577 over the course of my working relationship with them.

I'd received a total of $12,130 in advances from Upper Class over the preceding decade. This is the only money I ever got from them. I could only account for $76,197 in expenses, based solely on our correspondence. Upper Class was prodigious at getting grants to help cover costs. They got a Starmaker domestic marketing grant for $41,958 in 2006 for *Breaking Kayfabe*. They got a $12,500 AFA marketing grant in December 2012. They received MuchFACT grants for five of my videos, usually around $20,000 each. They got a $10,000 business development FACTOR grant on August 26, 2013, which was right before they started ignoring my emails. From October 2006 to March 2013, Upper

Class received a total of $123,048 in FACTOR funding related to my career. And that's just what I know about. Each of my albums sold a couple thousand copies each and the first two were very inexpensive to record. I found it hard to understand how I still hadn't recouped my deal.

Something wasn't adding up. It made me think of every time they took money that had nothing to do with music: my poet laureate honorarium, my *Canada Reads* appearance fee, my consulting fee for contributing design ideas to the Kingsway LRT in Edmonton. I thought about how they were always adamant that I deposited show and merch money into their account as soon as possible. It often felt like the label was on the precipice of collapse. Money would go through them and then disappear without a trace or any accounting, presumably after being "reinvested" into my music. Upper Class was a black hole, a rickety structure built on a flimsy foundation that also happened to contain my career.

Seeing how they worked with clients also made me suspect something was off. When it came to paying others on my behalf, they were consistently late. They really pushed the idea of net 30 to the limit. I was always getting emails asking if I could talk to Upper Class about late payments. They ignored the designer of the album cover for *Hope in Dirt City* for almost a year over the five hundred dollars they owed her. DJ Nato told me he was reluctant to work with me anymore after Upper Class failed to pay him for recording the horns on the same album. DJs who backed me up live would hit me up long after the shows ended, wondering when they'd be paid. One of my tour managers cc'ed me on an email almost four months after a tour had ended saying he still hadn't been financially compensated. Upper Class was always trying to get shit done as cheaply as possible, getting interns or college students to do design work for free. Their lack of professionalism reflected poorly on me.

I started working with my managers when I was just a kid, seeing them as surrogate parents who would guide me through the slings and arrows of the record business. My music manager once told me in an email that it would be a long time before I would ever recoup the costs for making my music, so having to wait wasn't a surprise. But it's very uncommon for management to absorb all the money from live shows and merch, both of which are traditionally considered the primary source of revenue for musicians. They never gave me any accounting and there was no transparency about what was happening with the money. I asked my business manager what my debt was once and she said, "You don't wanna know." They kept me in the dark and watched me work ceaselessly towards some unattainable, undefined goal, a constantly moving target that I could never reach. As my managers, they had a fiduciary duty to look out for my best interests but they always chose the company over me. And when things got bad, they abandoned me with no support or direction.

That's the thing about signing a deal in which your label and management are the same entity. There's no system of checks and balances. If your booking agent, management, and label are all different people, they keep each other honest and advocate for you from whatever their position is. Maybe this is why Upper Class would chastise me when I'd tell my booking agent what my merch sales numbers on a tour were to show him my most passionate markets. They were possessive and secretive about information. They were weirdly evasive. I downplayed all these red flags in my mind, thinking that maybe my managers were just in over their heads a little. I had been too distracted by the constant wave of performances, sessions, and professional obligations to get to the bottom of what was happening.

I don't completely blame Upper Class for their actions and decisions because they created this structure based on the industry that they worked in. It's learned behaviour that they got from working at a major label. The contracts they had me sign back then were considered industry standard at the time. But what does that mean if the record industry is inherently exploitative and extractive? Look at the language of my record contract. It talks about the "worldwide exploitation of the Artist's recording services." My albums became "the sole and exclusive property" of Upper Class. It was in their rights to "exploit" my music. In the industry, record labels own "master" recordings and all derivative copies of these recordings until recently were referred to as "slaves." These connotations are even more charged when you consider the racial dynamic at play in many of these arrangements.

The stories of Black artists being taken advantage of by labels and management are countless. Motown used to pay musicians with fur coats and Cadillacs in lieu of the long-term profitability of royalties. Chess Records made Chuck Berry give disc jockey Alan Freed and the record company's landlord a cut of the publishing royalties for his song "Maybellene." Record industry giant Morris Levy made millions from his publishing empire, often giving himself writing credit for songs created by Black artists that he didn't actually write. Nat Tarnopol gave writing credit for "Doggin' Around" by Jackie Wilson to his own son, Paul, who had not yet been born at the time of recording.

These tales of exploitation have become synonymous with an industry that is widely known for its duplicitous nature. In his book *Black Talk*, Ben Sidran lays out the racial dichotomy clearly: "the black musician has, himself, been the *product* in the music business . . . although his music is often accepted, his person is invariably exploited." As A Tribe Called Quest's Q-Tip said on "Check the Rhime," "Industry rule number 4080: record company people are shady!" Record contracts are designed to be as labyrinthine and indecipherable as possible. It's rarer to find an artist who doesn't have these types of stories than to find one who does.

My lawyer Jared and I continued going through all the relevant correspondence. Upper Class had ignored at least eighty-six emails from me between September 2012 and August 2015. Around the same time, I went to my booking agency's website and noticed that my name had been removed from the list of artists they represented, presumably due to a lack of activity. This is how I found out that I was no longer one of my agent Steven Himmelfarb's clients. I officially didn't have a label, PR, management, or any booking agents. I didn't have anything left to lose.

At the end of September, Jared connected me with a litigation lawyer named Ren Bucholz who was willing to work on my case at a reduced rate. I emailed Upper Class formally asking for a proper accounting on October 21, 2015. After two weeks of silence and a subsequent follow-up email from me, my business manager responded saying she didn't have the "reports ready to go" and suggested we get on a call. I asked her to send the accounting before we talked over the phone. I received a call from her for the first time in three years. She left a message saying that she had just realized that I lived in Toronto and that she wanted my address to mail me some voided SoundExchange cheques she had failed to send me months prior.

On November 12, Ren sent Upper Class a letter demanding the accounting. My lawyers and I got into protracted legal discussions with the business manager and her lawyer about extricating myself from the contracts and retaining my publishing and masters. Never at any point did Upper Class provide any accounting to me. I'm still digging out from under years of mismanagement today. At press time, Upper Class still receives 50 percent of the publishing on my first three albums and owns the masters, even though they're no longer active as a label and the business manager is out of the music industry.

Why couldn't my management just be honest and forthright about what happened? Why did Upper Class string me along for years when they clearly couldn't handle managing my career? I stayed with them because I didn't want to be disloyal. They plucked me out of obscurity and had proven that they were able to make things happen. I figured that they'd right the ship eventually, that they'd figure it out. I felt like each show I played brought me closer to breaking even and the psychological freedom that would come with it. But Upper Class just keep moving the goal posts. It was like I had Stockholm syndrome. Any time I got paid directly for DJing or writing an article, I felt guilty for keeping the money, like it didn't really belong to me. I worried that the label would get angry if they found out. I was scared to talk to anyone about my situation for fear of reprisal. I felt so much shame and embarrassment for years, but I finally decided that I was ready to leave at last. I was free to release music elsewhere and formally move on with my career.

I cold-called James Trauzzi, the VP of marketing and A&R at Last Gang Records at the time, to see if he'd be down to meet me to talk about music. We met up for drinks at Three Speed on Bloor West and I explained where I'd been for the past four years. Beaten down by my previous label situation, my confidence level was pretty low, but I was driven to make something happen. I met up with James, Chris Moncada, and Ricardo Chung at the Last Gang office in Liberty Village in early 2016 and I was reminded that the Cadence Weapon name still had some significance. I had been trying to get away from it, but it still carried some weight in the Canadian music scene. They encouraged me to focus on rapping and try working with some outside producers and collaborators. Ricardo sent me some tracks from a producer from Oshawa named Gibbs who had really strange elastic beats.

I started working on demos over the beats by Gibbs. I wrote openly about my struggles and experimented with more contemporary styles of rapping. We made dozens of songs, primarily recorded at Dream House Studios in Toronto's Chinatown with an intrepid young engineer named Calvin Hartwick. Hit like a ton of bricks by both the collapse of my previous management team and the shockingly high cost of living in Toronto, I was incredibly motivated to make this potential opportunity work. I was determined not to be a Canadian rap footnote. Recording at night, I sustained myself with freelance writing, DJ gigs, and voiceover narration for VICELAND shows *Payday* and *Mister Tachyon*.

As I stacked up songs, I signed with Last Gang's parent company eOne to release a track I'd recorded back in 2014 as a single. "My Crew (Woooo)", recorded with my friend Tyler in Montreal, premiered on Zane Lowe's *Beats 1* radio show on Apple Music two days after my thirty-first birthday on February 23, 2017, springboarding me back to relevance. When I rap "Thanks to Kaytranada" in the second verse of the song, I really mean it. If I didn't have that track, I probably never would've gotten in the door with Last Gang.

The first time Kaytranada and I met was when we DJed together at Cabaret Underworld with Prince Club on February 2, 2013. I'd been hearing his instant classic remix of Janet Jackson's "If" all over town. I watched his set and was totally blown away by what he was playing. I honestly thought I was watching the second coming of J Dilla. I talked to him afterwards.

"What was all that music you were playing?" I asked.

"Mine," he said. "I made it."

My response: "Wow, we need to work together." He sent me a link full of beats over Twitter, all of them ridiculously cool and completely singular. I was like a kid in a candy store. The first one I picked, he said someone else had dibs on it already. That track ended up becoming "GLOWED UP" with Anderson .Paak. The second beat I selected became "My Crew (Woooo)."

There was something hypnotic about the instrumental. It sounded both unlike anything I'd ever heard before and also instantly familiar. The music felt alive. It was contemporary but also alien. It was probably the hardest beat I'd ever had a chance to rap on up to that point and I knew I had to do it justice. I spent a long time writing to it. I wanted to knock it out of the park. When I recorded it with Tyler, we decided to experiment with Auto-Tune, something I had been vehemently opposed to in the past. My verses were more stylistically dynamic and playful than they were on my older work, twisting and shifting from line to line. I wanted to live up to the quality of the beat. It brought the best out of me.

By the time the song was released, Kaytranada's 2016 Polaris Music Prize–winning album 99.9% had transformed him into one of the most in-demand producers in the world. It was the right track at the right time as well as a complete departure from anything I'd released previously. I was lucky he hadn't decided to give the beat to anyone else in the three-plus years it took for me to finish and release the song.

It was the perfect way to reintroduce myself to a music world that had changed dramatically over the five years since *Hope in Dirt City*. I mean, Apple Music didn't even exist back in 2012. Streaming had completely changed the music industry, helping it recover from the internet piracy era. Canadian rap was unrecognizable, reshaped by OVO's global success. This song with Kaytranada was an example of me being on the ground floor with an artist and not squandering the opportunity to make something with them. Kevin Calero directed a flashy video for the song that dropped in May 2017. Shot in Montréal, Kevin secured a giant slingshot that had been used by Denis Villeneuve for his film *Arrival*. I was suspended by a harness and rapidly shot backwards across the large studio.

Working without management or a booking agent, I spent much of that year doing everything myself for the first time since I'd dropped out of university to be a rapper. I did extensive research and connected with producers, photographers, visual artists, directors, and collaborators in person and on social media. I was forced to become more organized and proactive. I contacted potential booking agents, show promoters, and collaborators myself, scoring some gigs in the process. My first shows after nearly four years of inactivity were Wavelength, Arboretum, Up + Downtown, Night\Shift, and M for Montréal. I tour-managed myself as well as booked and coordinated my own travel logistics and lodging. I kept fastidious accounting records. I negotiated deals on my own. I got the album recorded, engineered, mixed, and mastered myself. It was empowering to realize that I was capable of doing this administrative side of things that had been largely obscured from me in the past.

After working tirelessly for two straight years, I released my fourth album *Cadence Weapon* on January 19, 2018, on eOne Music Canada. I decided to make the album self-titled because it represented a new beginning for me. I always thought it was a vibe when an established artist would drop a self-titled record later in their career. After everything that had happened with Upper Class, I literally had to restart my career from the ground up. Considering the larger role I had taken on in managing myself, this album represented an unfiltered yet refined version of Cadence Weapon.

Self-reliance and knowledge of self are major themes on this record. I also touch on systemic racism, sexism, gentrification, and mortality. For an album that felt so personal to me, it's ironically my first release to not feature any of my own production. After moving to Toronto, I let more people into the process, jammed more, and had many in-person sessions. I feel like there's more life in these songs, just a sense of freedom and joy. The album starts with a sample of my dad on the radio, talking about me being born. He says prophetically, "If I don't get ya, my son will." Equipped with contemporary beats from notable producers like Kaytranada, Jacques Greene, FrancisGotHeat, and Harrison, I matched the more professional production with stronger rhyming technique and sharper songwriting.

Suddenly, I was back like I'd never left. My self-titled album made it onto the 2018 Polaris Music Prize longlist; I got a new booking agent and toured North America in the fall. I was somewhat surprised that folks were actually happy to see me back in the picture. The landscape had shifted. The Canadian music scene had become more diverse than it had been when I first started and rap was at the forefront. Fans would come up to me and tell me they listened to *Breaking Kayfabe* when they were in high school. Most of the rappers and bands who were around when I'd started had disappeared. Against all odds, I survived and now I was perceived as an elder statesman from a bygone era.

As an artist, you have to learn to manage the ups and downs, the ebb and flow. Sometimes you're gonna be hot or cold in the eyes of the outside world, but the actual truth always resides within yourself. The music industry feeds on youth and novelty, happy to discard anyone perceived as being past their sell-by date. Certainly no one suspected that I had more music inside me or that I could adapt to the changes to the industry and become relevant again. But deep down I always believed in myself and knew I still had something meaningful to offer to the world. That belief in myself is what kept me going.

The whole process of hitting rock bottom and nearly losing my career helped to make my temperament more balanced. Now, I never get too high or low about anything. Over time, I became more patient. I take things as they come and continue to work at my own pace. But I also don't take anything for granted.

European tours and international record deals don't grow on trees. And once you lose that stuff after having it, it's nearly impossible to get it back. Easy come, easy go. Trust me, I know. Perhaps the first act of my career happened because I was destined to tell my story. Maybe some young artists will be able to avoid going through a situation like what I went through because they read this. Nothing would make me happier than if that turns out to be true.

12

TRAPPED

In the summer of 2017, you couldn't go anywhere without hearing "Mask Off" by Future. The second single from the Atlanta rapper's self-titled album, the song went six times platinum and made it to number five on the *Billboard* Hot 100. Metro Boomin's epic instrumental grabs you with its wistful flourishes of flute sampled from Tommy Butler's "Prison Song." But it's the first lines of the chorus that made the song impossible to forget: "Percocets, molly, Percocets / Percocets, molly, Percocets." Sounding like a lobbyist for Big Pharma, Future monotonously repeats the names of these two drugs in a way that celebrates the mundanity of addiction, cycling between prescription and illegal drugs with a resigned sense of familiarity.

During the verses, he rifles off a stream-of-consciousness laundry list of chemical imagery ("Drug houses, looking like Peru . . . pink molly, I can barely move"), stumbling towards a combination of intoxication and luxury that he makes feel inextricably inter-twined. The most telling line in the song is "my guillotine, drank promethazine," a reference to the double-edged nature of his recreational use of prescription codeine cough syrup that can have lethal results after prolonged use.

But Future doesn't drink the stuff anymore. In a 2016 video interview with Clique TV, he admitted that his artistic image wasn't exactly in line with his personal reality:

> *I'm not like super drugged out or a drug addict. My music*
> *may portray a certain kind of image and I know it's some*
> *people that might be super drugged out and they listen to*
> *the music like, "Ay, thank you, you speaking for me," and*
> *then some people that's not [super drugged out] that feel like,*
> *"Man, I don't have to do drugs, I can listen to Future and*
> *feel like I'm on something" and don't have to try [drugs].*
> *I don't do it for you to really have to live that type of*
> *life . . . I feel like [drugs are] the number one thing*
> *everybody likes to talk about.*

In an interview with Genius promoting his 2019 album *The Wizrd*, Future claimed that after he quit, he was scared to let his audience know: "I don't want to tell nobody I stopped drinking lean, I didn't want to tell them because I felt like then they was going to be like, 'Oh, his music changed because he ain't drink-ing lean no more.' Or 'I can hear it when he changing.'"

An artist writing vividly about something they aren't living isn't anything new. No one necessarily expected Neil Young to be actually riding llamas back in 1979. What's interesting is the fact that the author of "Dirty Sprite" and "Codeine Crazy," a man who once bragged "I just took a piss and I seen codeine coming out," was worried what people might think about this music coming from a sober person.

This is the paradox at the heart of trap music.

A subgenre of rap that originated in the southern United States, it's hip-hop music that merges the spirits of punk rock, outlaw country, and the blues. And like so much Black music in America, its value is directly connected to how tangible the Black pain behind it is.

Trap music comes from the term trap house, Atlanta slang for a residential building where drugs are manufactured and sold. Trap houses are usually in poor, predominantly Black neighbour-hoods, sometimes operating out of abandoned, vacant buildings called bandos. The origin stories of why the word *trap* is used vary. Some say it's because the houses typically have only one way in and out. Others have said it's related to drug users being trapped by the cycle of addiction. In an interview with PBS's *Sound Field*, Dr. Lakeyta M. Bonnette-Bailey says, "It's about a lifestyle where you're dealing drugs and it's a trap . . . that you can't really get out of."

Sonically, trap music was the next evolutionary step for south-ern rap following crunk and snap music in the early 2000s. Trap is informed by gangsta rap from the West Coast as well as a hodgepodge of regional sounds that broke out to larger audiences in the '90s. The dark horrorcore of Memphis's Three 6 Mafia is one of the primary influences on trap music as well as the Miami bass sound of 2 Live Crew. Pimp C's funky live compositions for UGK, DJ Screw's slowed and throwed mixtapes, and the early

Rap-A-Lot Records catalogue dictated the sound of Texas rap. Mannie Fresh's hyperactive strip club symphonies for Cash Money Records battled Master P's No Limit Records for New Orleans bounce supremacy. Organized Noize's strange and soulful beats for Dungeon Family in Atlanta competed with Jermaine Dupri's well-tuned pop experiments at So So Def Recordings. Mix that all together and you have the foundation for the trap sound.

The first time I remember hearing an artist substantially refer to the trap on a mainstream rap record was on "SpottieOttie-Dopaliscious" from OutKast's 1998 album *Aquemini*. Big Boi ends his "smokin' word" verse with a fearful rumination:

> *But the United Parcel Service and the people at the post office*
> *Didn't call you back because you had cloudy piss*
> *So now you back in the trap, just that . . . trapped*

On the next song "Y'all Scared," André 3000 asks an important question after his treatise on drug addiction: "Have you ever thought of the meaning of the word *trap*?"

Both of these references make the trap sound like a place that you ended up, not somewhere that you actually wanted to be. But around the turn of the millennium, the lyrical perspective shifted in Atlanta rap. A new generation of locals started making music for trappers by trappers. It wasn't just the fact that they rapped about dealing drugs, these new artists expressed an unprecedented pride in being mere foot soldiers. These weren't street corner kids pretending to be kingpins. This was dope boy music.

The minutiae of the low-level drug trade had rarely been expressed with this level of specificity. New York street emcees in the '90s rapped about pitching on the corners, but the manufacturing process was typically only hinted at. Trappers in Atlanta sounded like they recorded verses to pass the time away from cooking crack on the stove. New York emcees like Jay-Z usually only spoke about dealing drugs in past tense, reminiscing about the regretful period before they became rich enough to stop. The mafioso verses of the Notorious B.I.G., Raekwon, and Ghostface in the '90s were fantastical and violent with the grandiosity of a big-budget action flick. Listening to Atlanta trap music was closer to watching an uncompromising drug documentary that you couldn't look away from.

In Atlanta, the trap itself became the subject matter. Featuring genre-defining production from DJ Toomp, T.I. was the first rapper to bring the trap to the mainstream when he named his 2003 album *Trap Muzik*. Young Jeezy took over the underground with his mixtapes with DJ Drama (*Tha Streets Iz Watchin* and *Trap or Die*), subsequently bringing his hard-worn street tales to Def Jam on his 2005 debut album *Let's Get It: Thug Motivation 101*. In the songs, Jeezy discussed supply chain, pricing, and distribution. Promotional shirts with his Snowman logo on them sold like wildfire, getting banned from schools after the drug symbolism was discovered.

But the true driving force behind the ascent of trap music was Gucci Mane. Born in Bessemer, Alabama, and based in East Atlanta, he named his 2005 debut *Trap House* and followed it up with dozens of similarly named albums and mixtapes: *Trap-A-Thon*, *Back to the Trap House*, *Trap Back*, *Trap God*. Flooding the streets with countless mixtapes that progressively raised his profile using a strategy popularized by Lil Wayne, he took the assembly line system of the trap house and applied it to the music industry.

Gucci rapped and trapped without empathy. He mentioned adversaries and customers by name on record. There was no token final album track where he would find religion and atone for his sins. His music was unapologetic and a generation of disfranchised D-boys could relate. Gucci was an erratic, quasi-mythical figure who frequently ran afoul of the law, and many of today's biggest rappers spring directly from him as if they were alien symbiotes that spawned from Venom in the *Spider-Man* comics: Young Thug, Future, 2 Chainz, 21 Savage, Migos. And nearly all of the most influential trap producers cut their teeth working with Gucci as well: Shawty Redd, Zaytoven, Drumma Boy, Southside, Mike WiLL Made-It, Sonny Digital.

Gucci Mane's protege Waka Flocka Flame created the ur-text for what a mainstream trap album should sound like with 2010's *Flockaveli*, helping producer Lex Luger go from a kid making beats on Fruity Loops in his mom's basement to one of the most in-demand producers of the decade. There was no hedging with mainstream pop features or other previously established regional sounds. You can hear all the defining characteristics of trap music present on this record: distorted 808 kicks pitched up and down, rolling triplet hi-hats, horror movie synths, and an overall melodic profile that suggests something like triumphant darkness.

Waka turned background adlib vocals into an art form. Rather than merely doubling the main vocal for emphasis, as was previously the custom in rap, Waka created a call-and-response session with himself. It was like a frenzied musical self-high-five.

Before, rappers used adlibs to subtly emphasize and support the primary vocal. Waka's adlibs were often as loud as or louder than his verses. Turning what was typically considered an afterthought into the main event, he prefigured the Migos sound that took over the pop world three years later and helped to inspire a recording trend that's still being imitated today.

◆

In 2016, Red Bull Music Academy sent me to Atlanta to interview two of the progenitors of the mixtape scene that helped propel trap to the mainstream, DJ Drama and Don Cannon. Our interview took place at Patchwerk Recording Studios. There was once an outlaw mystique associated with selling unlicensed mixtapes, culminating in a 2007 police raid of Drama's studio on bootlegging and racketeering charges. But by the time of our interview, trap mixtapes had firmly been legalized, moving off the streets and the open web onto the iTunes Store by major labels. The walls at Patchwerk were completely covered with gold and platinum plaques.

During the day, I went for a walk to get a feel for the area around the studio. I passed a disused, trash-filled motel that looked like it had been abandoned for years. Like many other American cities, Atlanta seemed to be built for cars and not much else. The only other person I encountered was an emaciated man lying prone in front of House of Prayer Pentecostal Church. He was shirtless and looked like Black Jesus on the cross. Whenever I'm in the States, the lack of a social safety net is made very apparent. This country can inspire you to reach the highest heights but will also let you fall all the way to the bottom. Around the corner was the upscale streetwear store A Ma Maniére. I went inside and there was a reverential emptiness to the space, like a museum carrying the priceless garments of a long-lost civilization.

Atlanta has a languorous pace to it. It's like a southern drawl in the form of a city. Everyone moves slowly and deliberately. Lush, massive trees are everywhere, swaying listlessly and climbing impossibly high. Here it feels like the day can easily get away from you without anything happening at all. And yet there is also an overbearing sense that danger could strike at any moment. Donald Glover's *Atlanta* captures this spirit particularly well. Everything is all good until it suddenly isn't.

I went to a nearby suburb called Decatur to profile Awful Records, the indie rap collective that spawned artists like Father, Zack Fox, and Abra. Well-trained dogs skipped around the clutter lining the living room. There was a dusty Dirt Devil covered by pieces of a broken bedframe. A glossy photo of Gucci Mane had prominent placement beside a door, the trap god taking pride of place where you might expect to see a watercolour of Jesus. Among the detritus were reminders of the label's DIY ethos: a pink camcorder, various lighting equipment, a makeshift bedroom studio.

When it was time to leave, my Uber arrived, rolling slowly down the street in search of the correct address to pick me up from. A little too slowly. Ethereal said something about how people shouldn't drive like that around here. You could feel the tension in the air. When I got into the backseat of the car, I mentioned that I was from out of town to my driver, and he warned me that everyone in Atlanta had a gun so I shouldn't get into an argument with anybody. Including him. He was packing as well.

Later that evening, I arrived at Graveyard Tavern in East Atlanta Village to watch DJ Drama, Don Cannon, and Speakerfoxxx play tracks. Posted up at the back entrance of the club was a police officer brandishing a shotgun. In Canada, it wouldn't be normal to see a cop working security for a club, let alone openly holding a firearm outside of one. Were bars getting robbed that frequently? A few days later, I went with the Red Bull Music Academy crew to Magic City, the strip club that is considered a sacred place for the Atlanta music scene. The security was more stringent than at the airport. A billboard promoting *Savage Mode* by 21 Savage and Metro Boomin hung proudly above the building.

Famous for chicken wings that are so good that basketball star Lou Williams allegedly endangered the NBA's COVID-19 bubble just to grab some, Magic City is also known as something of a southern rap R&D department. DC from '90s group Tag Team was one of the first DJs at Magic City. His song "Whoomp! (There It Is)" first gained popularity at the club before selling over 3.5 million copies and hitting number two on the *Billboard* Hot 100 in 1993. From that point on, a symbiotic relationship developed between rappers, DJs, and strippers at Magic City.

Rappers would pay the DJs to play pre-release versions of their songs to see which ones resonated with the dancers at the club. OutKast used to bring over an unfinished track, get it playtested at Magic, and then head back to the studio to complete it based on the response. The strippers and DJs at Magic City are kingmakers, trap prognosticators who get paid for their Herculean feats on stage and their savvy behind the decks but also happen to be some of the best A&Rs in the music industry. If a song becomes a hit at Magic City, it won't be long before it's a hit everywhere else in the world.

Monday night is when the Atlanta rap scene typically congregates there (immortalized by Jeezy on "Magic City Monday"), but I was at Magic on a Wednesday. Hump day is open mic night, when aspiring rappers pay twenty dollars each to perform on the catwalk with the women dancing around them. Hoping to catch the eye of a big-name producer like Zaytoven (who was in attendance) or one of the ascendant local rappers throwing ungodly sums of cash in the air, these generic trap stars glumly performed their bland songs for an unenthused audience. Even when the dancers were in action (which looked more like Olympic-level gymnastics than a striptease), there wasn't much attention paid to them. Most of the guys were gawking around, looking to see which artists were in the building.

◆

If you wanted to find a prime example of how white America engages with trap music, *Noisey: Atlanta* would be the perfect microcosm. Produced by VICE in 2014, it was hosted by nerdy white journalist Thomas Morton, who functioned as a surrogate for the average American rap fan. We follow him as he profiles the founding fathers and upstarts of the burgeoning Atlanta trap scene. The documentary series fixates on only the most lurid, violent details, hovering over bubbling crack pots and gleaming artillery without stopping to consider the humanity of the people forced to use these tools.

A promotional image for the series features a faceless Black man wearing a white tee and gold chains with a gun in his hand. On *Noisey: Atlanta*, Black people in Atlanta are treated with the anthropological lens of *National Geographic*. Like a white teenager listening to Spotify's RapCaviar playlist, Morton and VICE can pop in, take what they want from the culture and move on when they lose interest. But like the young Black boy who urged the IFC camera crew to leave his Katrina-ravaged New Orleans neighbourhood when Born Ruffians and I were dragged there on a ruin porn field trip, the subjects on camera don't have the luxury of being able to leave.

By the middle of the '10s, the trap had been slowly insinuating itself into American culture for several years. Like pressure building on a dam, this breakthrough was the result of previous hip-hop incursions into the mainstream, moments that made a dent but never quite formed a hole large enough for the whole scene to pass through. There were *Krush Groove* and *Beat Street* in the '80s as well as MC Hammer, Vanilla Ice, and *The Fresh Prince of Bel-Air* in the early '90s. *8 Mile* and *Chappelle's Show* (especially his impersonation of Lil Jon that went viral before going viral was a thing) made an impact in the early '00s. Midway through that decade, southern rap was no longer considered a niche concern: OutKast won Album of the Year at the Grammys in 2004 and Three 6 Mafia received the Oscar for Best Original Song in 2006.

This was the environment that primed us for the trapocalypse we find ourselves in today. Kanye West was an early adopter of the emerging trap sound in the mainstream, working with genre pioneers DJ Toomp and Young Jeezy on his single "Can't Tell Me Nothing" from his 2007 album *Graduation*. Lex Luger's ascent following *Flockaveli* led him to produce hundreds of songs that came out in 2011, none more important than Kanye West and Jay-Z's "H.A.M." The song peaked at number twenty-three on the *Billboard* Hot 100. The duo also used trap elements on other songs from their collaborative album *Watch the Throne*, most prominently on "Niggas in Paris," which won Best Rap Song and Best Rap Performance at the Grammys in 2013.

The commercial acceptance of trap by established figures in hip-hop benefited artists from Atlanta more substantially over the next couple years. Nicki Minaj made "Beez in the Trap" with 2 Chainz. Mike WiLL Made-It found great success with his cinematic beat for Rihanna's "Pour It Up." Migos created one of the most imitated sounds in rap music with their nimble triplet flows, inspiring Drake to jump on the remix for their song "Versace." The group later popularized dabbing, turning the dance move into a cultural phenomenon.

One of the biggest mainstream moments for trap was Beyoncé and Jay-Z's "Drunk in Love," which won Best R&B Song and Best R&B Performance at the 57th Grammy Awards. The pop world was taking notice. Miley Cyrus's album *Bangerz* was executive-produced by Mike WiLL Made-It. Katy Perry, Lady Gaga, Ariana Grande, Lorde, and Taylor Swift all released songs featuring trap elements in the 2010s. During the same decade, a hybrid of electronic music and trap was being produced by artists like Girl Unit, Rustie, and TNGHT. The success of Baauer's chart-topping 2012 smash "Harlem Shake" helped pave the way for what is now referred to as EDM trap.

Sounding like a cross between U.K. dubstep and Atlanta trap, EDM trap often repurposes the sonic elements of trap music while removing the rapping and the pathos. Black people occasionally turn up on a sample or as a brief feature appearance. Everything that makes trap music feel euphoric has been streamlined here and designed for maximum programmed thrills. It reminds me of a Michael Bay action film or a theme park ride, all of the highs without any of the comedown.

During the second half of the decade, trap spread around the U.S.A. and into other countries, continuing to mutate. A sub-genre called drill was developed in Chicago and later spread to London, New York, and Toronto, creating a soundtrack for the pervasive inner-city tension in those metropolitan centres. Hailing from New Jersey, Fetty Wap and his irresistibly melodic "Trap Queen" was one of the most popular songs of 2015. Anuel AA, Ozuna, and Bad Bunny are some of the leading stars of the Latin trap scene. Hugely successful groups like Blackpink make trap-influenced K-pop. There's French trap, eastern European trap, African trap. What was once music for trappers by trappers in Atlanta has become universally adopted in just a few short years.

Another shift in trap came with the advent of SoundCloud rap in 2017. Young rappers were gaining massive followings with songs they'd upload to the music streaming platform. Their version of trap was scrappier and rawer than what was happening in the mainstream. Songs like XXXTentacion's "Look at Me!" had an insouciant, punkish, lo-fi edge to them. Most of the scene was based in Florida, home of trap-influencing Miami bass, 2 Live Crew, and Slip-N-Slide Records. There was an industry frenzy to scoop up SoundCloud rappers, and Florida artists such as Kodak Black, Lil Pump, Ski Mask the Slump God, and Smokepurpp all signed major label deals.

Their ascent further changed the dynamic of how rappers engaged with drugs. Kids who grew up listening to hedonistic trap pioneers like Juicy J and Gucci Mane were coming of age, and this new generation was determined to push the sound and their consumption to the next level. Many early emcees in the '80s were decidedly anti-drugs. By the end of that decade going into the mid-'90s, the prevailing stance was to immortalize the hustlers that emcees grew up idolizing by composing alluring yet cautionary tales about dealing drugs. Around the turn of the century, most street rappers were already over it, world-weary at an early age, reminiscing about their checkered pasts from the deck of a yacht or the back row of a private plane.

Atlanta's trap boom shifted the focus to water whipping over the stove and slanging on the corner without a conscience in the mid-'00s. But from that point on, the dealer slowly became the customer. Houston rappers were the first to recreationally drink codeine cough syrup and rap about it, turning it into a way of life and inspiring a new sound. Songs like D4L's "Scotty," where Fabo gets "geeked up" and suffers from paranoia and hallucinations over a club-ready beat, influenced artists like Young Thug and Migos. Future's "Dirty Sprite" acknowledged the life-threatening potential of drinking lean but might as well be a jingle for the purple stuff. Whereas rappers like Scarface and Eminem once rapped with poignancy about being trapped in the clutches of drug addiction, the younger generation was more inclined to celebrate their chemical dependency.

With the rise of the SoundCloud rappers, drug abuse was plat-formed in the mainstream. Pill popping had become pop friendly, the modern equivalent of Joey Ramone singing about sniffing glue. Lil Peep rapped about "Drugs in my nose, good drugs in my cup" on "Benz Truck (Гелик)." Lil Pump danced around with Charlie Sheen and claimed, "I been poppin' pills since I was seven," in the video for "Drug Addicts." Chicago rapper Juice WRLD had a massive hit with "Lucid Dreams," where he sadly crooned about dependency: "I take prescriptions to make me feel a-okay." His Dem Franchize Boyz–referencing chorus on "Lean Wit Me" came off like a battle cry for the medicated generation:

> *Lean with me, pop with me*
> *Get high with me if you rock with me*
> *Smoke with me, drink with me*
> *Fucked-up liver with some bad kidneys*

In June 2017, the *New York Times* called SoundCloud rap "the most vital and disruptive new movement in hip-hop." By December 2019, it published an article mourning the scene's end. Lil Peep was found dead on his tour bus in Tucson, Arizona, of an accidental overdose on November 15, 2017. XXXTentacion was murdered outside of a motorsports shop on June 18, 2018. Over eight thousand fans attended his funeral at the BB&T Center in Sunrise, Florida. Juice WRLD died on December 8, 2019, suffering a seizure from an accidental overdose of codeine and oxycodone after landing at Midway International Airport. His final moments before the seizure were posted on social media. In the press for *Wrld on Drugs*, his 2018 collaborative album with Future, Juice WRLD mentioned that he had been inspired to start drinking lean by listening to Future's music.

Like the drugs that inspired it in the first place, trap music can be addictive. It's the kind of music you make after walking out of your bulletproof SUV, having survived a barrage of bullets from your rival, like Young Dolph did before he made "100 Shots." Despite often being associated with downers like lean, trap really gives you a boost like cocaine. It can push you to the next level

during a Peloton session. Today, it soundtracks the world's greatest athletic achievements on television and the most inventive
exploits on TikTok. It's been used as a marketing tool, such as
in the title of the political podcast *Chapo Trap House*. People
want the euphoric feeling you get after escaping poverty and
cheating death but want to ignore what it took to get to that
point. They want the Negro spiritual without having to live
through slavery.

Trap music has become the soundtrack to urban life in America,
the omnipresent hi-hats shuffling in and out of earshot at all
hours of the day. In 2017, a forty-nine-year-old white man
named Michael Dunn fired ten shots into the Dodge Durango
of a Black seventeen-year-old named Jordan Davis because the
boy refused to turn his trap music down. Two years later,
Michael Paul Adams, twenty-seven, followed Elijah Al-Amin,
seventeen, into a Circle K in Peoria, Arizona, stabbed him, and
slit his throat because he "felt threatened by the music" Al-Amin
had been playing in his car outside. Adams claimed the music
made him feel "unsafe" because he'd allegedly been attacked by
rap music listeners in the past. He expressed in court documents that "people who listen to rap music are a threat to him
and the community."

It seems that there's something inherently threatening about
trap music's naked portrayal of Black pain that some white folks
don't like being reminded of. Trap evokes an atmosphere of
dread and paranoia that constantly surveilled Black folks around
the world can all appreciate. Just like rock and roll before it, trap
music was frequently portrayed as a source of moral panic until
it was commodified and appropriated. U.K. drill music in particular has been blamed for knife crime to the point that artists

like Digga D are forced by court order to send their music and lyrics to the police for approval within twenty-four hours of uploading. Black pain has been the engine driving the music industry since its inception. The establishment shudders if that pain seems too realistic, while the majority of young white listeners can't get enough of it.

The white American music audience's fascination with the outlaw mystique of the Black musician is nothing new. In his book *Black Talk*, Ben Sidran could have easily been describing the contemporary appeal of trap music when writing about the Jazz Age of 1920s America: "Whites gravitated toward black music and black culture in general because they felt it expressed the abandon and hedonism toward which they liked to think they were moving."

That Black artists can turn their pain into art in the face of persistent economic and social inequality is a miracle in itself. These songs are more than merely catchy. They often reach centuries back to the motherland, calling directly upon African cultural memory. You can trace Quavo's adlibs back to the hollers of field slaves. Gospel organ takes pride of place in many trap songs. The ring shout lives on in Kanye West's Sunday Service performances. Call and response is a common part of any hip-hop show and exists in the DNA of every African-American musical form.

In Samuel A. Floyd Jr.'s book *The Power of Black Music*, the author discusses how blues singers created their songs "by combining fragments and verses from the hundreds or thousands of formulas that were floating around in black communities everywhere." This sounds remarkably similar to dances moving from hood to hood via TikTok or rap flows gaining popularity and being quickly adopted by rappers around the world today. It reminds me of how samples become hip-hop standards and are used across decades by numerous artists as a form of homage, how old school rap references become like speakeasy passwords for acceptance into the Black underground. Trap music is part of the continuum of Black American music, sharing many of the same successes and pitfalls of the styles that came before it.

◆

I returned to SXSW in 2018 to promote my self-titled fourth album. It was the fifth time I had attended the festival in Austin, Texas. Attendance seemed to be increasing exponentially on an annual basis. Each time I arrived, it felt progressively more chaotic with larger crowds and a more substantial corporate presence. Major labels and their artists started booking performances to align themselves with SXSW's hipster cool factor, siphoning attention away from the emerging acts that the festival was initially designed to support. Kanye played the Fader Fort stage in 2010. During SXSW 2015, an inebriated aspiring rapper named Rashad Owens was evading police after a traffic stop when he plowed into a crowd of revellers, killing four people and injuring another twenty. To me, it had felt inevitable that something like that might one day happen during SXSW. The growth was out of control.

Things seemed chiller in 2018. You could walk on the streets a bit more freely. It seemed like many tech companies and publications weren't seeing the value in hosting an event at the festival anymore. That wasn't the same story for labels. There seemed to be more bands than ever at SXSW, trying to grab attention any way that they possibly could. Walking down 6th Street, I came across a flash mob: a group of dancers formed a circle and

Memphis trap rapper BlocBoy JB emerged out of the middle. He was riding high on the recent success of his Drake collaboration "Look Alive," as well as his viral hit "Shoot" and the associated dance that came with it. He did the "Shoot" dance in the circle and then the flash mob disbanded and moved to another location to repeat the roving advertisement. That dance was later appropriated without accreditation by Epic Games in *Fortnite*.

Rappers were everywhere, thirsty for attention, popping into my field of vision like the human embodiment of internet spam. There were rappers rapping on every corner of 6th Street, essentially busking without even passing the hat around. I saw rappers and their hangers-on walking around while wearing electronic sandwich boards, becoming human billboards, a mini Times Square. I saw rappers with Steadicam operators and boom mic technicians following them closely as they roamed the streets. Making it big with trap music was a gold rush and it was as if every rapper in North America came to Austin with their pickaxe.

It is true that to stay relevant in rap music, you have to keep up with the trends. The industry moves at a rapid pace and no one wants to be left behind. My approach has always been to remain aware of what was in fashion so I could consciously avoid what was popular whenever possible. I always want to know what's popping so I know exactly what I need to subvert. It's fun to take bits and pieces of the dominant form of the moment and roll them into what I'm doing though. My self-titled album occasionally draws from the trap sonic palette on songs like "Soju" and "Large." But I never feel pressure to change my subject matter or do things just because they've become popular in the mainstream. Music is a conversation, but you don't have to repeat what everyone else is saying in order to be understood. I try to let the art guide my decision-making process. Throughout my career, I would say I've been ideologically stubborn but always stylistically flexible.

I was booked to play a hip-hop festival in Montreal called Metro Metro in the summer of 2018. Taking place on the exhibition grounds in the shadow of the seldom-used Olympic Stadium, some of the biggest trap artists in the world were tapped to perform. Future, Juice WRLD, and Cardi B were some of the big names in attendance. A festival that featured mostly trap was still a relatively uncommon occurrence in our country, despite the success of events like Rolling Loud happening down south. Online commenters expressed disbelief that the festival would take place at all. It was also rare for me to share a bill with contemporary rappers, instead of being the speck of colour in a sea of indie rock bands. My sister Gena made the trip up from New York for it. She locked eyes with Waka Flocka Flame backstage and they shared a laugh.

Walking the grounds of the festival, I took in the assemblage of the audience. The crowd was heavily weighted with French-Canadian teenagers who rapped along to every word of the songs. *Every* word. I was struck by the outfit synchronization I was seeing, a common feature of today's large-scale music gatherings. Sets of *les jeunes filles* wearing matching neon-green bikinis and around-the-way-girl attire. White bros decked out in Lil Yachty braids studded with colourful red beads. The very same braids created to protect sensitive African hair thousands of years ago. The more time I spent at Metro Metro, the more I felt like an uninvited guest at a Halloween party where my culture was the costume.

Certainly, it's typical for music fans to take on the pose of their preferred genre. If it was a metal show, it would likely be an ocean of leather and jean jackets with the sleeves cut off. But when it comes to white fans engaging with Black music, there can be something about it that feels extractive. On my recording trips to Los Angeles, I'd bounce around the vintage shops along Melrose. The walls were usually lined with the ephemera of decades of Black experience: Million Man March T-shirts, Malcolm X jackets, deadstock limited edition Jordans, retro Polo Ralph Lauren rugbys that Raekwon would've worn. The clientele seemed to be a mix of rich white children and Black rappers and their entourages. Inside and outside of these spaces were actual rappers and aspiring rappers and rapper-adjacent individuals creating content about the rappers.

There's a cottage industry around trap that feels inexhaustible. The recently opened Trap Music Museum in Atlanta features a cotton-candy-pink replica of a trap house built for Instagram photo ops and something called the Escape the Trap Escape Room. It still seems like the majority of the press is struggling to interface with the dominant Black music form of our time. Music websites publish uncritical puff pieces that function solely as label-sanctioned advertorial content, pumping out interchangeable blurbs about the trapper of the moment. Mainstream publications either cover a trap artist months after they were first relevant or skip out on covering them entirely unless a murder is involved. I'm reminded of Ben Sidran's assessment of the clueless white jazz critic from *Black Talk*: "the white intellectual approaching black culture with the best intentions can be, and often is, fooled . . . he fools himself further if he thinks he can predict what will and what will not constitute the 'taste' or the leadership of black culture."

I suspect that trap music will soon go the way of crunk and snap, perhaps getting fully subsumed by drill or whatever comes after it. Black music has historically held a chameleonic character, always moving and changing at the very moment it has been recognized. Not only do Black musicians in America have to contend with navigating the vulnerability of their personal quest for survival in their art, but they also have to constantly shift the paradigm to dodge the inevitable spectre of cultural appropriation. When I listen to trap music, I have trouble ignoring the pain that naturally informs it. Even Young Dolph couldn't stay triumphant for long—he was gunned down in Memphis on November 17, 2021. The prison bids, the overdoses, and the posthumous releases loom larger than the bottomless kick drum that threatens to swallow all of twenty-first-century life when played at an appropriately loud volume.

13

PARALLEL WORLD

Following the release of my self-titled album, I started to rebuild the infrastructure around my career. I signed with a new booking agent who understood me as an artist, a legitimate label that believed in my music, and a Canadian PR team adept at presenting my work to the public at large. Momentum was developing and my music was being introduced to a new generation. At the beginning of 2020, I had some great opportunities lined up. I started off the year in Los Angeles, where I DJed at the Ace Hotel, had a couple recording sessions, and took some meetings. I spent all of February in Montréal acting in the play *Please Thrill Me* at La Chapelle Scènes Contemporaines. I was invited to the Banff Centre twice: to collaborate on the Mâmawapihk project for Fort Edmonton Park in January and to be a guest mentor for the Banff International Songwriter Residency in March.

In late March, I was booked to perform at SXSW and at the Nasher Sculpture Center in Dallas when the COVID-19 pandemic took hold in North America. Just as my career was getting back into gear after a long absence from the public eye, there was a once-in-a-lifetime global pandemic paralyzing the world. I flew back to Toronto from Banff; new restrictions were being added on a daily basis as understanding of the virus grew. Pearson Airport looked like a scene from *Deep Impact*, with cars lined up as far as the eye could see, frantic drivers waiting to collect their frightened loved ones. Unnerved and faced with an unprecedented level of uncertainty, I hunkered down, moved into my partner Sara's home, and tried to stay present.

Would I ever perform a live concert again? I had no idea. I told myself that I wouldn't work on anything for as long as possible. The viability of my music career felt insignificant when compared to the human race dealing with a deadly, rapidly spreading invisible disease that threatened our very existence.

During lockdown, we had a lot of time on our hands. We baked bread and experimented with new recipes. We watched every movie and TV show available, including multiple iterations of the *Real Housewives* franchise. Every weekend I DJed over Twitch for a small group of my fans in a series that I called Quarantunes. I'd play them all the songs I'd discovered over the previous week of online digging, as if I was preparing for a party that might never happen. It helped me to re-establish a connection with people in the outside world. I found lots of weird '80s pop songs but this exercise also encouraged me to stay up to date with the new grime and drill songs coming from the U.K., genres that largely informed the sound of music I eventually made.

One unexpected by-product of the pandemic was how it exposed the flimsiness of institutions that once felt too big to fail. Time-honoured businesses quickly went bankrupt. When George Floyd was murdered on camera by a police officer named Derek Chauvin in May, I thought it would be treated as another blip in the tradition of Trayvon Martin and Michael Brown. More Black death for the history books. Floyd would posthumously be painted as the villain despite being the victim, and we'd go right back to the status quo.

But something surprising happened. A world unencumbered by the typical distractions of work and routine watched in horror and said, "Enough is enough!" They took to the streets en masse and discovered the power of collective action. Other musicians and I got involved in our communities and used our excess time to organize socially and politically. Folks questioned authority for the first time, openly wondering about the necessity of armed police in their communities. People looked in shock at ballooning police budgets and wondered if our tax money could be put to better use. I watched virtual city council meetings and was baffled by the lack of creativity exhibited by our municipal leadership. I was horrified by online eviction blitzes where scores of vulnerable people were cruelly kicked out of their homes during an unprecedented worldwide health crisis.

I started thinking deeper about the institutional reasons for why things were the way they were. Television news shows were discussing concepts like microaggressions and structural racism. NBA players had civil rights slogans on the backs of their jerseys during games. Issues that I had observed as a Black person throughout my life were being acknowledged and taken seriously by the mainstream media for the first time. Corporations from

Nike to Sephora felt pressure to show that they too believed that Black Lives Matter. It was against this backdrop that I got back into creating. I started writing this book, looking back at the first decade of my career as the world stood still. Around the same time, I began collecting lyric ideas and themes in the Notes app on my phone.

The songs were inspired by the world-building bravery of Michaela Coel's *I May Destroy You*. Reading Reni Eddo-Lodge's *Why I'm No Longer Talking to White People about Race* encouraged me to rap about sociopolitical issues in a way that was informative and accessible. I watched old comedy specials by Chris Rock and Richard Pryor, examining how they succinctly satirized complex racial issues through humour. I listened to classic albums by artists who successfully balanced funk with a social message: the Clash, Marvin Gaye, Public Enemy, Gil Scott-Heron, Nina Simone, Sly & the Family Stone, Linton Kwesi Johnson. I studied rap albums from recent years that were lyrically dense and sonically cohesive: JAY-Z's *4:44*, Mac Miller's *Swimming*, Kendrick Lamar's *DAMN*.

I would jog around Toronto. Running through the industrial landscape north of our apartment, lyrics came to me with great regularity. The forward momentum stirred something in me. I would stop multiple times to jot some words down or record a voice note, the words tumbling out of my brain like boulders rolling off of a cliff. I felt a great sense of urgency to speak to the strange times that we were living in. I began canvassing for beats from producers I knew, booking three-hour night sessions with my engineer Calvin at Dream House Studios to record the songs as soon as I finished writing them.

I increasingly found myself agitating for social causes online. I wrote an article for *Hazlitt* about the transit-based gentrification caused by the Eglinton Crosstown LRT construction project happening in Toronto's Little Jamaica neighbourhood that had led to the shuttering of dozens of Black-owned businesses. In my research for that piece, I learned more about other disenfranchised primarily Black communities in Canada like Africville and Hogan's Alley. I wrote a tweet comparing the hundreds of thousands raised for the GoFundMe page created in support of Adam Skelly's Adamson Barbeque restaurants that flouted lockdown restrictions with the meagre contributions to the GoFundMe created by Reclaim, Rebuild Eg West for Black business grants in Little Jamaica, leading to thousands of dollars being contributed to the latter fundraiser. I released a remix album on Bandcamp and raised hundreds of dollars for the Canadian Association of Black Journalists.

How could I advocate in a similar way with the music I was making? Some themes started recurring in my new songs: Black Canadian history, racial profiling, surveillance, gentrification, systemic racism, perception versus reality. In a mad dash to the end of 2020, I collected the tracks that would make up *Parallel World*. The album title was inspired by the idea that two people can be walking down the same street in the same city but live completely different lives based on what race they are. I pictured myself walking across the street from the well-intentioned white folks in my old neighbourhood of Roncesvalles. I also wanted to create a sonic world for people to live in as a form of musical escapism from our contemporary circumstances.

When making this album, I locked into a level of focus that I hadn't experienced since the creation of *Breaking Kayfabe*. I felt like I was back living in my mom's attic, combing the internet for new music and researching ideas all night. Without the distraction of live shows, travel, or other obligations, I had a singularly obsessive approach to making *Parallel World* that probably wouldn't have been possible without the pandemic. This bled into how I chose to present the album to the audience as well. I was disappointed that I hadn't made the themes of my self-titled album clearer and thought about how to do a better job of that with *Parallel World*. Also frustrated with navigating social media algorithms that only allowed me to reach a fraction of my audience unless I paid for ads, I started a newsletter on Substack and wrote openly about the process of making the album, a throwback to the blog era that I had gleefully taken part in. My career was coming full circle. The newsletter was a major success, building anticipation for the album and, in a surprising turn of events, even being directly referenced by journalists during interviews. This time I refused to be misunderstood.

I created the album almost totally remotely with musicians like Jacques Greene, Backxwash, Jimmy Edgar, Martyn Bootyspoon, Fat Tony, Casey MQ, and Little Snake. I would send voice notes over text and email to share ideas with my collaborators who were based not only all across Canada but in the States, England, and Australia. As lockdowns were lifted and then resumed at seemingly random intervals, the process of making the album often felt like a race against time. I worried that if I didn't finish the record soon, Dream House Studios would be closed for lockdown and my record would be left in limbo.

The album was mixed in December, mastered in January, and released on April 30, 2021, eleven days after I received my first shot of Pfizer's COVID-19 vaccine. I felt a sense of optimism and hope for the future that had been absent for much of the preceding year. Many artists struggled with whether to release new music during the pandemic or to wait until live shows were a reality again. I felt like the urgency of *Parallel World*'s subject matter would be felt more strongly if it came out as soon as possible. The album was received warmly by critics and fans, and thanks to new health and safety restrictions and a rise in vaccinations, it became safe for me to play some festival shows that summer in Edmonton, Montréal, and Ontario.

In an unpredictable career filled with false starts, sporadic success, and jarring failures, I had finally put out the right album at the right time. On July 15, *Parallel World* made it on the shortlist for the 2021 Polaris Music Prize, my first record in almost a decade to receive that distinction. The Canadian music landscape had changed dramatically since I was nominated for the inaugural Polaris Music Prize in 2006. Back then, most of the nominees were white indie rock bands and I was the lone Black electro rapper making acerbic underground hip-hop that didn't have a precedent at home or abroad. In 2021, this dynamic had been reversed: the slate of nominees was more racially and sonically diverse than ever. Rather than being an outlier, I fit in perfectly. The sociopolitical topics and experimental sonics that informed *Breaking Kayfabe* had slowly seeped into the mainstream, making today's press and audience more likely to appreciate the context surrounding my new album.

On September 27, I won the 2021 Polaris Music Prize for *Parallel World*. After a decade of working for free under my old management and label, I had earned a fifty-thousand-dollar cash prize. Like most of my life milestones during the pandemic, I learned the news over Zoom. In my acceptance speech—delivered virtually instead of in front of an audience at a gala—I gave props to my artistic communities in Toronto and Montréal and promised to organize voter registration events around the Toronto municipal election and the Ontario provincial election in 2022. Echoing my lyrics on "Play No Games," I reminded everyone that Canada's prime minister, Justin Trudeau, had worn blackface so many times that he couldn't remember them all and had still been rewarded with a third term.

The last part of my speech was something that I had visualized in my mind for years. I knew what I would say if I ever won anything. I shouted out Edmonton and Alberta, emphasizing how you don't have to be from Toronto to make Canadian art that matters, that the experience of young Albertans was valuable. I concluded my speech by saying, "The prairies got something to say!" And then I sat there, having won one of the biggest prizes in Canadian music. I thought back to when I first came to Toronto in the early 2000s, all bright-eyed and enthusiastic with my Nudie Jeans on. Local musicians would make the tired crack "Sorry to hear that!" when I said that I was from Edmonton. Just like I did when I first started rapping about my community, I hoped to encourage and inspire younger artists by representing my city and being true to where I came from.

Nothing would make me happier than seeing a prairie rapper reference my speech ten years from now when they're taking home a big national award. The last line of my speech was itself a reference to André 3000's famous acceptance speech from the 1995 Source Awards when OutKast won Best New Rap Group. A duo from Atlanta unexpectedly won a major award in the thick of the tense, charged atmosphere of the East Coast–West Coast rap rivalry in the mecca of hip-hop, New York City.

OutKast were booed lustily as they walked to the stage. A defiant André stood at the podium and ended his speech with "The South got something to say!" These iconic, audacious words emboldened Southern rappers to see themselves as more than regional curiosities. The scene became a force to be reckoned with. Southern rap went on to define the direction of hip-hop culture for decades to come.

I related to that moment, found it empowering, and essentially sampled it for my own speech. What's more hip-hop than that?

ACKNOWLEDGEMENTS

Writing a book is something that has lingered in the back of my mind for quite some time. I didn't know what it would be like until I actually started writing it. The process involved unearthing some trauma around the music industry that I hadn't dealt with or told anyone. Making *Bedroom Rapper* was incredibly challenging but it was also one of the most rewarding experiences I've ever had and I couldn't have done it without a solid support system.

Shout out to everybody at McClelland & Stewart and Penguin Random House Canada. Thank you to Jared Bland for meeting with me and believing that I could do this.

To my editor Haley Cullingham: thank you, thank you, thank you! This book wouldn't be here without her empathetic, measured hand guiding me along the way. In the words of Sly Stone, thank you for letting me be myself. She is truly the Cool Edit Pro.

Thanks to my copy editor Crissy Calhoun for her attention to detail and razor sharp instincts. Special thanks to Linda Friedner, Tonia Addison, Blossom Thom, Kimberlee Kemp, Chimedum Ohaegbu, Matthew Flute, Kim Kandravy, and Terra Page.

Thanks so much to my literary agent Martha Webb at CookeMcDermid for her guidance and for helping to bring this whole thing to fruition. Thanks to Jen Agg for making the connection.

Elements of the Poet Laureate chapter were adapted from a lecture I gave at the Banff Centre for Arts and Creativity for the International Songwriter Residency. I'd like to thank them for having me and for giving me the space to develop these ideas. I wrote sections of this book at Artscape Gibraltar Point and would like to thank them for providing an idyllic environment to create in.

To my wonderful friends who read chapters and fragments of this book along the way, thank you for taking the time: Laura Broadbent, Samantha Henman, Anne T. Donahue, Cam Maclean, Patrick Leonard, Tamara Lindeman, Rachel Shaw, Sean Nicholas Savage, Sebastian Cowan, Miriam Gallou, Jared Leon, Molly Nilsson, Philippe Aubin-Dionne, and Jane Penny. Thanks to Stephanie Bailey for encouraging me to write a book about my music career when a memoir wasn't something I had yet considered.

To those whose conversation and advice helped me on the journey of completing this book, thank you deeply: George Elliot Clarke, Natasha Ramoutar, Fariha Róisín, Sean Michaels, Vivek Shraya, Dan Werb, Sinead Petrasek, Sophie O'Manique, my high school English A.P. teacher Mr. Barton Leibel, Laura Dawe, Patricia Boushel, Owen Pallett, Rio Mitchell, Ashley Obscura, Simona Lepadatu, Anthony Obi, Mihaela Poca, Alex Hughes, Scott Pilgrim, and Julia Hart.

To my manager Jon Bartlett and everyone at Kelp Management for showing me that an equitable partnership is possible in the music industry. Thanks to my booking agent Ouss Laghzaoui for his sage advice and steadfast belief in me. Shout out to everyone at MNRK Music Group and Indoor Recess for their hard work in helping to translate my musical vision to the public.

Thank you to my family. Mick, thanks for always having my back. My sister Gena: you've been like another parent to me. I appreciate you! My sister Sierra: it's been amazing to see you grow up. Thanks for keeping me hip. To Uncle Brett and Aunt Dani, thanks for showing me what a life in art can look like. To the Miles, Lipscombe and Pemberton families, love you all! R.I.P. T.E.D.D.Y., Rollie and Marianne Miles.

Finally, I want to thank my partner Sara Mojtehedzadeh for her unconditional love and support as I worked on this book over the past two and a half years. Her brilliant advice, compassionate encouragement and keen eye helped me immeasurably. I became a better writer just by being near her and I became a better person by having her in my life. I love you, Sara.

SUGGESTED READING

Jeff Chang, *Can't Stop Won't Stop: A History of the Hip-Hop Generation*

Dan Hancox, *Inner City Pressure: The Story of Grime*

Bill Brewster and Frank Broughton, *Last Night A DJ Saved My Life: The History of the Disc Jockey*

Tim Lawrence, *Love Saves The Day: A History of American Dance Music Culture, 1970-1979*

Simon Reynolds, *Energy Flash: A Journey Through Rave Music and Dance Culture*

SUGGESTED LISTENING

Aceyalone – *A Book of Human Language*

Beastie Boys – *Paul's Boutique*

Birdapres – *Catch An L*

Buck 65 – *Vertex*

Cadence Weapon – *Breaking Kayfabe*

Cadence Weapon – *Afterparty Babies*

Cadence Weapon – *Hope in Dirt City*

Cadence Weapon – *Cadence Weapon*

Cadence Weapon – *Parallel World*

Cannibal Ox – *The Cold Vein*

Daft Punk – *Discovery*

De La Soul – *Buhloone Mindstate*

Dizzee Rascal – *Boy In Da Corner*

Freestyle Fellowship – *Innercity Griots*

Ghostface Killah – *Supreme Clientele*

Grimes – *Visions*

Hip Hop Weiners – *All Beef, No Chicken*

J Dilla – *Donuts*

John Smith – *Pinky's Laundromat*

Mac DeMarco – *Rock and Roll Night Club*

Madvillain – *Madvillainy*

OutKast – *Aquemini*

Shout Out Out Out Out – *Not Saying / Just Saying*

Silly Kissers – *Love Tsunami*

The Streets – *Original Pirate Material*

TOPS – *Tender Opposites*

Various Artists – *Disco Not Disco* series

LISTEN TO THE *BEDROOM RAPPER* PLAYLIST

Spotify
https://bit.ly/bedroom_spotify

YouTube
https://bit.ly/bedroom_YT